Heartwood

Published by Melbourne Books
Level 9, 100 Collins Street,
Melbourne, VIC 3000
Australia
www.melbournebooks.com.au
info@melbournebooks.com.au

Copyright © Rowan Reid 2017

First published 2017
Reprinted 2019, 2021

All rights reserved. No part of this publication may be reproduced, stored in a retrieval system, or transmitted in any form or any means electronic, mechanical, photocopying, recording or otherwise without the prior permission of the publishers.

Photography: Cover and opening tree chapter photos by Cormac Hanrahan. All others by Rowan Reid unless otherwise stated.
Artwork: All wildlife drawings by Michelle Stewart.
Cover image: Seedling of Australian Silky Oak on a Sydney Blue Gum log.

Title: Heartwood: The Art and Science of Growing Trees for Conservation and Profit
Author: Rowan Reid
ISBN: 9781925556117

 A catalogue record for this book is available from the National Library of Australia

Heartwood

The art and science of growing trees
for conservation and profit

Rowan Reid

MELBOURNE BOOKS

The Author

Rowan Reid (B.For.Sci. & M.For.Sci.) is a forester amongst farmers. His passion for trees began as a child in the coastal eucalypt forests of southern Victoria and has led to a life teaching and working with farmers around the world. Rowan won the 2001 Australian Eureka Prize for Excellence in Environmental Education for his farmer course (The Australian Master TreeGrower), which he continues to deliver around Australia and internationally (Africa, Timor Leste, Indonesia etc.). A Senior Lecturer at the University of Melbourne for 20 years, Rowan continues his academic teaching and research as a Senior Fellow of the university and the managing director of the Australian Agroforestry Foundation (a not-for-profit organisation). Since the publication of *Agroforestry in Australia and New Zealand* (1985), Rowan has written or co-authored eight other books and is an internationally recognised leader in farmer education and extension.

Most importantly, Rowan is also a farmer and tree grower in his own right, with a family farm in the Otway Ranges of southern Victoria where he helped establish one of Australia's most successful Landcare groups, the Otway Agroforestry Network. More than 10,000 visitors have toured his Bambra Agroforestry Farm, which is set up as a 42-hectare outdoor classroom for farmers, scientists, students and tree lovers, and a living laboratory for his own learning.

Contents

Introduction
The Third Wave — 8

1
Messmate Stringybark — 22
Eucalyptus obliqua

2
Blackwood — 36
Acacia melanoxylon

3
Mountain Ash — 54
Eucalyptus regnans

4
Coast Redwood — 72
Sequoia sempervirens

5
Australian Silky Oak — 90
Grevillea robusta

6
Manna Gum — 110
Eucalyptus viminalis

7
Shining Gum — 126
Eucalyptus nitens

8
River Sheoak — 146
Casuarina cunninghamiana

9
Sydney Blue Gum — 164
Eucalyptus saligna

10
Poplars and Willows — 182
Populus and *Salix*

11
Black Walnut — 202
Juglans nigra

12
Red Ironbark — 224
Eucalyptus tricarpa and *Eucalyptus sideroxylon*

13
English Oak — 242
Quercus robur

14
Spotted Gum — 260
Corymbia maculata

15
Australian Red Cedar — 278
Toona ciliata var. australis

Acknowledgments — 298

Index — 299

Introduction

The Third Wave

There are three types of waves at my home surf break. The fastest is the 'bar wave', which forms a long straight wall of water that breaks to the right across a shallow sandbar. Rather than try and ride it, most board-riders are happy just to watch as it barrels through the inside. Being in the minority as a 'goofy-footer', right foot forward, I'm on my backhand when riding a right-breaking wave, which makes it even harder to make it through to the rip without wiping out and risking a face full of quartz. When I was much younger there was the occasion when I did take on a bar wave and get myself into the zone. I'd hold the outside rail of my board with my left hand and tuck my head back under the lip. If I was lucky, a section might throw right over me; a tube or barrel. Once lived, being inside a pipe of water becomes one of those frozen-in-time moments that stays with you for life, particularly if you only get to experience it a handful of times.

The easier option is the 'peak wave'. It rises directly in front of the electricity pole between the surf break's two neat bitumen car parks. In my teens, there was just a tangled web of goat tracks pushed into the Coast Beard-heath scrub (*Leucopogon parviflorus*) by surfers in kombis and surfies in panel vans. But I never needed a car to get to my home surf break. In the year I was born, Mum bought a bush block on the sand dunes overlooking the beach and built her first house—she was just twenty-five years old.

The right-hander off the peak wave is good enough for most but there is another option: the elusive 'third wave'.

As I write, it occurs to me that I don't have any other name for it. I've not spoken to anyone about it before and have never heard any of the other surfers in the crowd mention it, which makes me wonder whether anyone else can see it. Surfing is an individual pursuit, with each board-rider making their own judgement on the best place to position themselves. For me, this means paddling past the crowd clustered around the take-off area for the peak wave and on to a spot directly in line with a patch of Drooping Sheoak (*Allocasuarina verticillata*) that runs up the hill behind the second car park. This act alone often draws resentment from those who think I'm trying to take up an inside position, but they misunderstand. It's not arrogance that takes me inside the crowd. I'm not a good enough surfer to pull that off. I'm not following any person. I'm following the patterns I see in the ocean.

With time, I've learnt to read the water and I'm sure I've found a better wave. It's usually the second or third in the set and rises between the take-off

Riding my elusive third wave at my home surf break on the Great Ocean Road.

areas for the bar wave and the peak to form a steep, wide crest. It provides a fast take-off to the right onto a solid wall of water from where I can cut-back to pick up the energy as my wave rises onto the sandbar. If I get it right, the power in the wave throws me forward onto a long playful face that takes me through to the rip.

The third wave is clearly the best that my home surf break can offer me, not so much a compromise between two extremes—the bar wave or the peak—but something altogether different. We have become accustomed to defining our world, and even ourselves, within the context of opposing dualisms—goofy or natural, left or right, faith or reason, art or science. By doing so we may be missing something, the third wave. This is particularly evident in my field.

I am a forester, or should I say a forest scientist. Not that the clarification will reassure some. Everyone knows forests are for *either* conservation *or* production, to be saved *or* plundered. This polarity helps people, whatever their ecological understanding, make sense of the complexity that is inherent in the natural world and in our own relationship with it. They can take a side, feel part of a tribe, and express a collective opinion with confidence. For some the dichotomy goes deeper than just an opinion, it becomes an identity—'I am a conservationist'—making it almost impossible to challenge their views without offending the person.

If there are only two sides to the forest debate, which side am I on? If I am not a conservationist, then maybe I am an industrialist or an exploiter? Had I spent years studying oceanography, aquaculture, fish population management and the dietary and economic contribution of fisheries to people, both rich and poor, you wouldn't call me a fisherman, even if I occasionally threw out a line or enjoyed a plate of salmon.

In my time, Australian forest scientists have never enjoyed the public respect afforded marine scientists. Of course, we largely have ourselves to blame. In the 1980s there were the huge clear-felled logging coupes in the native forests around the Eden woodchip export facility, in southern New South Wales, which heralded the beginning of the forestry wars. During the 1990s vast areas of public native forest in Tasmania were deemed unproductive and converted to monoculture eucalypt plantations. Then, to cap it off, we had a decade of dodgy plantation investment schemes that collapsed spectacularly when the global financial crisis hit in 2009.

When I made my career choice I was a teenage surfer wearing desert boots and cords. I travelled the Great Ocean Road in Mum's kombi with 'Solar not Nuclear' stickers on the back window, and grew a few plants in the backyard of Dad's suburban manse. I had been drawn to the coast by the waves and what the 1970s surf culture represented—being close to nature and non-conformist whilst celebrating individual expression—but the trees, with their roots firmly grounded in the earth (realism) and their canopies reaching for the sky (optimism), lured me into the forest. For me, being *in* the forest was not about knowing it, utilising it or even saving it, it was just about being *with* it.

Places, particularly natural environments, hold greater meaning for those that know them, play in them or work in them, than a visitor can ever discern. My childhood coastal playground—the surf break, the beach and the forest behind it—is just real estate to most, but for me it became much more. I've built a relationship, a history, with this place that makes it personal; a narrative that I relive, and develop further, every time I paddle out into the ocean or walk in the bush. Over time, I have seen the landscape change and have come to appreciate that forests are as fluid as the ocean, whereas for the traveller or tourist visiting my place for the first time, their understanding of it is static, much like a picture in a tourist calendar.

Every experience, no matter how unremarkable, will start to splice the fine threads of one's life in with those of the landscape. You may find that the landscape becomes part of your own story and that you can even leave a little of yourself in the enduring story of the land, in its spirit. I've seen it in so many of the farmers and Indigenous landholders I've met. I have felt it myself. A place need not be outstanding—boasting the best waves, the tallest trees or the most beautiful views—for it to become special to the person who feels they are a part of it, and it of them.

I chose to study forest science to learn more about the landscape that I wanted to become part of me. From the stunted, wind-beaten Messmate Stringybark (*Eucalyptus obliqua*) growing on the slopes overlooking my home surf break, to the strong Red Ironbarks (*Eucalyptus tricarpa*) over the ridge—where my dog and I would walk when I needed time alone—and up into the

I have learnt to see forests as dynamic systems. This Red Ironbark forest behind our beach looks very different to when I was a teenager.

ranges to where the Mountain Ash (*Eucalyptus regnans*) grow as tall as any tree can. Through my teenage years, the trees of the Otway Ranges didn't need Latin names to mean something to me. But as I learnt about their biology and ecology I started to understand things that I already knew and resonated with. Like how eucalypts, because of their unprotected leaf buds, tend to take on a shape that reflects the environment in which they grow. Like what was happening to me.

I also began to develop an eye with which to read, and ride, the waves of change in a forest. Though some of the stages are ugly, such as those following a wildfire or cyclone, I learnt to look beyond the devastation for evidence of the ecological processes that will drive change. Processes that mean the mix of plant and animal species we can find in the forest, or the lack of them, continues to change. Whilst there is change, no matter its pace, every stage has purpose. The bare blackened soil and dead stags of a burnt Mountain Ash forest have as much ecological legitimacy as the mature forest that was there before the wildfire, or the temperate rainforest that would have replaced it had it not been burnt. The elimination of one group of species provides an opportunity for another. It is not a question of what has happened, but of what will happen in the future. Just as it was for me.

What followed was no backflip. I didn't suddenly forsake my teenage idealism and change sides. I like to think I remained true to myself and to the places that define me, and that this has allowed me to move beyond the dualism inherent in the world of forestry in my search for something more satisfying.

Heartwood

left: The shearing shed on John Peter's Tubbo Station beside the Murrumbidgee River in NSW. Tubbo was held by our family until the 1980s.

opposite: The clearing of forests for farming has exacerbated soil erosion and dryland salinity.

I did consider following my heart and seeking a career working in the native forests of the Otway Ranges. But, while walking, working, surfing and living in and around the hills I made the decision that if the future of our public forests was to be determined by a political contest between opposing ideologies, there would be little opportunity for me to contribute. Besides, the real environmental frontline was not at the forest blockades, but at the farm gate.

The primary reason Australia is the world leader in flora and fauna extinction, and continues to see a decline in almost all measures of soil and water health, is not logging for timber but the clearing of our forests and woodlands for agriculture. It seemed to me that as long as our public native forests were protected from land use change, the native flora and fauna species that depend on them would most probably survive poor logging practices and even worse conservation policies. It was the agricultural landscape that needed my science. I would be a forester amongst farmers.

Farmers manage more than sixty percent of the Australian land mass. Most is in the semi-arid areas where leaseholders have traditionally grazed livestock on a mix of native plants, including shrubs, grasses and herbs. My great grandmother's uncle, John Peter, was among the first to recognise the feed value of the native Saltbush (*Atriplex* species). The son of a Scottish farmer, he arrived in Australia in 1832 and was managing a grassland property near Goulburn in New South Wales when a devastating sheep disease broke out across the region.

Through trial and error he found that he could keep losses down by giving stock access to clean pastures and rock salt. Seeing an opportunity to profit from adversity, Peter encouraged his boss to take up a grazing licence on the Saltbush Plains along the Murrumbidgee River—further inland than any other squatter thought viable at the time—and then took up ten miles of river frontage even further west for himself. He was just twenty-five years old.

Over the next thirty years, John Peter accumulated leases over more

than one million acres of 'virgin' country, which carried a similar number of sheep, and became one of the most successful pastoralists in the colonies.[1] But he never became an Australian. He returned to his homeland childless with the fortune he'd made milking the wealth of a foreign landscape—a landscape that its first people had spent thousands of years preparing for his arrival. Fortunately, for me at least, Peter did bring his young sister Elizabeth out from Scotland. She married a local farmer and left a daughter in Australia, my great grandmother, to continue the family line.

The livestock and the pests that the Europeans introduced—goats, camels, brumbies, rabbits, foxes, cats and donkeys—have modified the vegetation structure of the arid rangelands, exacerbating wind erosion and biodiversity loss. Yet, despite more than 150 years of exploitation, wherever the native vegetation has not been purposely cleared or over grazed, the ecological integrity of the pastoral lands remain largely intact.[2] By using modern technology to manage grazing pressure, such as remotely operating water points and gates, and reintroducing the indigenous practice of early season burning, more progressive pastoralists are showing that, even in our driest landscapes, profitability and environmental improvement are not necessarily mutually exclusive.

Saltbush and other native fodder shrubs still have a role to play in sustaining the arid lands, both commercially and environmentally. I'm also interested in the potential for the strategic harvesting and regeneration of native timbers such as Beefwood (*Grevillea striata*), Sandalwood (*Santalum spicatum*), Cypress Pine (*Callitris* species), and bushfoods like the Kakadu Plum (*Terminalia ferdinandiana*) and Quandong (*Santalum acuminatum*). Why? Because the real risk facing the vast rangelands of Australia is not the commercial utilization of the indigenous vegetation but the perception that it has no commercial value.

Australia's greatest environmental tragedy—one that might only be eclipsed by the impending, and somewhat related, impacts of climate change—

is occurring on the privately owned farmland outside the pastoral zone.[2] From the Atherton Tablelands in Far North Queensland, down around the east coast to Victoria and Tasmania, and across the Nullarbor to the southwest of Western Australia, over 100,000 farming businesses, mostly families, own more than fifty million hectares of rural Australia. Having been deemed to be of no commercial value, almost all the native vegetation on these farms was cleared generations ago to make way for pastures, crops and horticulture. It is true that the clearing helped build the nation and that modern agriculture plays a critical role in sustaining the communities that are working the hardest to restore the country. But there is no doubt that the loss of native forests and woodlands from our farmland remains the single greatest cause of land degradation, water quality decline and biodiversity loss across the continent, and is a significant factor in our contribution to climate change.

My great grandfather John Archibald Campbell, grew up in his father's central Victorian pub during the gold rush of the 1850s and was twenty-five years old when he bought a small farm not far from John Peter's Tubbo Station on the Murrumbidgee River. He soon married Peter's niece Jane, whose father, a contemporary of Peter's, encouraged him to sell up and head further north in search of quality native country. Just north of Walgett he purchased what became our family farm, Dungalear Station, and shore 100,000 sheep in his first year (1885) without having to clear a single tree.

When explorer Major Sir Thomas Mitchell crossed the same plains fifty years earlier he wrote in his diary (21st January 1832):

> *Penetrating next through a narrow strip of casuarinae scrub, we found the remains of native huts; and beyond this scrub we crossed a beautiful plain; covered with shining verdure, and ornamented with trees, which, although 'dropped in nature's careless haste,' gave the country the appearance of an extensive park.*[3]

Such descriptions are common among the writings of early explorers. Once considered wild and untamed, it is now accepted that most of rural Australia was a purposefully managed landscape, an estate that provided a full range of values: food, fuel, shelter, culture and spirituality. Blinded by ignorance and buoyed by a sense of entitlement provided by British law, my ancestors saw a welcoming landscape.

Tragedy struck my family during the Great War. My great grandfather's two eldest sons died within five weeks of each other during active service in France, which led to the death of their distraught father before Christmas that

My family 'farmed' the native country on Dungalear Station near Walgett, NSW, for almost one hundred years.

same year. Thankfully the conflict was over before his third son, my grandfather, was old enough to enlist. After studying in England, the young John Campbell returned to Australia and purchased Dungalear from his father's estate. He was twenty-five years old.

The farm became his passion until his own premature death at forty. My grandmother, who I knew well, never shared her husband's interest in agriculture, so it may not have surprised her to learn that one of the conditions of my grandfather's will specified that Dungalear could not be sold until she herself had passed on, thus deferring any decision to my mother's generation.

A manager was employed to run the farm, and I grew up with the stories about the huge wool cheques during the Korean War, the introduction of the wool floor price and the inevitable rising wool stockpile. There were also stories of the losses incurred due to drought, fire, rabbits and flood. Our annual pre-Christmas dinner with the cousins always started politely enough but, fueled by wine and whisky, Mum and her brother would invariably clash over politics and his plans for the farm.

My uncle was keen to move the farm into the modern era by clearing more native vegetation for cropping. Mum, often with tears in her eyes, would grasp any rational argument she could summon to stop him calling in the bulldozers. It was only recently, after her death, that I realised why she was so determined to protect the indigenous vegetation. She knew that clearing Mitchell's 'native parkland' would sever the last few strands of connection that any descendant of the local Indigenous clans might have had with their country.

Her ancestors had used a foreign law to take title over this land and forced those that were already there to stop their traditional farming practices. They had bought their labour and compliance with blankets, sugar and flour and, possibly, turned a blind eye to atrocities. If there was any chance of a reconciliation it would be built on the foundation that was the native vegetation. It was the scaffold that carried their songlines.

In 1986, forty-six years after my grandfather's death, my family's farming history finally caught up with me. Claire and I had been hitch-hiking through Scandinavia, dodging the pickpockets around the Mediterranean and visiting relatives in England before we boarded a direct flight from London to Jomo Kenyatta Airport, Nairobi. Being in Europe, where forests only exist because of their value to people, had helped me envisage what a future of forests in the farming landscape might look like back home. But it was in Kenya that I was to see a pathway that I could follow to help achieve it.

My visit to the headquarters of the World Agroforestry Centre in Nairobi was as much a rite of passage as the months I'd spent backpacking in Europe. Their research was exploring how planting trees on the smallest farms could serve the needs of the poorest farmers—for food, fodder, firewood and fertiliser. Then, a Kenyan forester, Eli Mwanza, who had studied with me in Melbourne took us into the highlands where I met subsistence farmers who, with barely an acre of land from which to feed their family, could still find the time and the space to plant more trees. Always thinking of home, I could clearly see that commercial forestry, the act of planting trees for profit, could be made an attractive option for Australian farming families, but that the reasons, means, products and markets would need to change. Forestry on farms would look different from what government and industry were doing.

My plans were coming together. I would create a place where farmers, students and the public could learn about trees and wood, and see new opportunities: somewhere independent of government and industry; a place built on passion but based on science; a working forest farm that would make planting trees, and even the act of cutting them down, attractive to farmers. My forest would not be a *museum* of trees—like an arboretum or a botanic garden. Neither would it be a demonstration of someone else's interpretation of 'world's-best-practice' commercial forestry. I wanted to challenge this dualistic thinking and celebrate the breadth of opportunity that lies between these extremes; I wanted to show that there could be a third wave. First, I would need some land.

My Mum's cousins Jack and Betty lived in Nairobi and my parents just happened to be visiting. Claire and I planned to spend a few days with them before heading off to explore more of Kenya. That's when Mum told me that while I'd been away she and her brother had sold Dungalear. Then, knowing of her father's passion for the land, she asked if I had any interest in taking my share early, to buy a farm of my own.

In East Africa—a landscape that had, like ours, been degraded by European colonisation—Mum was giving me an opportunity to start a new farm in her father's memory. I knew immediately that in accepting such a gift, I would also be accepting a share of the burden that my mother had largely carried alone. As a teenager, I knew this as inherited guilt. Now I was being given the opportunity to make decisions based on a more constructive narrative:

Travelling through rural Kenya in 1986.

one that follows neither the guilt of the black armband view of Australian history nor the denial-infused nostalgia of the white blindfold.

I was being given an opportunity to help create a third way: A future where nothing separates my own unborn grandchildren from the descendants of the traditional owners of this land. A future in which Aboriginality is not defined by the colour of our skin or a proven direct ancestry, but by a shared history we all inherit and through a connection with, and love for, the country on which we walk.

That night, as I fell asleep with the options playing over in my mind, a guard walked around the garden protecting us with a bow and arrow. No one seriously expected he would fight off any well-armed home invaders but maybe he could sound the alarm before he fled to protect himself. Yet, I felt safe and slept well. I dreamt of a treeless valley divided by an eroded creek, and when I woke I held on to the image in my mind until I was sure I was fully conscious. I had a sense that I had dreamt of a real place and, if so, I would find it somewhere close to my childhood home, in the hills of the Otway Ranges. I'd left Australia in search of a future and I found it in a girl that chose to meet my plane in Copenhagen and a dream I had in a cottage in Nairobi. I knew I'd be heading home to start a family, build a career and plant some trees. I was twenty-five years old.

Years later, I walked into a University of Melbourne lecture theatre with my chainsaw and set it down in front of the lectern. I'd been invited to give a guest presentation to an environmental science class. It's a wonder I got a chainsaw past campus security, but I'm glad I did. I enjoy an argument that challenges

top: I took this photo on our Otway Ranges farm in early 1987 in the days before we took possession.

bottom: Our Bambra Agroforestry Farm after 13 years of tree planting, in 2001.

beliefs, ideologies and customs; both my opponent's and my own. My topic: *Can cutting down trees help save the environment?* My approach: Confront the stereotypes, focus on the outcomes and demonstrate that when it comes to managing our rural landscapes it is not the methods, or the tools, that are important, but the motives and knowledge of the person making the decisions.

My arguments were based on my science and from what I had learnt from hundreds of farmers I have worked with over the years across Australia and around the world. My confidence came from my own experience as a tree grower on a small farm in the Otway Ranges.

Poet Robert Frost famously wrote: '*Two roads diverged in a wood and I - I took the one less travelled by, and that has made all the difference.*'[4] What if he missed something? What of the path through the undergrowth, a path *not yet travelled*? As we approach the environmental, social and productivity limits of our conventional systems, it's time for a fresh approach. Modern forestry began with the harvesting of market-ready trees from the existing native forest. Then there was the development of large scale monoculture plantations by government and corporations.

Now there is a third wave rising: A suite of approaches to growing new forests that are not primarily commercial but make good business sense. They don't look like conservation, yet improve biodiversity and reduce land degradation. They are not compromises. They are not negotiated points along some tug-of-war line between two opposing ideologies. They are elegant solutions, appropriate for each owner, their place and the time, which provide a balance of conservation, aesthetics and profit. Together they can deliver much more than can be achieved by simply dividing up the landscape between competing interests.

CEO of World Vision Australia Tim Costello quotes a South American philosopher who argued that what we need, in his case to help the poor, was not a revolution or a reformation but

> *'a new and powerful tale, one so persuasive that it sweeps away the old myths and becomes the preferred story, one so inclusive that it gathers all the bits of our past and our present into a coherent whole, one that even shines some light into the future so that we can take the next step forward.'*[5]

While we're not dealing with world poverty here—although there is certainly a role for trees in meeting that challenge—the growing and harvesting of trees for conservation, aesthetics and profit, as celebrated in this book, is a new story for most landholders, foresters and environmentalists. A story that is being written right now by tree growers around the country who have had the courage to blaze a new path and are now emerging with a clearer view of an alternative future for our rural landscapes. A story that argues that the felling of a tree for its timber is not necessarily a step back; it can be a leap forward, a revelation, *'a new and more powerful tale'*.

Australasian Gannet (*Morus serrator*)

---

1. Paul de Serville, *Tubbo: The great Peter's run*, (Melbourne: Oxford University Press, 1982).

2. State of the Environment 2011 Committee, *Australia state of the environment 2011. Independent report to the Australian Government Minister for Sustainability, Environment, Water, Population and Communities* (Canberra: DSEWPaC, 2011).

3. Thomas L. Mitchell, *Three expeditions into the interior of eastern Australia: With descriptions of the recently explored region of Australian Felix, and of the present colony of New South Wales*, (London: Boone, 1839).

4. Robert Frost, 'The Road Not Taken.' In: *Mountain Interval* (New York: Henry Holt and Company, 1916).

5. Tim Costello, *Tips from a Travelling Soul Searcher* (Sydney: Allen & Unwin, 1999).

Chapter 1

Messmate Stringybark
Eucalyptus obliqua

Messmate Stringybark was my first eucalypt. As a youth, it was part of my life and my learning. I taught myself how to pick the grain and swing an axe splitting foot-rounds for firewood and would use its stringy bark to light the fires that warmed me up after a mid-winter surf. When it came to learning the Latin names, *Eucalyptus obliqua* was the first I could recall. Lectures on the taxonomy, biology, ecology, history and wood qualities of Messmate Stringybark tangled with my childhood experiences and provided a comforting feeling that my chosen discipline was a perfect mix of the classical (science, economics and technology) and the romantic (emotion, art and desire).

Eucalypt-type trees first appeared more than ten million years ago, but their dominance within the Australian landscape only goes back about 100,000 years with the retreat of the rainforests that once covered our continent. Hastened with the demise of the megafauna and the increased frequency of fire that accompanied the arrival of humans about 50,000 years ago, natural selection, isolation, hybridisation and random mutation has driven differentiation of the eucalypts into three genera (*Eucalyptus*, *Corymbia* and *Angophora*) and more than 800 species.

In science, the Messmate Stringybark became the first eucalypt when, in 1788, the French botanist, Charles-Louis L'Héritier de Brutelle used Linnaeus' rules of botanical nomenclature to formally describe a specimen collected from an island off the south coast of Tasmania during Captain Cook's third Pacific expedition. Being the first to formally publish gave L'Héritier the right to name not only the species—with a reference to the oblique asymmetrical leaf—but also the genus: a Greek-derived reference to the 'well-covered' flower buds (eu meaning 'well' and kalyptos meaning 'covered'). But what did he really know about the tree? L'Heritier had never stood in a Messmate Stringybark forest, never sought warmth from a Messmate fire or sheltered under a roof supported by a Stringybark beam. He didn't *know* the Messmate Stringybark like those of us who lived with it.

The early European settlers in the Otway Ranges found Messmate Stringybark relatively easy to saw and dry. It performed well in the weather, if kept off the ground, particularly in comparison to the other southern eucalypts on offer. But then, Messmate Stringybark was never considered a furniture grade timber because of its predisposition to bleed kino. Kino is the thick red-brown liquid (condensed tannins) that is often seen weeping out of the wounds of some eucalypts, forming gum pockets and veins through the wood. Indeed, the bush name *Messmate* might well have been a reference to the poor bugger

preceding page: Claire and I beside the old Messmate Stringybark on our farm.

right: Kino bleeding out of the trunk of our Messmate Stringybark.

working down in the sawpit who would be covered with a mix of sawdust and the tacky red gum which, combined with his sweat, would stick to his skin like glue. That's just my reasoning, but it seems as plausible as the explanation provided by Joseph Maiden, the NSW Government Botanist, who, in 1917, said it was 'because it is associated with or mess-mates with other stringybarks.'[1] As if the bushies working in the forests knew or cared about the promiscuity of the trees they were harvesting.

I like to think there is something to be learnt from the common names given to so many of our Australian trees, especially by those who worked with and amongst them. Names often provide insights about where a species could be found or its utilitarian values that a gentleman botanist might have easily missed.

There are common names that indicate the characteristics of the soil or its suitability for agriculture (Swamp Gum, Flooded Gum), the physical properties of the wood (Steel Gum, Steel Box), its uses (Brown Mallet, Coachwood), ease of hand splitting (Bastard Box), similarity with other new-world timbers (Southern Mahogany), the oil content of the leaves (Peppermint) or whether the sap was sweet enough to be fermented into alcohol (Cider Gum). It makes you wonder what names like Diehard Stringybark, Bollywood, or Cut Tail Ash might refer to. No doubt there are good stories behind them all.

The presence of kino in native forest Messmate Stringybark is often interpreted as being an indication of past fire, injury or insect attack. Yet, when milling our planted Messmate Stringybark, which have not experienced any of these abuses, I find bands and pockets of kino between the growth rings. I think they developed during periods of intense moisture stress. It is common for trees to shrink a little in diameter in a dry season if they are unable to draw sufficient water to maintain cell saturation. Uneven shrinkage between the outer and inner layers of the trunk can sever the wood along the annual growth rings causing a curved 'ring-shake'. In English Oak (*Quercus robur*), ring shakes are known to occur more frequently on well drained sandy soils that are prone to late summer drought.[2] Without a kino-like glue that can fill the void and bond the wood together, boards cut from an affected English Oak tree just fall apart, making the timber useless. Narrow veins of kino in Messmate Stringybark have no effect on the strength of the timber, and, with the recent trend of celebrating the naturalness of our native woods, the presence of kino is increasingly being recognised as a feature, rather than a defect, in high quality furniture.

As a forest science student, I did a summer with the Queensland Forests Department working in the pine plantations around the Glasshouse Mountains. The experience could have led to a secure government job but when the offer of a cadetship came up I didn't apply. I could see that my future would not be in government or the industrial plantation sector. Ian, my university study mate, did and he moved north to take up the job and start a family. In our first year on the farm he visited and presented us with a seedling to mark the occasion. Having spent our university swat vacs studying and surfing together at my home surf break, it was no surprise that he chose a Messmate Stringybark. We had a little ceremonial planting to christen our new venture and left it at that. As Ian moved around the Sunshine State and up through the bureaucracy, his tree grew. As it did I directed its growth and shaped its future by pruning the branches from the stem and ensuring it had plenty of room to expand its canopy.

Twenty-five years after Ian planted the tree it toppled over in a wild spring storm. The Messmate Stringybark had grown a straight clear branch-free trunk more than six metres long and was over 50 centimetres in diameter at breast height (1.3 metres). The roots on one side were lifted clean out of the ground and extended high over my head as I stood in the hole and examined the root structure. The bulk of the roots had spread out through the surface soil seeking the easy-to-find moisture and nutrients. There was no major taproot, just a few small sinker roots coming off the main laterals that would have reached down into the heavy clay soils in search of backup moisture to get the tree through the driest seasons.

Over the years we have lost quite a few of our young trees to windthrow. It started happening soon after I'd finished pruning the best of our eucalypts up to six metres, creating what my neighbours referred to as my 'lollipop farm'. Over the next two or three years the strong equinox winds and heavy spring rains left many trees lying on the ground, wrenched over to expose half their root system. I began searching for a reason, maybe even a solution. An experienced arborist suggested I'd planted J-rooted seedlings or used a poor planting technique that had twisted the roots and made them unstable. A forester who was more familiar

Ian's 25-yr-old Messmate Stringybark blew over in a wild spring storm. Fortunately, I had pruned the tree so I could salvage a sawlog.

with dense unpruned plantations simply pointed out that the wider spacing and pruning must have opened the trees up to the wind.

I dismissed both suggestions because my own observations didn't support either. The best I could come up with was that pruning may have increased the proportion of stiffer heartwood in the stem, thereby reducing flexibility and concentrating the bending force at the point where the tree was anchored in the soil. Although I was able to measure the effect of pruning on heartwood formation and could find studies that seemed to confirm that heartwood increased stem stiffness, I was never entirely comfortable with the reasoning. In science, being prepared to change your mind is a sign of strength.

Years later it was an engineer, rather than a botanist, who helped me understand why trees with a tall branch-free trunk are inherently unstable.

Ken James' office was just down the hall from mine at the University of Melbourne. As an engineer his interest in trees was structural. Using sensitive instruments pinned into the trunk he could measure the strain in the stem as a tree swayed in the wind. We would demonstrate this to our students by tying a long rope to a big solid tree in the university gardens and getting them to pull on it while Ken's data logger mapped the imperceptible movement of the lower trunk.

By using data collected during windstorms, Ken was able to show that branches sway independently of the main trunk and thereby act as mass dampeners, dissipating the wind energy and reducing the dynamic stress on the stem.[3] Apparently, engineers rely on a similar principle when they place large water tanks in tall buildings to reduce sway due to strong winds or earthquake. If the building moves the liquid sloshes around the tank, like a branch on a tree, dissipating the energy.

Ken's research provided a much more plausible explanation and he had data to prove the link: by pruning all the branches off the lower stem I had reduced the mass dampening effect thus increasing the dynamic load on the main trunk and therefore the risk of the stem snapping or the whole tree toppling over.

Ken's theory also explained something else that had intrigued me since a solo hitchhiking trip I'd taken around the southwest corner of Western Australia after my first year at university. I made a point of visiting the giant Karri forests (*Eucalyptus diversicolor*) where I climbed the sixty-metre-tall Gloucester Tree fire tower. On the wall of regional forest offices around Australia one usually finds a huge map with protractors pinned at the location of each tower. When a sighting of smoke comes in, a coloured string is stretched out from each tower location along the reported bearing. To accurately pinpoint the location of a rising column of smoke you need compass bearings from at least two towers, three is better. Where the strings cross marks the source.

In the Otways the fire towers are strategically located on the highest vantage points along the range, but in the Karri forests there are few hills that allow a 20 or 30-metre-tall steel tower to achieve an uninterrupted view over a 60-metre-tall forest. So, rather than try to build a tower taller than the forest, the Western Australian foresters decided they'd use the trees instead.

The Gloucester Tree was 'built' in 1947. With just climbing boots and a belt—no ropes—one of the local foresters, Jack Watson, scaled the huge tree to assess its suitability. At a height of 58 metres he found he had a clear view over the distant forests, and so marked the point on the trunk. With a girth of more than seven metres near the ground and several large branches blocking his way, just scaling this tree was an extraordinary feat.

Then George Reynolds, another forester, climbed his way up, knocking off any branches as he went and banging in steel pegs. This created a circular staircase up to the viewing point, where he then *topped* the tree to create a 58-metre branch-free pedestal.

Some old film footage, which I first saw in the Pemberton timber museum, shows a scene that would have been similar to the final moments of the beheading of the Gloucester fire tower tree.

We see the tree's head begin to move and the climber let go of his axe, which was tied to a long rope, then grab his climbing belt and pull himself hard up against the trunk—the aeroplane brace position. As the massive canopy begins to topple, the trunk is pushed back by the weight. Then, as the head falls, the branch-free trunk shakes violently. The climber looks like an ant desperately hanging on to a tuning fork. While he protects his head from being beaten against the tree, the axe flings around on the rope, threatening to take off a limb—his own this time. Had George understood Ken's theory he may well have decided to cut off the branches on the way down rather than on the way up!

To complete the tower they built an observation cabin on top of the stump and it was then someone's job to sit up there in the heat and the wind during days of extreme fire weather. By the time I arrived there in 1980, the Gloucester Tree had resprouted branches down the full length of its trunk. Ignorant of the theory of mass-dampening, I confidently climbed up to the top and stood up in the cabin sixty metres above the forest floor, proud of my

The Gloucester Tree was 'built' in 1947 and is still operational as a fire tower. Photos show the tree in the 1950s (left), 1970s (centre) and when I visited in the early 1980s (right). Images from 1950s and 1970s courtesy of the Western Australian Department of Parks and Wildlife.

achievement. Even so, I do remember being unsettled as the tree swayed in the wind. I now know that it would have been far worse for the fire-spotter back in those early years when the tower was just a branch-free pole. Knowledge changes the way we understand our past experiences.

The time I'd invested in pruning Ian's tree was like taking out life insurance on its uncertain future. If it happened to die, fall over or be burnt, or if I ever decided to cash in my policy, I'd be able to recover a sawlog from the trunk. Without pruning, it would have grown into a heavily branched open-grown tree that would have only been good for firewood. In any event, I would get plenty of that from the spreading canopy up above the clear branch-free bole. Fortunately, Ian's Messmate Stringybark was a good diameter for milling when it fell. I cut the six-metre-long pruned log into two short logs and milled them on our portable bandsaw into one-and-a-half-inch quartersawn boards and stacked them to dry in the shed.

The terms quartersawn and backsawn refer to the original orientation of the board as it was within the log. A perfectly quartersawn board is cut such that the growth rings run from face to face, exposing the radial plane on its widest face. The face of a backsawn board shows the tangential surface, with the growth rings essentially running from edge to edge. In most tree species, this difference in orientation is significant and can mean that two boards cut from the same log look and perform very differently. For example, quartersawn

boards are less susceptible to splitting and warping during the drying process than backsawn boards and move less in use (as flooring or furniture) in reponse to changes in humidity. This is due to differences in radial and tangential shrinkage. From freshly cut green timber, Messmate has a tangential shrinkage (along the growth rings) of about eleven percent and a radial shrinkage of five percent.[4] As a result, backsawn boards (which have a tangential face) are more prone to cupping and checking (the development of fine splits) as they dry, than quartersawn boards which have a radial face.

Once dry, timber will continue to swell and shrink with changes in humidity (as described by the unit tangential movement of a species, which is the percentage dimensional change in the wood for a one percent change in moisture content).[5] The humidity inside our houses and offices can vary from twenty-five percent to more than eighty percent over the course of a normal year, particularly in coastal areas, leading to changes in the moisture content of dry timber from about eight to sixteen percent. This means that a one-metre-wide solid table top made up of backsawn Messmate Stringybark (which has a unit tangential movement of 0.36 %) could vary in width by as much as thirty millimetres over the course of the seasons whereas, if the boards were all quartersawn, movement would be less than half that. Because the shrinkage rates are unequal on each face, a backsawn board will also be more prone to cupping, whereas a quartersawn board will remain flat. No amount of clamping and nailing will prevent the boards from moving—if it did, then the timber would split—which is why it is important to design both floors and furniture to allow for this movement.

Many of the boards in Ian's Messmate Stringybark were perfectly clean—free of branch knots, rot or other defects—but some contained kino veins. Local Otway craftsman, Robert Marr, makes a feature of kino veins in his line of Messmate Stringybark art deco furniture. I invited him over to have a look at our air-dried timber. He had never used young fast-grown planted eucalypt timber before and I was keen to get his feedback, and to see a piece of furniture made out of our timber for sale in the local gallery.

To complement our farm-grown Messmate Stringybark, Robert also

left: Ian's Messmate Stringybark log ready to mill. You can see the darker brown heartwood and fine rings of kino.

centre: I milled the Messmate Stringybark into quartersawn boards and air-dried them for more than a year.

right: Robert Marr used the timber, along with some London Plane (drawer fronts) and Black Walnut (handles), to make a coffee table. Image courtesy of Robert Marr.

took some boards of London Plane (*Platanus orientalis var. acerifolia*) that I'd milled from a log rescued from the chipper by a forester working for the Melbourne City Council. The London Plane can grow into a huge tree if it's given space so it is quite common for healthy specimens to be removed in urban areas. In Europe, the timber of the London Plane is called Lacewood. The heartwood is a creamy white colour with large medullary ray cells that give it a beautiful grain.

He used the Messmate for the structure and the Lacewood for the drawer fronts. Robert reported that the timber of both species dried and dressed well. 'Do you have some Black Walnut for the handles?' he asked. I gave him two pieces I'd cut from one of our twenty-eight-year-old Black Walnut trees (*Juglans nigra*) the previous winter. A couple of weeks later he sent through the first photos of his three-species, art deco coffee table complete with kino feature. Trees can live on through their wood well after they have died.

There is one Messmate Stringybark that I won't cut down. When Claire and I discussed buying the farm we sat under a large old Messmate Stringybark looking back over the eroded creek to where the house now stands. Back then the tree was strong and healthy but time has taken its toll. On one occasion, I was presenting the growth data from my spacing trial located beside the old tree to a group of students when, without warning, one of its huge limbs crashed to the ground. It was a hot dry afternoon in late summer, and there was no wind. Another lecture began.

As regularly as there are news stories of bushfires 'destroying' a native eucalypt forest (which, of course, is never the case), there are the tragic reports in the summer papers of people being killed or injured by a large eucalypt branch falling on them 'without warning' on a hot afternoon. The witnesses are always surprised: 'but there was no wind!' The local council, caravan park owner or government department might release a statement saying that the tree had been inspected by a professional arborist prior to the accident and there was no indication of any potential risk. It must have been a freak of nature or an act of God. But what if it wasn't either?

Mature eucalypt trees can pump as much as 500 litres of water on a warm sunny day out of the soil and up their stem and branches and out through their leaves. Faced with dry summers and regular droughts most Australian tree species have adapted means of controlling their water loss, such as the thick waxy cuticle covering eucalypt leaves that trap in the moisture. But the tree needs to breathe, drawing in carbon dioxide and expelling oxygen, to drive the process of photosynthesis. Energy from sunlight is used to break the chemical bonds of water (H_2O) and carbon dioxide (CO_2) thus allowing the elements to be recombined into a simple sugar (glucose: $C_6H_{12}O_6$) that can be transported around the plant to fuel growth. The waste product, oxygen (O_2), is released back into the atmosphere. The chemical reaction can be described as $6CO_2 + 6H_2O \ggg C_6H_{12}O_6 + 6O_2$.

Small valves (stomata) in the leaves control the release of water vapour and the flow, in and out, of carbon dioxide and oxygen. Yet, photosynthesis only uses a very small proportion of the water that the tree draws up from the soil. Most of it just flows through the tree, maintaining the turgidity of cells, transporting nutrients and sugars, and regulating temperature. The flow of water from the roots to the leaves and out through the stomata is largely driven by evaporation. As water vapour escapes from the leaf, surface tension and osmosis draw more water up through the saturated cells in the stem to replace it.

When the air around the leaf is very dry, the stomata close to avoid moisture loss, effectively shutting down the process of photosynthesis until conditions are more favourable. Similarly, if there is no moisture available in the soil, the roots will shut down to protect the tree from desiccation. Problems arise when the leaves continue to transpire despite the roots being closed, thus increasing the tension in the water columns within the trunk.

In some species, particularly those with fine pores embedded in a matrix of short dense fibres, the negative pressures (tension) in the water column can become so great that the water in the stem vaporises. Because vapour molecules lack the cohesive attraction of their liquid relatives, the suspended column suddenly collapses causing an implosion that sucks all the water out of a section of the branch.

This cavitation of the water column in trees is common and, if contained, has little physical effect on the tree. But what we witnessed in the old Messmate Stringybark was the catastrophic failure of the water column that fed a whole branch, causing the phenomenon European and North American arborists call 'summer branch drop'.[6]

In the two cases that I have witnessed there was a clearly audible dry cracking sound before the branch fell and, on inspection, the wood around the break appeared dry and corky, as if it had been both sucked dry and crushed. Both the branches that I witnessed fall were healthy and appeared to have been firmly integrated into the main stem. There was certainly nothing that I could see in the structure or form of the fallen branches or the surviving stem that might have warned of the impending failure.

My interest in the science of tree branch failure led to me spending a day observing the proceedings of the Victorian Coroner's Court. The case involved the death of a child as a result of the failure of a branch of a eucalypt in a city garden. While the lawyers, with the wisdom of hindsight, challenged the arborist who had assessed the tree as safe not long before the tragedy, my interest in the underlying plant physiology suddenly seemed a little too academic. I wondered how my own understanding of the science of trees might hold up in court. Being only an observer, I had the luxury of being able to review my understanding and change my theory, without consequences to anything more than my academic reputation. For the family of the victim, and the young arborist, there was only loss and regret, and a pain that would stay with them for life.

Our grand old Messmate Stringybark lost more than one large branch during the drought and now looks tired and worn. Trees don't have a natural lifespan in the same way animals do. There are no vital organs to wear out, they simply reach a point where they cannot recover from the successive battle scars. When continuing or repeated stress or decay occurs faster than the tree's ability to regrow the leaves, roots and wood cells that provide critical functions, it will decline, usually dying back from the highest leading shoots. But I can see signs of fresh new growth right at the top of our old Messmate Stringybark so I'm hoping it will survive for some years to come.

But it will die one day. So, in anticipation, I collect its seed and plant its progeny. Then, when the time comes, if I am still here myself, I'll fell the old dead tree and salvage some quartersawn boards from its weary trunk and dry them in our solar kiln so the tree, and its story, can live on, carrying with it our memories and creating new ones. Already, our old Messmate Stringybark has taken on a meaning for me beyond its physical presence, ecological values or the shade it provides. When it came to spreading my Mum's ashes, the old Messmate Stringybark was the obvious choice. For it was under its branches on a warm, still mid-summer afternoon in early 1987 that Claire and I agreed on a future; we would buy this farm, build a house, plant some trees and start our family here. An opportunity, a life, which Mum helped me to realise.

Rufous Bristlebird (*Dasyornis broadbenti*)

1   Joseph Henry Maiden, *Forestry Handbook Part II. Some of the Principal Commercial Trees of New South Wales* (Sydney: William Applegate Gullick, Government Printer, 1917).

2   Andrew Price, A *Shake in oak: an evidence review*, Forestry Commission Research Report (Edinburgh: Forestry Commission, 2015).

3   Ken James, 'A Study of Branch Dynamics on an Open-Grown Tree,' *Arboriculture and Urban Forestry* 40 (2014): 125–134.

4   Shrinkage rates for many Australian and imported timbers can be found in: Keith R. Bootle, *Wood in Australia – Types properties and uses, 2nd Edition* (Sydney: McGraw-Hill, 2005).

5   For figures on the unit tangential movement of Australian timbers see: National Association of Forest Industries, *NAFI Timber Data file P1 - Timber species and properties, Revised Edition*. 2004.

6   There is some contention as to the physiology of summer branch drop. The explanation I have provided may not explain all cases, but I believe it has merit with respect to eucalypts and oaks that unexpectedly drop healthy branches on a calm afternoon late in the dry season.

Quartersawn, backsawn and shrinkage

Craftsmen and builders may declare a preference for either backsawn or quartersawn boards because of the effect that the orientation of the growth rings in a piece of timber has on its stability and appearance.

Backsawn timber (as shown in figure 1), sometimes called crown or flat cut, is sawn so that the faces of the board are tangential to the annual growth rings. In practice, timber is regarded as backsawn if the growth rings meet the face of the board at an angle of less than forty-five degrees. **Backsawn** boards tend to have a wavy, cathedral grain on the face.

Quartersawn timber (as shown in figure 1) shows the radial surface of the log with the growth rings running from face to face. Quartersawn boards tend to show the growth rings as lines running along the length of the timber.

As timber dries it shrinks in length, width and thickness. The **shrinkage** in length is so small, less than 0.2 percent, that it is not important. However, the tangential (along the growth rings) and radial **shrinkage** (across the growth rings) are much higher (up to 13 %) and can have a bearing on how a piece of timber behaves as it dries (cracking and warping) and its stability in use with changes in humidity. Another important consideration is the difference between the tangential and radial shrinkage (figure 2).

For Messmate Stringybark, the tangential **shrinkage** from green (freshly sawn) to kiln-dried (12 % moisture content) is more than ten percent, whereas the radial shrinkage is less than half that (around 5 %). Because the length of the growth rings differs across a **backsawn** board the timber will tend to cup away from the side that was closest to the centre of a log (figure 3). In a **quartersawn** board the length of the growth rings is more constant so the timber will tend to hold its shape as its moisture content changes.

In practice, most boards are a mix of **backsawn** and **quartersawn** timber. In this case, it is the extent of contraction during drying and the ratio between tangential and radial shrinkage that will have a bearing on how the board behaves. Unless **quartersawn**, species that have a tangential shrinkage greater than about eight percent, or a tangential/radial shrinkage ratio of greater than about 1.5, are very difficult to dry without twisting and warping.

Table 1 shows the shrinkage rates for some of the timbers that I grow. Based on this information the only ones I would consider backsawing into boards wider than, say, 100 millimetres are Blackwood, Black Walnut, Spotted Gum, Coast Redwood and Poplar. All these have a tangential shrinkage of less than seven percent. English Oak and Silky Oak do have relatively low tangential shrinkage rates but, as I describe later, these oak-type timbers should be **quartersawn** because of their prominent ray cells.

figure 1

figure 2

figure 3

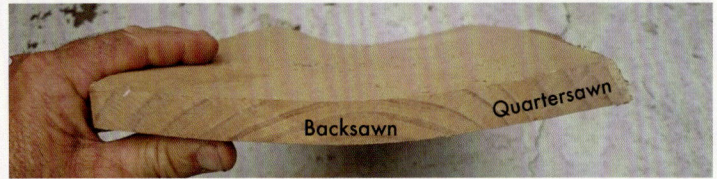
figure 4

The shrinkage rates for a range of timber species

Species	Radial Shrinkage (%)	Tangential Shrinkage (%)	Ratio of Tangential to Radial
Mountain Ash	6.5	13	2.0
Manna Gum	6	12	2.0
Southern Blue Gum	6	12	2.0
Messmate Stringybark	5	11	2.2
Shining Gum	5	9	1.8
Sydney Blue Gum	5	9	1.8
River Sheoak	3	8	2.7
Red Ironbark	3.5	7	2.0
Spotted Gum	4.5	6	1.3
English Oak	3	6	2.0
Poplar	2.5	5.5	2.2
Silky Oak	2	5	2.5
Black Walnut	3	4.5	1.5
Radiata Pine	3	4.5	1.5
Blackwood	1.5	4	2.7
Australian Red Cedar	2	4	2.0
Coast Redwood	1.5	2.5	1.7

Source: Keith R. Bootle, *Wood in Australia – Types properties and uses, 2nd Edition* (Sydney: McGraw-Hill, 2005). table 1

figure 1: The original orientation of backsawn and quartersawn boards in the log.

figure 2: The direction of tangential (along the growth ring) and radial shrinkage in timber.

figure 3: Backsawn boards will shrink more on the face closest to the outside of the tree. This will cause the board to cup. Quartersawn boards are more likely to retain their original shape when dried.

figure 4: A sawn board of River Sheoak that contains both backsawn and quartersawn timber. As it dried the part of the board containing backsawn timber warped whereas the quartersawn section retained its original shape.

Chapter 2

Blackwood

Acacia melanoxylon

I would dearly love to harvest at least one big Australian Blackwood that I've planted and tended myself. At first glance it seems achievable. Blackwood grows naturally, like a weed really, right across the farm and there are still a few big trees left up in our native bush. A reasonable-sized one fell over one winter so my son Tristan and I pulled its two-metre-long butt log out of the gully with the logging winch. It cut well on the bandsaw and the colour was beautiful: true to the rich chocolate hues that Robert Brown, the botanist for Matthew Flinders on the *Investigator*, drew on in his naming of the species in 1813 (in Greek *melas* means 'black' and *xylon* means 'wood').

The Tasmanian settlers just called it 'Black Wooded Acacia'. They loaded rough sawn boards into the hulls of the returning supply ships to test its commercial potential back in the motherland. Before there was any wool to export, wood was often used as ballast for the journey home, and that's how the strange dark Van Diemen's Land timber was initially accepted in England. It wasn't until the 1851 Great Exhibition at the Crystal Palace in Hyde Park that the Brits finally recognized Tasmanian Blackwood, alongside Australian Red Cedar (*Toona ciliata*), as our contribution to the world's premium furniture timbers. But even then, there was a problem.

Unlike the evenly coloured and predictably black African Blackwood (*Dalbergia melanoxylon*) being shipped in from Mombasa, our Blackwood was not always black. The official Great Exhibition catalogue lists a sideboard by cabinetmaker John Brown from Launceston with a note referencing the variability in the colour in the boards coming from across the island:

> *The timber of the Acacia melanoxylon is considered to be more deeply veined and tinted on the northern than on the southern side of the colony. It is called Blackwood in Launceston and Lightwood in Hobart Town.*[1]

Since then, subject to the fashion of the times, the variability in colour of our Australian Blackwood has been both its strength and weakness. That this variability extends to its performance in plantations makes Blackwood one of the most frustrating species in my farm tree catalogue.

Blackwood grows naturally from the Adelaide Hills in South Australia right around the southeast corner of the continent and up the east coast to the Atherton Tablelands, just inland from Cairns. In most areas, it is a nondescript bushy shrub with a rounded canopy, multiple stems and heavy branches that wouldn't provide so much as a candlestick. But, on the right site—with deep soils, fresh water and shelter from drying winds—Blackwood can develop into a good size tree with a large clean mill log. The tallest I've seen were in the native swamp forests of northwest Tasmania, just across Bass Strait from my home surf break. The largest I've measured were in a 100-year-old plantation near Rotorua in New Zealand, which I took as evidence that Blackwood could be domesticated. The Blackwood I grow is the one I know best, that which grows naturally in the Otway Ranges.

In the same year that I began my degree at the University of Melbourne my older brother Tom took up a walk-out, walk-in option on an Otway Ranges ridge-top dairy farm with a small herd of Jersey cows. I spent my weekends working with him on the farm and my weekdays learning about the tall Mountain Ash and Blackwood forest that once covered it. I got vacation work with the local government forestry office assessing logging regeneration, measuring pine plantations and labouring on the summer fire crew. But I also spent time with farmers, hearing their views about trees and forests and witnessing their passion for their place in the same landscape.

Paddy and Betty O'Connor were running their own herd of Jersey cows twice a day through their dairy on the next farm down the Wild Dog Road. Paddy welcomed my brother to the district and took on the challenge of

preceding page: Milling one of our fallen native Blackwoods on our portable horizontal bandsaw.

left: Blackwood growing under a canopy of Mountain Ash along the Otway Ridge.

right: Paddy O'Connor beside a native Blackwood he left as a paddock tree for stock shade and timber after clearing out the overstorey of Mountain Ash.

teaching him how to milk cows, build fences and cut hay. When I turned up from university, Paddy set about teaching me a thing or two about forestry as well.

For my lesson on Blackwood he took me up to a spur he'd cleared himself. I looked out across the lush dairy pastures, sheltered by scattered paddock trees, as Paddy explained how he had cut out the understorey and all the tall eucalypts, leaving the best-formed Blackwood to develop in full sunlight. Having spent his life in the hills, Paddy naturally knew of its fine timber. He also knew Blackwood as a valuable farm tree. It provided dense shade that kept the cows cool in summer, its tough bark resisted the most inquisitive heifer, grass grew well under its canopy and it didn't drop branches. In the gullies, Blackwood created a dense shade sufficient to suppress the introduced blackberry, and their roots suckered freely, which helped control soil erosion.

Also, while Paddy might not have understood the biochemistry, he knew Blackwood was a legume, just like the peas he grew in rotation with turnips to provide summer feed and rejuvenate his pastures. Legumes form a symbiotic relationship with *Rhizobium* bacteria, resulting in root nodules that extract nitrogen from the air and make it available to plants. The trees then cycle nitrogen rich organic matter back into the soil through their leaf litter and fine root turnover, which significantly improves soil structure and fertility.

The Blackwood trees that Paddy chose to retain had grown up in the shade of the Mountain Ash and would have been tall and thin with a long clear branch-free trunk when he finally sowed down his Rye Grass and clover. Given full sunlight and nothing more than shallow rooted pastures to compete with, the trees quickly put on more leaf and spread their canopy to take advantage of the extra resources. More leaf meant more sugars flowing down the stem and a dramatic increase in the diameter growth up the lower trunk. Fifteen years later, Paddy stood proudly in front of a tree almost twice his width, demanding I take his photo. He then told me about his plans to work with his son to rebuild the old farm sawmill. I sensed I was getting a lecture more valuable than anything I'd sat through at university and from someone who'd learnt from the bush rather than books. While the scientists were trying to domesticate the Blackwood to grow in plantations, Paddy had already tamed the wild ones.

My challenge in recent years has been to just get our Blackwood seedlings above head height. When we first planted seedlings in our bare paddocks we had no problem getting them up and going. But, as our tree cover increased, the wallabies moved back in. They love the feathery juvenile leaves and nitrogen-rich phyllodes.[2] For years, I struggled with how I'd combat the wallabies. Colleagues working in the plantation industry suggested I apply for a licence to shoot or poison them but I couldn't do that every year. Besides, at about the same time, my daughter Jessica's love of animals had led her to become a vegetarian, and she may never have forgiven me. Fencing out the steep hill country from wallabies would be both impractical and expensive. I needed a simple solution that I could use repeatedly to get my Blackwood seedlings safely up above browsing height.

During our European backpacking trip, I'd seen four-foot-tall tubes made of UV-stabilised corflute supported by one-inch wooden stakes being used to protect English Oak seedlings from sheep and deer. I'd got a few from the Australian importer for a trial but found that they weren't ideal for Blackwood. The problem was one of stability: oaks grow slowly in height and the stem hardens off and becomes woody each winter, making them stable. My Blackwoods growing in the tubes remained soft and limp and their growing tips were often damaged by the wind as they emerged out the top of the rigid tube. The same seedling growing without a tall rigid guard, which effectively acts like a stake holding the tree upright, would be able to sway in the wind. This movement encourages thickening of the stem through a physiological process known as thigmomorphogenesis, which makes the stem more stable. There were other challenges too. Sheep rubbed on the rigid guards and they were knocked around by kangaroos and wallabies so I was continually straightening them up. I also found a few dead birds that had gotten trapped when they chased insects down the tubes.

I needed a tall guard that would move a little in the wind so that the seedling could naturally develop a more stable trunk. If it had a soft edge at the top it wouldn't damage the tender shoots as they emerged out of the tube. A flexible guard would be of little value to sheep as a rubbing post and would bounce back upright if knocked. And, it had to be cost effective and easy to construct.

I settled on a design that used a 1.2 metre length of plastic sleeve (with a 13 centimetre diameter when open), which I purchase in a continuous roll and cut to length. I support the sleeve with a 2 metre length of 20 millimetre diameter electrical conduit that is pushed into the damp soil about 50 centimetres deep, right beside the seedling. Three cable ties pushed through the plastic and around the conduit at the top, bottom and middle hold the sleeve in place. Unlike the rigid corflute, the light plastic doesn't provide a perch for small birds and I am yet to find one trapped in the sleeve.

I've developed my design further in response to a few issues. For example, if the seedling is very small I might add a short stick on the opposite side, just to hold the plastic sleeve away from the stem and guide it up the tube. For the post, I now use an 8 millimetre diameter fiberglass rod which is easier to push into dry gound. We have also lost some seedlings in the sleeves due to excessive heat so I now try to ensure that there is a small gap at the bottom to allow cool air to be drawn in and up the sleeve on a hot day.

Although regular inspections are required, particularly on windy sites, I have found the guard to be effective for many species. The notable exceptions are some of the eucalypts like Shining Gum (*Eucalyptus nitens*), whose fleshy blue juvenile leaves are particularly susceptible to fungal attack, or those species with very large leaves that clog up the tube, blocking the natural cooling mechanism, such as London Plane.

left: Blackwood seedlings developing in my flexible tree guard. Soon after planting (left), and after two years (right).

opposite: I know it is possible to grow large Blackwoods on farms. This plantation on a farm in New Zealand is just 20 years old. The tree has a diameter of 52.5 cm and the basal area of the plantation is 18 m²/ha.

Blackwood loves the humid environment inside the sleeves and shoots out the top within a few months after planting. Once the seedlings are about two metres tall they will have developed their own stability so I can remove and reuse the post. I leave the plastic sleeve on the stem for another season to prevent sheep from chewing on the young bark but then take care to cut it off before it gets too tight. These individual guards allow me to plant Blackwoods without incurring the cost of fencing. Being able to maintain sheep grazing is an advantage as it helps to reduce the weeds and control the fire hazard. Because the guards provide some initial shelter from the elements, I can also spread the trees out more than you might in a conventional plantation, which offsets some of the costs. It's not a solution for everyone—they won't work on rocky ground for example—but without these guards I simply wouldn't be able to grow Blackwoods on our bush slopes.

When I cut down my home-grown Blackwood I'll use a standard tree-felling method that begins with cutting a scarf out of the trunk on the side where I want the tree to fall. Whenever I cut down trees or cut up logs, I find myself pausing to examine the various parts of the tree and how they all work together to contribute to the growth and survival of the living organism and the wide variety of products that trees provide us. This starts as soon as my freshly sharpened chainsaw begins to tear through the dry outer bark.

Tree bark is mostly made up of layers of cork cells, specifically produced to protect the inner bark and cambium from the elements. It also contains the remains of the cells that once formed the conductive tissue (phloem), through which sugars produced by the leaves flow down the stem. As the cork cells mature, their cell walls are often impregnated with a waxy substance (suberin) and their cavities filled with tannins, resins and minerals that enhance the durability and waterproofing properties of the bark. Though it will take only seconds for the chain to cut through the bark, the high concentration of abrasive calcium and silica will mean the cutters will have already lost some of their edge.

Bark itself can be a useful product. With no English Oak available, the first Europeans in Australia were on the lookout for a tree with bark that could provide quality tannin for making leather. While Blackwood was a credible candidate, the most promising species in southeastern Australia was the closely related Black Wattle (*Acacia mearnsii*), the bark of which contains about forty percent water-soluble tannin. Vegetable tannins are phenolic compounds with the special property of being able to precipitate animal proteins, making them useful for cleaning and preserving animal skins. The tannin is extracted by leaching the shredded bark with hot water and when the concentrated liquor is dried into a powder, the extract becomes a highly valued and easily transported commodity.

One old-timer in our area told me how, as a young kid growing up on the farm between the two World Wars, he used to make up bundles of freshly stripped Black Wattle bark and sell them to passing traders. By then the industry was well past its prime. These days we import tannins from South

Africa and China where it is still manually harvested from Australian Black Wattle plantations.

Neither me, nor my chainsaw, will notice the point when we sever the cambium layer of my home-grown Blackwood. The cambium is a thin band of living tissue sandwiched between the bark and the wood that produces new wood cells on the inside and bark cells on the outside. The type and number of wood cells produced varies through the growing season. During favourable conditions in early spring, high concentrations of carbohydrates result in the formation of the large 'earlywood' cells. But as the tree's photosynthetic activity slows during dry or cooler conditions, the concentrations fall, resulting in small thick-walled 'latewood' cells. It is the thin bands of dense latewood cells running between the thicker layers of earlywood cells that we see as growth rings.

In well-watered temperate regions, evergreen trees like Blackwood will produce one growth ring each year, making it possible to determine the age of a tree by counting the number of annual rings. Further north, in the drier inland areas or along the tropical coast, tree growth responds to rainfall rather than temperature so the same species can produce a number of growth rings in any year or, if conditions are very dry, maybe none at all.

If the cutters on my chain are set correctly, the saw will bite into the white sapwood inside the cambium and immediately begin to throw out large chips behind me. This part of the tree is essentially pure wood (cellulose, hemicellulose and lignin) with nothing in it that will dull my chain. The vast majority of the earlywood and latewood cells in the sapwood zone are dead and empty with small open pits that allow water and nutrients to move from cell to cell. Larger dead cells, called vessels or pores, link end to end to provide a pipe to move water quickly up the stem of the living tree. All trees also have cells that run horizontally. These dead ray cells allow nutrients and sugars to move back and forth from the cambium into the sapwood.

There are a few living cells in the sapwood zone. Their main role is to store energy in the form of starch. When required, the starch can be converted back into sugars to drive growth. Maple syrup is an extract of the early spring season sap flow of the North American Sugar Maple (*Acer saccharum*). The sugar-tappers simply drill a hole into the sapwood zone to release the sweetened water which is then concentrated into a syrup.

As I finish the base-cut for the scarf, the chainsaw will be about one third of the way through the trunk. So I'll be well into the heartwood when I remove the saw, place it against the bark higher up the stem and cut down on an angle to release the wedge-shaped biscuit, leaving a neat open 'smile' in the trunk. Then I'll put the chain-break on, rest, and review my work.

The heartwood of all trees is made up of cells that were once part of the sapwood band but have since been impregnated with various chemical compounds and crystals that give each species its unique heartwood characteristics and properties. The rich natural colours of the heartwood of Blackwood come from the tannins and phenolic compounds deposited into the

Cross section of 4-yr-old Blackwood showing the growth rings and the development of heartwood.

inner sapwood cells as they are retired from their role in storing carbohydrates and carrying water up the stem. The process of heartwood formation in trees is complicated, I don't fully understand it. But I am interested in learning about when and what triggers the transition from sapwood to heartwood and what I can do to influence the process—even the resulting heartwood colour.

When my Blackwood trees were just four years old, a small group of foresters visited the farm to see what I was up to. I explained how I expected to be able to produce furniture grade Blackwood sawlogs in thirty or forty years. 'You won't produce much dark-coloured heartwood in thirty years, the logs will be full of sapwood', said one. He had worked in native forest harvesting and had seen hundreds of Blackwood logs carted off to mills. By just looking at the end of freshly cut logs and counting the number of growth rings within the sapwood zone he could see that it took more than ten years before the colour changed. There would be no heartwood in my four-year-old trees and none for many years to come.

I'd seen the same native logs, but I had also gained some experience from growing Blackwood myself. I couldn't resist the temptation. Picking up the chainsaw and donning my helmet, I cut one of my perfectly good four-year-old Blackwood trees off at waist height. I then turned the saw upright and cut down through the centre of the stem to expose the full width of the trunk from its core out to the bark. It showed four clear circular growth rings and a band of dark-coloured heartwood in the centre that was more than three centimetres wide, or about a third of the total stem diameter. There were only two growth rings, or about two-and-a-half years' growth, within the sapwood band.

I pointed out that trees do not know how old they are. How they grow in any particular season and the wood produced simply reflects their size, shape, health and the prevailing environmental conditions. We all knew from our first-year plant physiology classes that the role of the sapwood was to move water up the stem and I put it to them that this function alone provided an explanation as to when a tree might retire the sapwood and convert it to heartwood. A fast-growing tree has more foliage and therefore requires a wider sapwood band to maintain an adequate supply of water. But, once there was sufficient sapwood for the task, a healthy tree of any age would begin to form heartwood rather than carry the cost, in energy terms, of maintaining an ever-increasing width of sapwood.

Regarding the colour of the wood, as the heartwood boundary moves outwards there is no opportunity for the tree to add any more compounds to the inner heartwood that could change its colour. Any further change in colour could only occur if the chemicals already present changed their form over time. Although I didn't know then what impact growth rate might have on the heartwood colour of my Blackwood, the hues in my freshly cut four-year-old sample were reassuring.

Early research reports from South Africa, where Australian Blackwood has been grown in plantations for more than fifty years, suggest that the darkest wood is found in trees growing on sites with a definite cool dormant season, high spring rainfall and deep organic soils.[3] More recently, Tasmanian researcher Gordon Bradbury analysed wood samples cut from sixteen families of Blackwood that were grown in pure plantations on two very different sites: one a high quality, well-watered krasnozem soil and the other a low rainfall site with poor soils.[4] He found no significant difference in heartwood colour between the two sites for trees growing in monoculture plantations. I was particularly interested in his finding that growth rate, per se, had no impact on wood colour or density. However, Gordon found that Blackwood growing amongst a dense eucalypt nurse crop did produce lighter coloured heartwood which may relate to increased moisture competition.

Genetically, the colour ranking of the sixteen families of Blackwood in the trial remained pretty much unchanged across the two sites, suggesting that we may be able to identify and propagate clones of Blackwood that consistently produce dark-coloured heartwood.

One of my graduate students, Jason Summers, took root cuttings from several naturally growing trees on our farm as well as from other regions, and at different times during the year, tested their vegetative propagation potential in different soil mediums. He found that root cuttings collected in autumn struck well in a well-drained nursery media containing vermiculite. I planted out some of the cuttings and we now have a little clonal trial of our own.

After fifteen years, as expected, the clones appear to have a very similar form and growth rate. I'll wait a little longer before I cut them down to see whether their wood colour is also consistent. In the meantime, I'm constantly

Blackwood guitar showing a fiddleback grain on the quartersawn face.

on the lookout for any Blackwood tree on the farm that has an interesting grain pattern, such as bird's-eye or fiddleback. Fiddleback is a tiger-stripe pattern resulting from a wavy grain and is best seen on quartersawn boards. Bird's-eye is a teardrop-type pattern that appears only on the back-sawn face. Imagine finding a drought-resistant, well-formed, locally-indigenous Blackwood that could be easily propagated from root cuttings and consistently produced clones with dark-coloured heartwood and an interesting grain.

With the scarf removed, I'll use the tip of my chainsaw to make two marks in the bark on each side of the trunk to delineate the hinge-wood I plan to leave. For a tree 50 centimetres in diameter, I leave a hinge about 5 centimetres wide between the scarf and the back-cut to ensure the tree can only fall one way: over the cut scarf. By placing the horizontal back-cut about 5 centimetres above the bottom of the scarf, I can ensure that the tree will not jump backwards off the stump as it falls. As I cut into the back of the tree, I'll watch the kerf left behind the saw carefully. If it starts to widen then the tree is beginning to move. If it closes on the saw it means the tree is leaning backwards and I might need to insert a wedge to keep it upright.

This final cut into the trunk of my large Blackwood will reach the centre of the tree and may even cross the pith. The pith is a ribbon of dead cells that runs up the middle of the trunk with offshoots that follow up the middle of each branch. The cells originate from growth that occurred at the growing tip as it passed that point in the trunk or branch, marking the biological centre of the stem circled by all the growth rings. The extent to which the pith is in the true centre of the trunk depends on how straight the main stem was when the

left: Our young pruned Blackwood. In the early years, the aim is to develop a straight branch-free trunk that can act as the scaffold for growing high quality timber.

opposite: The decline in the availability of large clean native Blackwood logs means farmers should have a ready market for farm-grown trees. This log was amongst the last of the sawlogs harvested from public native forests in the Otways.

tree was growing and the shape of its canopy. If, due to competition, shading, topography or latitude, there is more active leaf on one side of the canopy than the other, you might expect to see more wood growth on that side of the stem leading to the pith becoming more off-centre over time. This asymmetrical growth is common in conifers growing at higher latitudes, including in Tasmania, and can be used to determine which is the north side of a tree or stump.

In Blackwood, it is rare to find the pith running straight up the centre of a log because the leading shoot on the young sapling tends to wander a little and often dies back due to frost, drought or insects, allowing a secondary bud to take over as a leader. This will leave a kink in the stem that can be 'read' in the pith left behind in the log.

If the intention is to produce high-quality furniture timber, it is important that the pith is not included in sawn boards for two reasons: the colour, density and texture of the pith cells are quite different to those of the true wood, and timber shrinks around the pith as it dries so any piece that includes it is likely to develop radial splits.

With the back-cut complete all I will need to do is bang in a wedge to open it up a little and watch the top of the tree for signs of movement. If I get it all right, the tree will shift its weight over the hinge to the tipping point. The wood in a live tree has a degree of flexibility not seen in dead or dry wood so the tree will bend over quite a bit before the weight of the canopy takes over. Once

it starts to fall, I'll move away to one side for my own safety. My Blackwood won't crash to the ground like a tall forest giant. The broad canopy of my open grown tree will offer a degree of wind resistance, slowing the rate of fall and cushioning the impact.

I've still got much to learn. Tree felling is dangerous and I sometimes make a point of quietly reading through extracts from coroners' reports of chainsaw fatalities, just to make sure I never get complacent. Using my tractor driven logging winch helps. I can tie the cable to a point about four or five metres up the stem and use the remote control to apply just enough tension to hold the back-cut open and pull the tree over the hinge so I don't need to bang in wedges and I can stand well back as the tree falls. I also try to follow the advice I got from an experienced eucalypt faller and sawmiller in New Zealand. He told me that, even after years of experience, he puts his chainsaw down after every tree and takes a moment to inspect the cut stump so he can carefully replay the fall in his mind.

Once the tree is safely on the ground I'll cut a high-value sawlog out of the branch-free trunk and extract any small sawlogs from within the canopy that might be worth milling into craftwood or even woodturning blocks. Then, depending on where it lies, I'll either clean up the branches for firewood or leave them on the ground to provide wildlife habitat and slowly decay. In a forest, nothing is ever wasted.

I am looking at other species of wattle that might be better suited to our warming climate. There are more than 800 species of Acacia in Australia but only a handful get large enough to be regarded as useful for sawn timber. River Cooba (*Acacia stenophylla*) can grow into a substantial tree in semi-arid regions

Hickory Wattle—a drought tolerant alternative to Blackwood.

of the Riverina in New South Wales and has established well on our farm, but I don't really know how a low-rainfall species will adapt to our humid conditions. We'll see. And, though I'm tempted by the prices being paid for its lumber, I doubt it's worth the weed risk of introducing the Koa (*Acacia koa*) from Hawaii.

One Acacia that I am enthusiastic about, at least for now, has the encouraging name of Hickory Wattle (*Acacia falciformis*). It grows naturally on the cold, dry tablelands of southern New South Wales. I was introduced to the species by a tree grower from Yass, just north of Canberra, who supplements his farming income by collecting, cleaning and trading native seeds. When I visited his farm in 2005, John Weatherstone had already recognised the timber potential of Hickory Wattle and had established a small plantation from seed he'd collected from a promising wild population.

First, he showed me a sample of the dark-coloured timber, which looked to me just like a piece of Blackwood, and then we went out to see his trees. I was amazed by their form. The young trees had a strong central leader and small near-horizontal branches, almost the antipathy of the Blackwood I knew. The long sickle-shaped phyllodes were bluey-grey, suggesting an adaptation that afforded some protection from both frost and drought. I left with a small handful of seed and planted out my first seedlings a year later.

True to form, the trees look fantastic—tall with small horizontal branches. I cut open one of our larger trees to inspect the wood; it was beginning to form a deep orange coloured heartwood. In his 1917 *Forestry Handbook*, Joseph Maiden, the NSW Government Botanist, reports the timber is 'very durable and very tough' and adds that the trees, even on dry sites, are 'usually sound, and not attacked by grubs'.[5]

Planting a non-indigenous Acacia raises an ethical dilemma. Although the Hickory Wattle will not hybridise with the Blackwood, it will probably become naturalised. Knowing that we are changing the climate, what should we do? Persist with local indigenous species, despite the fact that we know they will be unable to cope with the increased moisture stress, or explore more tolerant species that fulfil the same ecological and economic niche? I guess, having planted Hickory Wattle, I have decided to adapt in the face of the changes that are beyond my control. I guess I'll learn as I go.

A year after I'd cut down the young Hickory Wattle, I noticed fresh shoots on the stump and more emerging out of the soil from the roots. Young Blackwood coppices and suckers like that but I didn't know that Hickory Wattle did the same. I've now guarded one of the shoots and will grow it into a new tree. I expect it will grow faster than a seedling, but we'll see. There is always something to learn when growing your own trees. I may have started with a dream of harvesting a large local-Blackwood sawlog that I had grown and tended myself, but I'm prepared to end up somewhere quite different. Such is the journey of a tree grower.

Gang-gang Cockatoo (*Callocephalon fimbriatum*)

1   London. Great exhibition of the works of industry of all nations, *Official descriptive and illustrated catalogue, 1851* (London: Spicer brothers, 1851).

2   Although all wattles have true feathery leaves when young, many, like the Blackwood, develop photosynthetically active phyllodes, which look like leaves but are more like flattened stems.

3   C.M. Harrison. 'The relative in influence of genetics and environment upon certain timber quality characteristics of *Acacia melanoxylon* in South Africa,' *Forestry in South Africa* 17 (1975): 23-27.

4   Gordon J. Bradbury. 'Environmental & genetic variation in blackwood (*Acacia melanoxylon* R.Br.) survival, growth, form & wood properties.' PhD thesis, University of Tasmania, 2010.

5   Joseph H. Maiden. *NSW Forestry Handbook Part II, Some of the principal commercial trees of New South Wales*. (Sydney: Government Printer, 1917).

The components of a tree trunk

The dry **outer bark** surrounding the trunk is made up of dead cells impregnated with extractives, including tannins, resins and oils, and minerals. They provide protection for the living cells of the inner bark, cambium and sapwood against moisture loss, variations in temperature, fire, insects and fungi. Some species, including many gum-bark eucalypts, shed some of their outer bark each year. Others like **Blackwood**, hold onto their bark, so, as the tree expands, vertical cracks tend to form along the trunk.

The **inner bark** provides additional protection for the cambium and includes living cells that produce a corky material, which fills the vertical gaps that develop as the tree expands in diameter. Within the inner bark there is a network of linked cells (the phloem) that allow the sugars, nutrients and hormones to flow down the stem, from the branches, to feed the growth of the trunk and roots.

The **cambium** is a thin layer of living cells sandwiched between the bark and the wood that produces new wood cells on the inside and new bark cells on the outside. Cambium growth results in an envelope of new wood being laid down over the existing woody stem within a thickening protective layer of bark.

The young wood cells produced by the cambium form a band of **sapwood** (the xylem). Most of the cells are orientated vertically and provide the pipe to transport water, nutrients, minerals and sugars up the tree to the canopy. Ray cells allow for the horizontal movement back and forth across the sapwood band to the cambium. A small number of living cells in the sapwood provide storage for carbohydrates that can be converted to dissolved sugars, as required, for growth.

The **heartwood**, often called the truewood, is made up of dead sapwood cells that have been impregnated with the extractives, such as minerals, tannins, oils and resins. This gives timbers their unique colours and durability.

The wood formed by the cambium when growing conditions are good tends to be lower in wood density (earlywood) than those produced as growth slows due to lower temperatures or a lack of moisture (latewood). The densely-packed cells in the latewood zone often appear as a dark narrow line, or **growth ring**, that separates the wider bands of earlywood. In temperate areas, it is common to have one growth ring laid down each year. This is not always the case in evergreen trees growing in a milder climate.

The **pith** is a thin thread of soft dead corky material that is close to the centre of the stem and surrounded by all the growth rings. Unlike all the other cells created at the cambium, the pith cells are formed at the growing tip by the apical meristem. In effect, the pith in the stem is the trace left behind as the tip of the tree or branch grew past that point.

Basic tree felling

Tree felling is dangerous and should only be undertaken by a trained operator. Different techniques are used depending on the size, shape, lean and location of the tree. To illustrate the steps involved I present a basic method of falling that may be appropriate for a straight, healthy tree.

The **scarf** is cut on the side of the tree where it is expected to fall and extends about one-third the thickness of the trunk. The opening allows the tree to lean over without being restrained by the stump wood.

The horizontal **backcut** is placed above the base of the scarf to ensure that the tree cannot jump backwards off the stump. It may reach to the centre of the tree and should leave an even strip of **hingewood** intact about one-tenth of the diameter of the tree. A wedge is often placed in the **backcut** to keep it open as the operator finishes the cut. When the chainsaw is removed, the wedge can be forced into the backcut to encourage the tree to fall over the scarf.

Chapter 3

Mountain Ash

Eucalyptus regnans

My brother Tom's dairy farm on the Otway Ridge was cut out of the Mountain Ash forests by settlers using nothing more than an axe and a match. One old-timer told me how his ancestors would half-cut all the trees on a slope then fell the biggest high on the ridge, setting off a domino reaction that would lay the whole forest to the ground. Any trees too big to fall were easily ringbarked by the fires used to clear up the debris. Some of the dead stags still stand as a monument to man's determination and Nature's great potential.

As a student of forestry I was fascinated by the great heights achieved by the Mountain Ash: the world's tallest flowering plant. I wanted to know how trees could lift water more than 100 metres off the ground and what factors determined growth rate and a tree's ultimate height. I had no way of knowing how old, or how tall, the Mountain Ash trees might have been before Tom's farm was cleared, but I could see that the branch-free stags left standing in his front paddock were much taller than the fifty-year-old regrowth forest that surrounded the farm. Based on the science alone, I have no doubt that the mild moist climate and deep soils along the Otway Ridge could have once supported the tallest trees in the world.

Records suggest that the tallest tree ever measured was a Victorian Mountain Ash. The 'Ferguson Tree' fell over in 1872 and is said to have been 435 feet, or 132.6 metres, tall. But it might be a tall story. The experts I trust tell me that the most credible record of the tallest Mountain Ash ever goes to one felled by a Gippsland farmer in the early 1880s, which was measured by his brother, a certified government surveyor, as being 375 feet (114.3 metres) long—the tallest tree not standing! That's less than the current record for the tallest living tree in the world, a Coast Redwood (*Sequoia sempervirens*) growing in a native forest in California called Hyperion, which was measured in 2006 at 115.55 metres by the American forest researcher and renowned tall-tree climber Stephen Sillett. But that's not to say that our Mountain Ash might not regain the title.

Tom Greenwood, the appropriately named arborist and former Australian Tree Climbing Champion, likes to spend his spare time climbing tall eucalypt trees, with ropes, and measuring them with a tape. With the first branch being more than 60 metres above the ground and a trunk diameter of over 5 metres, a giant Mountain Ash can't be climbed the way you might scale a branchy pine or shimmy up a coconut palm. To get a start, Tom shoots a fine line over a firm branch then pulls a climbing rope over. Then, using one-way

preceding page: I made this 'live-edge' timber table from one of our 25-yr-old Mountain Ash trees.

right: Tom Greenwood at home in the canopy of a tall eucalypt.

friction clamps—one attached to his foot and the other to his harness—he 'walks' up the rope to the branches. Once in the canopy, he climbs as high as the leading branches will allow then expands a telescopic pole, or even just a dead branch, up until it just touches the highest leaf. By dropping a tape down to someone on the ground he can get a near-perfect measurement of total tree height.

In 2008, Tom measured what was thought to be Australia's tallest living Mountain Ash. The tree was 'discovered' when Forestry Tasmania flew over the Huon Valley using aircraft fitted with Light Detection and Ranging (LiDAR) technology that captures a three-dimensional digital map of the ground surface and the top of the canopies. The data seemed to show one tree that was over 100 metres tall. Within a week Tom and Brett Mifsud, his tall-tree-measuring partner, were there to check.

While Tom scaled the tree Brett carefully measured the diameter at breast height (12.73 metres at a height of 1.3 metres) and, following the internationally-agreed tall-tree measurement protocols, determined the average ground level around the base. When Tom was as high as he was prepared to climb, he marked the trunk and measured the distance up to the tallest leaf. He then held the end of a 100-metre-long measuring tape and dropped it down to the ground so that Brett could take his measurement.

Until they could add the two together, neither Tom nor Brett knew whether they'd just measured Australia's only surviving 100-metre-tall tree. As he came back down to earth, Tom calculated what Brett's measurement would need

left: This mature Mountain Ash forest, in a closed water catchment near Melbourne, was killed in the Black Saturday fires (2009).

opposite: From regeneration to old growth. Natural thinning in Mountain Ash forests reduces the stocking rate from over 100,000 to less than 100 trees per hectare. From left: 3-yr-old regeneration, 65-yr-old plantation and native old-growth.

to be and was still about 50 metres up the stem when they started shouting the numbers to each other. Centurion, as it was later named, was 99.61 metres tall.

Tom and Brett still have hopes that Victoria might one day reclaim the title. In 2008, their search was focused on a small patch of Mountain Ash in a closed part of Melbourne's water catchment that was thought to have germinated following a wildfire about 300 years ago. Tom told me that Stephen Sillett was due to return to Australia the following year to measure the trees; he then invited me to join them. All summer I looked forward to watching them at work, but then, on 7 February 2009, the Black Saturday fires tore through the Wallaby Creek Catchment killing all the fire-sensitive Mountain Ash trees. There would be no record for Victoria, not just yet anyway.

When I finally got my chance to access the locked site, I walked amongst the huge dead stags towering over a new 'crop' of Mountain Ash seedlings. It was both eerie and exhilarating, like seeing the birth of a whale. I was witnessing a critical phase in the life cycle of one of the world's natural giants. Using Pythagoras' rules of geometry, I estimated that some of the stags beside the track were over 75 metres tall. Others looked much taller but on hearing the crack, then some seconds later the crash, of a falling branch, I decided against any further exploration.

The natural forests of the *ash* eucalypts wouldn't exist without fire. We even identify each stand of Mountain Ash and Alpine Ash (*Eucalyptus delegatensis*) by the year that fire killed the parent trees and triggered a new wave of regeneration. The fire creates an ash bed that makes regeneration possible. It eliminates competition, exposes the soil to full sunlight, releases locked up nitrogen and phosphorous, and sterilises the soil to allow colonisation by bacteria and fungi more suited to the sunlit conditions and less damaging to the seedlings. The fire also kills off the ants that would otherwise harvest the seed and the wallabies that might browse the seedlings. The tiny eucalypt seeds that give rise to these giants survive the intense heat within the safety of the dense woody capsules held high in the canopy. Death to the parent tree causes the capsules to dry and open, raining their seed down onto the prepared seedbed a few days after the fire, just when the ash has cooled.

    From the tens of millions of Mountain Ash seeds that germinate, about 100,000 seedlings per hectare might survive the critical first two or three years, giving an average spacing of about 30 centimetres between stems. This is when the real Darwinian struggle begins. Periodic measurements of even-aged Mountain Ash regrowth show how the number of live trees drops, quickly at first, down to about 3,000 trees per hectare by age ten, and continues to decline for the life of the forest. By age thirty there might be less than 1,000 live trees per hectare. Through natural attrition, less than 150 trees per hectare will survive the 100 years or so that must pass before any tree might reach a height that warrants a visit from a future Tom or Stephen.

    Over hundreds of generations, each with a selection ratio of more than say 10,000 to 1, evolution of the Mountain Ash has favoured the tallest individuals. What fascinates me most is that this process of survival of the fittest follows a very simple mathematical model that touches on one of the fundamental truths of biology, and possibly humanity: bigger organisms need

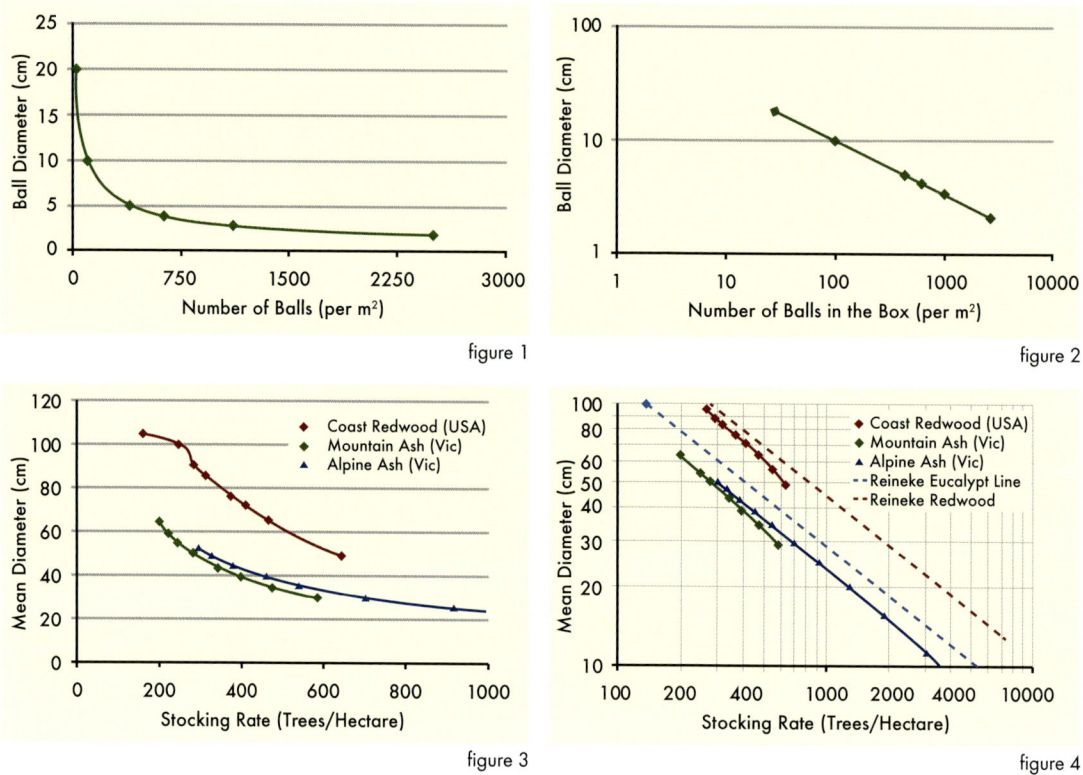

figure 1

figure 2

figure 3

figure 4

more resources—more space—so for some to survive and thrive others must die.

Imagine a shallow box exactly 1 metre square containing a single layer of tightly packed marbles, each 1 centimetre in diameter; the box would hold 10,000 marbles. If the marbles were replaced with five-centimetre-diameter billiard balls, the box would only hold 400. And so on. A graph of this relationship—with the size of the balls on the vertical axis and the number that would fit in the box on the horizontal axis—would show a curve that drops steeply at first then flattens out (see figure 1). There's nothing surprising in this except that if you convert both the axis of the graph to a logarithmic scale—in which each additional unit represents a tenfold increase in the size of the ball or the number in the box—the curve becomes a straight line (see figure 2).

The same linear relationship occurs in natural monoculture forests of Mountain Ash and Coast Redwood. If you plot the average trunk diameter, as an easy-to-measure proxy for total tree size, against the number of trees on a logarithmic scale, you get a straight line. Figure 3 shows data collected over many years from native forests of Mountain Ash and Alpine Ash in Victoria and Coast Redwood in California. In both cases, as the dominant trees grew larger in diameter, small trees died out, which resulted in a lower stocking rate.

In the 1930s an American forest researcher speculated that the gradient of the straight self-thinning lines in even-aged forests was the same for every tree species.[1] Only the position of the line differed, reflecting their relative tolerance to competition and the number of trees of a certain size that can fit on a hectare of land. For example, if the average diameter of the trees in a forest is 60

opposite: The relationship between the size of a ball and the number that can fit in a square metre shown on a regular graph (figure 1) and a logarithmic graph (figure 2). Real measurements of the average tree diameter and stocking of trees growing in natural forests show a similar pattern (figure 3 and 4). Source: Eucalypts[2], Coast Redwood[3].

right: Over-mature Mountain Ash lose their tops.

centimetres, the maximum number of live Mountain Ash trees that could fit on a hectare appears to be about 220 whereas if the trees were Coast Redwoods the maximum stocking would be over 500 (see figure 4). In effect, each Mountain Ash tree needs more than twice as much space as a Coast Redwood of the same diameter.

We also know that soil quality and climate have no bearing on the number of trees of a certain diameter that can fit on a hectare of land. Naturally, the deeper the soils and the higher the rainfall the faster the tree will grow, but this will only result in them reaching their natural limit sooner.

If one of our Mountain Ash ever does regain the world title I don't expect it will hold it for long. Just as they approach their maximum height, the tall eucalypts invariably become unstable and lose their top 30 or 40 metres. They survive by throwing out a mass of new shoots from the trunk, but these epicormic branches are poorly attached to the stem and have no hope of being able to carry the weight of a new canopy as large as the one that was lost. This is the final stage in a natural transition of the Mountain Ash forests from their tall mature phase to 'old-growth' status in which there might be only fifty huge-in-diameter-but-short-in-height topless trees per hectare.

Without what most people would consider a catastrophic event, like a wildfire, a massive landslip or, dare I say, logging, natural regeneration is impossible and the Mountain Ash will slowly die out, giving up their ground to the next phase in a natural succession. In the Otway Ranges this is a temperate rainforest, dominated by Blackwood and Myrtle Beech (*Lophozonia*

Heartwood

top: Our sheep grazing between our 2-yr-old Mountain Ash.

bottom: This photo was taken in 1992 when our Mountain Ash were 5-yrs-old. At the time, I didn't have a harness for high-pruning. I would not recommend this technique. Image courtesy of Andrew Campbell.

opposite: Our creek crossing in 2011 shows the large healthy 24-yr-old Mountain Ash just to the right of the gateway. It died the next year.

cunninghamii)[4], which totally blocks out the sun. In the darkness below, a new habitat is created and colonised by a suite of shade and moisture-loving animals and plants that have been lying low in the deep gullies awaiting their opportunity.

Mountain Ash was amongst the first eucalypt species we planted along our eroded creek. My aim was to mimic the native wet sclerophyll forests of the Otway Ranges by creating an overstorey of tall eucalypts for sawlogs that would shelter an understorey of slower growing native cabinet timbers like Blackwood. Though lighter in both colour and weight than most other eucalypts, the timber of Mountain Ash has the advantage of being non-susceptible to *Lyctus*, a tiny beetle that lays its eggs into the open pores in the dried sapwood of hardwood species. Pores, or vessels, are large open cells embedded in the sapwood that act as a pipe to move water up the stem.

When the larvae hatch they eat through the carbohydrate-rich sapwood before pupating and emerging through tiny holes in search of more unprotected sapwood. Heartwood is not affected because it contains no carbohydrates. Mountain Ash is naturally resistant because the pores in the sapwood are too small for the female ovipositor. This means the sapwood can be included in furniture and flooring without the risk of it turning to dust.[5]

Initially, our Mountain Ash grew well, even surviving the ten-year Millennium Drought. But then in 2013 following a series of record heatwaves, one of our largest trees succumbed. The first heatwave came in November 2012, resulting in the highest-ever recorded spring temperature in Victoria. That was followed by a second in early January when we registered the highest-ever

left: Milling our 25-yr-old Mountain Ash that died following the 2012–13 heatwaves.

opposite: This block of firewood shows how tangential shrinkage, around the growth rings, can cause radial cracks in timber.

minimum daily temperatures. But it was the third, in early autumn, which stunned meteorologists, farmers and tree growers. A special report on the heatwave by the Bureau of Meteorology stated:

> *Melbourne recorded nine consecutive days of 30°C or above from 4 to 12 March, all of which exceeded 32°C. This is the longest spell of days of 30°C or above in any month since records began in 1855.*[6]

When it died, at just under twenty-five years old, my Mountain Ash tree was 82.7 centimetres in diameter at breast height (1.3 metres) and about 25 metres tall. I left it standing for a year before felling. Once on the ground I measured my catch: The 6.2-metre-long pruned butt log had a large-end underbark diameter of 90.3 centimetres, a mid-log diameter of 65.3 centimetres, and a small-end diameter of 67.3 centimetres. That's right, the diameter at six metres up the tree was greater than the diameter at three metres. I call this the 'hourglass' effect and have seen it in many of our widely spaced pruned trees. It's caused by the higher concentration of carbohydrates in the sap flow at the base of the living canopy compared to lower down the stem, resulting in more diameter growth.

I made a conservative estimate of the wood volume of the pruned sawlog by using the underbark diameter halfway along the log. The equation for the volume of a cylinder is $\pi r^2 \times Ht$ (where π = 3.142, r is the radius in metres and Ht is the height in metres), which means that my log volume is 3.147 x

$(65.3/200)^2$ x 6.2 = 2.1 cubic metres (note I have converted the diameter in centimetres to the radius in metres by dividing by 200). The log was heavy and unwieldy so I cut it in two for milling. In total, the pruned log yielded 1.08 cubic metres of one-and-a-half-inch thick quartersawn boards, ranging from 10 to 24 centimetres wide and meant a green-sawn recovery rate of just over fifty percent. About five percent of the log would have ended up on the ground as sawdust. I would use the rest for firewood: this includes the 10-centimetre square core from the centre of the tree that contains the lower quality wood produced by the tree when it was young.

For drying I carefully stacked the sawn boards using 12 millimetre stickers to separate each layer. This allows air to reach the face of each board. By weight, a freshly sawn timber board can contain as much water as wood. The water is present as either 'free water' or 'bound water'. Imagine a paper straw full of water: the free water is that held within the tube that would simply drain out if released whereas the bound water is the moisture held in the paper itself.

Drying or seasoning timber involves extracting the moisture out of the wood to a point where the timber is fit for purpose. Firewood is considered seasoned when all the free water has been removed, leaving only water that is tightly bound to the cellulose fibres. This is known as the Fibre Saturation Point (FSP) and occurs in most species at a moisture content of between twenty-five and thirty percent.[7] As the wood dries below the FSP it will begin to shrink. Evidence of this can often be seen in the radial 'cat's-eye' like splits that form in the end grain of firewood.

I use an electronic moisture meter to check the moisture content of our firewood, particularly if I am selling it as 'dry'. Knocking two pieces together and listening to the sound can be just as effective. If the wood cells are empty of water the knocking sound will be clear and sharp, rather than a dull thud.

Mountain Ash wood is very hygroscopic: if left out in the weather it will absorb moisture out of the air. The heartwood of some of the other timbers we grow, such as the Sydney Blue Gum (*Eucalyptus saligna*) and Black Wattle, are better at resisting moisture uptake and can be stored out in the weather for longer. But then, it's just good practice to store firewood of any species undercover. I use an open-sided, clear plastic covered polyhouse which I load each autumn so I have dry firewood right through our cold wet winter months. This way I can get and keep the moisture content down to below twenty percent, which is perfect for burning, but not low enough for furniture-grade timber.

To achieve the highest value for our sawn timber I need to reduce the moisture content down to an even ten to twelve percent. Initially I expected I'd be able to do this by carefully air drying the timber in covered stacks, but in our environment, even after two summer seasons, I haven't been able to get the moisture content below about seventeen percent. It is also very difficult to air-dry hardwood timbers without causing cracking, warping and collapse.

Collapse refers to the flattening of the large thin-walled earlywood cells that lie between the dark growth rings, resulting in a 'washboard' effect across the surface of the board. It occurs during the early stages of drying when the cells are full of 'free' unbound water. I liken the process to sucking on that paper straw full of water: if you pinch the end a vacuum is created as the water is drawn out of the straw, causing the thin paper walls to collapse flat. The same occurs in wood when the free water is drawn out of the cells too quickly. The tall southern Australian eucalypts, including Mountain Ash, are particularly susceptible to collapse but it also occurs in many of the other species we grow, including English Oak, Coast Redwood and Poplar (*Populus* hybrid).

If the collapse is limited to the surface, the ripples can be planed off after seasoning without causing too much loss, but, severe collapse can reach deep into the board and create major distortions. Some sawmills treat their dry timber with steam to pop the cells back into shape. A few years back I milled one of our young River Sheoak (*Casuarina cunninghamiana*) and stacked the timber for air drying. When I opened the stack a year later almost all the boards showed some signs of collapse. To test whether the collapse was recoverable I put a small sample in a sealed plastic bag with a little water then placed it in the kitchen microwave. After about a minute the water vaporised and the cells popped back into shape. While reassuring, building a unit on the farm that would be suitable for steam reconditioning long boards would be difficult and expensive. Besides, reconditioning doesn't repair any cracks that may have developed. A much better option for small growers is to try and eliminate the risk of collapse by avoiding very low humidities during the early stages of drying that can induce high vacuum pressures in the wood cells leading to collapse.

I anticipated drying problems with our Mountain Ash so decided to fell and mill the tree in late autumn to avoid exposing the timber to the summer heat. I also draped black plastic over the sawn timber to maintain a high humidity within the stack. After a month or so, as winter set in, I removed the plastic and covered the stack with a roof of corrugated iron to protect it from the rain. This allowed the cool moist winter air to blow across the boards. By summer the moisture content of the surface of the boards was less than the FSP, which meant there was little risk of further collapse. My next concern was

left: Our new solar kiln ensures our timber has an even moisture content of between 10–12 percent.

right: I am using a moisture meter with strong prongs to assess the moisture content in the centre of a Mountain Ash board.

the development of drying cracks and distortion due to shrinkage as the bound water was drawn out of the cell walls themselves.

Small cracks, often called checks, occur when the moisture content of the outside of the board falls below the FSP and starts to shrink while the wood in the centre is still saturated. Drying timber is a balancing act. We need to establish a sufficient moisture gradient between the outside and the inside of the board to draw water out but not so great as to cause differential shrinkage. If the difference between the 'case' and 'core' moisture content is greater than about five percent, the difference in shrinkage can induce a stress sufficient to rupture the wood tissues. Rapid drying of the surface can also cause 'case hardening'. This is when the outer layers of the timber become so dry that they don't provide the continuous train of bonded water molecules required to draw out the moisture. Case hardening is common in very dense timbers, such as Red Ironbark, when they are air-dried in low humidity environments.

In our environment, with wet winters and very dry summers, I have been able to control the air-drying rate enough to reduce the risk of collapse and checking but I can't get the moisture content down enough to confidently sell timber as being suitable for furniture. So, I bought a kiln.

Timber drying kilns use added heat and humidity control to carefully entice the moisture out of the wood. While it is the humidity that determines the moisture gradient, the higher the temperature the greater the rate of moisture diffusion through the timber. I chose a kiln based on an insulated polyhouse. The kiln absorbs solar energy during the day, increasing the temperature of the timber stack, then cools down every night allowing moisture to condense on the surface of the wood. This helps equalise the moisture content across the board before the process is repeated the following day. Fans maintain air circulation through the timber stack while sensors and trigger switches allow me to control, to some extent, the temperature and humidity.

Our first load of timber in the kiln included my air-dried Mountain

top: We still have many large healthy Mountain Ash growing over an understorey of specialty timber species along our creek.

bottom left: In the winter after we harvested the Mountain Ash, I planted an Australian Red Cedar. This photo was taken in early 2017 when the seedling was two-and-a-half years old.

bottom right: I made this table from our Mountain Ash (breadboard end) and quartersawn Shining Gum (top) for our son Jarrod. The end board is fixed using dowels that allow the top to expand and contract with changes in humidity. At the end of summer the movement was about 6 mm (3 mm each side).

Ash along with some Southern Blue Gum (*Eucalyptus globulus*), Shining Gum, Messmate Stringybark, Blackwood and Black Walnut. It was the middle of summer and the temperature in the kiln would often rise to more than 50 degrees Celsius. Such temperatures would cause real problems if the timber was outside but, being in a sealed polyhouse, I could keep the humidity high enough to eliminate the risk of checking. Over a period of weeks I slowly reduced the humidity by changing the trigger point at which the automatically controlled vents exhaust the moist air and replace it with dry air from outside the kiln.

The result; stable, kiln-dried, quartersawn Mountain Ash timber from a tree less than thirty years old that could replace the timber used in furniture that is currently being sourced from 75-year-old native forests of the same species.

Back in 1987 Mountain Ash was considered a safe bet for our area. We didn't know then how rapidly climate change would affect our species choices. Neither was there much discussion about the potential role tree planting could play in locking up carbon. When it died, I could have left the tree to decay, returning its carbon to the atmosphere. But, I knew I could do better than that. By milling and drying the butt log, more than one ton of carbon dioxide has been locked up in furniture grade timber. For as long as the timber remains in service, the carbon is being kept out of the atmosphere. Even the firewood we produced has a contribution to make as a renewable carbon-neutral energy source that reduces our reliance on fossil fuels for heat.

A few months after I felled the Mountain Ash, I planted a new seedling beside the stump. It was an Australian Red Cedar from New South Wales. Whereas young eucalypts need full sunlight to grow, the shade tolerant rainforest tree is doing well under the canopy of the surrounding tall eucalypts. It is surprisingly drought tolerant. I'm now carefully pruning the young sapling and looking forward to harvesting, milling and drying its timber one day. Or maybe I'll leave it to the next generation to decide its future. Meanwhile, I'm still hoping that a few of our other Mountain Ash trees do survive and grow on to become 'old-growth'. Some of them are on track to reach more than 1 metre in diameter by the age of forty years.

Pied Currawong (*Strepera graculina*)

1   L.H. Reineke, 'Perfecting a stand-density index for even-aged forests,' *Journal of Agricultural Research* 46 (1933): 627-638.

2   C.J. Borough, W.D. Incoll, J.R. May, T. Bird, 'Yield statistics,' In: W. E. Hillis and A.G. Brown (eds.), *Eucalypts for Wood Production* (Melbourne: CSIRO, 1984): 201–225.

3   Gregory A. Giusti, Daniel Porter and Mathew Gerhardt, 'The Fritz Wonder Plot- -80 years of UC Forest Research.' Poster presented at: *A symposium for scientists and managers.* Pacific Southwest Research Station, Forest Services, United States Department of Agriculture. General Technical Report PSW-GTR-XX, 2011.

4   Myrtle Beech has recently had a botanical name change from *Nothofagus cunninghamii* to *Lophozonia cunninghamii*.

5   For information about the *Lyctus* susceptibility of the sapwood of different tree species see the Science and Practice section of the Red Ironbark chapter or Keith R. Bootle, *Wood in Australia – Types properties and uses, 2nd Edition* (Sydney: McGraw-Hill, 2005).

6   Commonwealth of Australia 2013. *Special Climate Statement 45 – a prolonged autumn heatwave for southeast Australia.* (Canberra: Australian Bureau of Meteorology, 2013).

7   For more on measuring the moisture content of wood see the Science and Practice section of the Shining Gum chapter.

How to grow tall trees

Height development in trees occurs at the top of the stem, unlike grass or bamboo, which push their leader up from below. If you bang a nail into the trunk it won't rise higher as the tree grows taller. The nail will remain at the same height and become embedded in the stem as the tree gains diameter.

In both natural forests and plantations, each tree species growing on a particular site will eventually reach a maximum height above which they can't grow any taller. This is due to the difficulty of maintaining a continuous supply of water to the growing tip. The tallest trees in the world, the Coast Redwoods along the coast of California or the Mountain Ash in the valleys of southern Tasmania, grow on deep rich soils in mild climates with high rainfall. Whilst we might be able to grow our trees faster in the early years, unless we can change the inherent soil structure and fertility, or substantially and permanently increase water availability through the drier months, there is little we can do as tree growers to make our trees grow taller than their natural limit for our site.

But we can ensure our trees grow to their full potential. I have often heard it said that to grow tall trees fast you need to plant them close together to 'force them up to the light'. Another suggestion was that by pruning the lower branches you can direct the tree's resources towards growth at the top.

Neither is true

Height growth occurs at the tip of the leading shoot, and each branch, where living tissue produces new cells, which then elongate to push the tip higher. When they die, these are the cells we see as the pith in the centre of the woody stem.

For a given species, the extent of height growth in any season depends on the light, temperature and humidity conditions immediately around the growing tip, and the supply of water, sugars and nutrients flowing up the stem. Even then, the sensitive leading shoot can die back if exposed to very dry or cold conditions or if the supply of water from the roots is interrupted. A new shoot may then take over when conditions improve. What growers can do to encourage height growth is improve the environment around the growing tip.

Trials examining the effect of plantation spacing on tree height and diameter growth show that trees do, indeed, grow taller if planted close together, but only up to a point (figure 1). I call this the mutual shelter effect. The presence of neighbouring trees increases the humidity around the growing tip and reduces exposure to damaging winds. Increasing the stocking rate above that required for mutual shelter does not increase height growth. In fact, at very close spacing competition for moisture can slow height growth. The same trials show how stocking, or particularly competition for light, affects average tree diameter. At high stockings, trees tend to grow tall and skinny whereas open grown trees can end up short and fat.

Because tree height growth tends to slow as the difficulty of lifting water to the growing tip increases, it is possible that trees initially affected by exposure will eventually catch up with their more sheltered neighbours (figure 2). The problem for sawlog growers like me is that the period of restricted height growth will result in heavier branching, which increases the time it takes to prune the tree. Cutting off the lower branches has no effect, either positive or negative, on height growth. This is also evident from the spacing trials. The self-pruning effect that occurs in a plantation at higher tree stocking rates does not reduce or increase height growth.

For sawlog growers, I recommend planting enough trees initially to provide mutual shelter then periodically thinning the plantation to maintain diameter growth. This will require close spacings on exposed sites. But, those planting in sheltered valleys or well-treed landscapes can adopt wider spacings confident that their young trees will grow as tall as they would in a dense forest.

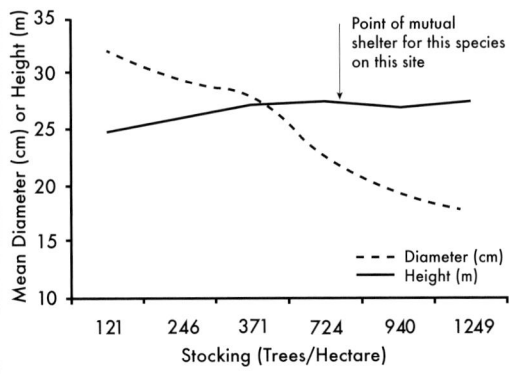

figure 1

figure 1: The effect of initial planting stocking rate on average tree height and diameter in an 11-yr-old plantation of Blackbutt (*Eucalyptus pilularis*) in NSW. Data cited in W.E. Hillis and A.G. Brown, *Eucalypts for wood production* (Melbourne: CSIRO, 1984): 189.

figure 2: Results from a Flooded Gum (*Eucalyptus grandis*) spacing trial in Queensland. At age 1.5 years, trees growing at a stocking of less than 1000 trees per hectare show signs of retarded height growth. By age 4.6, only trees growing at a stocking rate of less than 300 trees per hectare show retarded height growth. This suggests that the trees growing at the intermediate stocking rates have been able to catch up. Data from D.M. Cameron, S.J. Rance, D.A. Charles-Edwards, R.M. Jones and A. Barnes, 'Project STAG: An experimental study in agroforestry,' *Australian Journal of Agricultural Research* 40 (1989): 699-714.

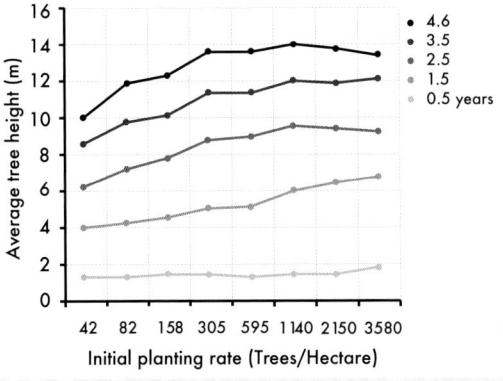

figure 2

Chapter 4

Coast Redwood

Sequoia sempervirens

It was snowing outside the community hall as a group of local farmers and I huddled around the fire pondering whether we'd go ahead with the planned measurement of the nearby Coast Redwood plantation. Mollongghip, near Ballarat in the central highlands of Victoria, is cold volcanic-red-soil country, potato country, *too good for trees* country! The native Messmate Stringybark forest was first cleared of timber to fuel the 1850s gold rush, but it was the need for food that stopped it growing back. For the early farmers, like the publicans and the prostitutes, there were riches aplenty in choosing to service the miners rather than be one.

The area produced another valuable product: water. With all the sedimentary soils being dug up and over for gold, the only sources of clean water for the burgeoning city of Ballarat were the creeks flowing off the red volcanic soils. But the problem there was farming itself.

The red colour comes from the high concentration of iron oxides, which, along with aluminium oxides, form strong bonds with the fine clay particles. This creates a deep, well-structured, stable, free-draining soil that has good water holding capacity. Perfect for potato growing. Following European farming methods, the settlers left their potatoes in the soil over the winter months, manually harvesting only what they could sell week by week. It was hard and muddy work that involved the whole family right through winter. It also increased the risk of erosion. After heavy rain the creeks ran red, filling Ballarat's new reservoirs with sediment.

The depth of the soils meant that the farmers were never too worried about losing a little off the top. They were being paid for the food they produced, not the purity of the water that flowed off their farms. The reduced life expectancy of the reservoirs, like the pink stains on the ladies' petticoats, was an externality—an off-site problem—something outside their immediate concern.

To filter the water the authorities began acquiring land around their dams and along the waterways that fed them, and planted trees. Exotics were preferred over natives because they provided less habitat for wildlife that might foul the waterways. The species that grew best were all American west coast softwoods including Douglas Fir (*Pseudotsuga menziesii*), Coast Redwood, Monterey Cypress (*Cupressus macrocarpa*) and what was then called *Pinus insignis*, now known as Radiata Pine (*Pinus radiata*).

Trees are broadly classified into two groups, hardwoods and softwoods, but the distinction is not strictly based on the density of their wood; the tropical

4 Coast Redwood

preceding page: By convention we measure diameter at 1.3 metres above the ground. Our largest 29-yr-old Coast Redwood was 80 cm in diameter.

right: The fertile, well-structured red soils around Mollongghip provide food and water. Trees planted along drainage lines by the water authority filter the runoff from farmland and control soil erosion (background).

Balsawood tree (*Ochroma pyramidale*) is actually a hardwood, while our tough native White Cypress Pine (*Callitris glaucophylla*) is a softwood. The terms originate in Europe and reflect the fundamental distinction between the oaks, which produce heavy, hard wood, and the pines and spruces which have soft timber. The true difference is in their biology: the conifers or cone-bearing trees were classified as *softwoods* while the flowering trees, including our hard eucalypts and soft rainforest timbers were the *hardwoods*.

With a seemingly endless supply of eucalypts, the early state government forest agencies began establishing softwood plantations to provide a source of light, easy to work, building timber. There are indigenous softwoods growing in all states but it was only in Queensland that natives were used: Hoop Pine (*Araucaria cunninghamii*) and, to a lesser extent, Queensland Kauri (*Agathis robusta*). In the south, the dominant plantation softwood is Radiata Pine from California. Coast Redwood was included in the early Victorian government plantation trials, but later rejected for being slow growing in its early years and too fussy with respect to soil and climate.

But timber was not the primary focus of the Ballarat water authority. For them, the Coast Redwood had a distinct advantage over the Radiata Pine; it was much more effective at controlling soil erosion. Our task for the day, if we could drag ourselves away from the fire, was to measure the plantation of Coast Redwood trees that was planted by the water authority in 1939 to improve water quality and produce timber. It was 2004; the trees were sixty-five years old.

left: The first signs of tunnel erosion are a series of holes in the topsoil linked together by a subsoil tunnel running down the slope.

opposite: As the tunnels grow larger, the surface soil collapses, creating gullies. This one formed under our planted eucalypts.

Ironically, on the driest continent on earth, soil loss and degradation due to excess water—waterlogging, runoff, flooding and rising saline watertables—continues to undermine the profitability and sustainability of our farming landscape. Almost every farm I have visited has some sort of water-related soil degradation problem. On our farm it is the erosion of the highly dispersible sodic clay subsoils, resulting in tunnel and gully erosion.

About thirty percent of the agricultural soils in Australia are sodic, meaning they have a high sodium content, and most of these are extremely dispersible when saturated. Tunnel erosion occurs when the sodic clay subsoils wash out from under the more stable surface soil. Eventually the subterranean tunnels become so large that the roof of topsoil collapses under its own weight, creating holes, then gullies, running down the slope.

You can test for dispersibility by dropping a dry clod of clay into a jar of water and just watching. A dispersible clay will slowly begin to break apart in a display of tiny explosions that send the fine clay particles into suspension. To confirm the diagnosis you can add a few drops of aluminium sulphate. If the soils are sodic the water will become clear within a few hours as the aluminium ions flocculate the tiny clay particles together so that they become heavy and sink to the bottom of the jar.

The dispersibility of sodic soils is due to an imbalance in the soil cations. Cations are positively charged elements and include calcium (Ca^{++}), magnesium (Mg^{++}), potassium (K^+), sodium (Na^+) and aluminium (Al^{+++}). Because it only

has a single charge, sodium forms a very weak bond with the negatively charged clay particles. When water is added, the bond can break, releasing sodium ions into the water and leaving the negatively charged clay particles to repel each other; hence the tiny explosions. Most gardeners are familiar with the concept of adding gypsum (which contains calcium sulphate) to heavy clay soil to make it more workable. The double-charged calcium ions form a stronger bond with the clay, enabling it to stay firm when the soils are wet.

Learning this, my attention shifted to what might have been the cause of the high sodium levels in our soils. The creek running through the next valley is saline, whereas ours runs fresh all year. Both catchments receive the same rainfall off the ocean which delivers a small, but over time significant, salt load. The original native forest would have transpired almost all the rainfall that percolated down into the subsoils. But the eucalypts and wattles only take up the water.

In the sandy clay loams, common in the next catchment, the salt remained as NaCl crystals. In our very fine clay soils, the negatively charged clay particles bonded with the sodium (Na^+–$Clay^{-ve}$–Na^+), releasing the chlorine as harmless chloride ions (Cl^-), which may have been taken up by the plants or just washed down the creek. The problem in the next catchment is that the tree clearing has increased drainage through the soil profile, dissolving the salt crystals and carrying the NaCl downslope into a rising watertable which is now causing dryland salinity problems along the creek. On our farm, the excess water steals the sodium ions back off the clay particles, causing the soil to swell and become highly dispersible.

In adjacent catchments, the same agent, salt, is causing two very different problems. Tree planting can provide a solution to both but maybe not the same trees in the same place. To search for a solution, I planted each of the drainage lines running down our sodic clay slopes with a different species. I tried Blackwood, eucalypts, Radiata Pine and Coast Redwood. Then, I waited and watched.

The eucalypts and pine grew fast and soon dominated their sites, suppressing the pasture. I fully expected the vigorous growth would dry out the subsoil and solve the problem. The Blackwood developed well enough, allowing good pasture growth between the pruned trees. The Coast Redwood were slow, very slow. But then I couldn't see what was happening under the ground.

I've since learnt that Coast Redwoods are one of the few softwoods that can store carbohydrates in an underground burl or lignotuber. Lignotubers are common amongst our dry-country eucalypts and can also form in some oaks (*Quercus* species), but only occur in a handful of softwood species. Other notable softwood examples are the ancient deciduous Gingko (*Ginkgo biloba*) from China and a couple of our own surviving Gondwanaland podocarps including the Western Australian Emu Berry (*Podocarpus drouynianus*).

Lignotubers are a survival adaptation that allows the young tree to regrow from the root ball if the stem is destroyed by fire or browsing. They even allow the tree to grow back after being harvested for timber. This means that when I do harvest my Coast Redwoods the root system will remain intact, continuing to hold the soil and providing me with a new tree. The fresh shoots will develop around the stump within a few months of cutting and all I'll need to do is thin them back to the strongest and straightest to grow into a new tree. I now know that the reason why our Coast Redwoods were slow to develop was that the seedling was putting energy into developing a lignotuber. After about five years our trees suddenly started growing taller and fatter and are now amongst the largest trees on the farm.

When the Coast Redwoods were eight years old, we experienced a very wet winter. Holes began appearing in the drainage lines under the pines and eucalypts and have continued to develop into deep tunnels and gullies. There are small tunnels developing under the planted Blackwood but they seem to be doing better than the larger pines and eucalypts. Of course, without a replicated trial I can't really make a definitive comparison. I did notice a few early signs of slumping under the Coast Redwoods but they never seemed to develop. What I've seen since has convinced me that the Coast Redwoods can control erosion of sodic clay soils.

Just last winter I went out during a heavy rainstorm to see what was happening under the trees. Below the eucalypts and pines, muddy water was pouring out along the base of the slope leaving a deep deposit of yellow clay across the creek flats. I followed the tunnels up the slope and could hear the

Coast Redwoods form lignotubers when they are young which continue to develop as they mature. I'm holding a 2-yr-old Coast Redwood seedling that has a lignotuber the size of my palm (left). Wade Cornell with an enormous lignotuber on one of his planted Coast Redwood in New Zealand (right).

water rushing below the surface as it worked its way around the thick shallow roots of the pines and eucalypts. But, less than 50 metres away under the Coast Redwoods, water was running clear across the surface. I dug into the ground to feel the soil. A deep dense mat of fine roots filled the soil profile, no tunnel could work its way through it.

What I couldn't see was what influence the tree roots might be having on the soil chemistry. As we know, sodic soils can be made less dispersible if calcium ions (Ca^{++}) are added to the soil solution. But rather than add gypsum or lime, the source of Ca^{++} can be in the soil itself (as calcite, a stable form of calcium carbonate $CaCO_3$), which is being held in an insoluble form. Plant roots add CO_2 to the soil directly as a byproduct of root respiration or via the decomposition of root exudates and added organic matter. Carbon dioxide reacts with the calcite releasing Ca^{++} into the soil solution thereby allowing it to replace the Na^+ bonded to the clay. Tree roots also release hydrogen (H^+), which assists in the process of breaking down the calcite.[1]

I don't know if this natural phytoremediation process is helping control the soil erosion under our Coast Redwoods. Maybe there is some experiment I can perform to test it. For now, I'm happy to continue planting Coast Redwoods to grow roots for soil conservation and trunks for timber.

They even provide habitat. On a number of occasions I have pushed the pruning ladder against the trunk and scared a Southern Boobook Owl out of the dense canopy. Although common, I have only ever seen the owls resting in our exotic trees. In summer, they like to spend the days hiding in the cool dense foliage of our English Oaks, and in winter, which is my pruning time, they move into the Redwoods.

For an Australian who is used to their red timbers—such as River Red Gum (*Eucalyptus camaldulensis*) or Red Ironbark—being hard, heavy and dense, Coast Redwood feels a lot like stained Balsawood. Its utilitarian value lies in its natural durability. In California, Coast Redwood has traditionally been used for decking, fencing, sleepers, bridge timbers, posts, shingles, doors, panelling, furniture and general construction. Concerns about the density and durability of timber from young trees may be justified. We do need more research to understand how genetics and management of Coast Redwood influences these factors. Nonetheless, the most important defect affecting the strength and value of plantation grown Coast Redwood is the presence of knots. Even in heavily stocked native forests in California, the Coast Redwood is very slow to self-prune. To produce clear knot-free timber from Coast Redwood you must either prune, or wait for it to occur naturally—in about 200 years!

  Fortunately, Coast Redwoods are fun to prune. The numerous small horizontal branches are easy to cut and the wounds heal over well. I prune all my Coast Redwoods annually to a stem diameter of 8 centimetres and continue until I reach a height of about 8 metres. The only problem is the prolific flush of epicormic shoots that tend to follow. If these are not removed in the next year or so they will develop into branches, negating any benefit to wood quality that pruning may have provided.

  Epicormic shoots are a common and natural response in many tree species, including many eucalypts, English Oak, Poplar, Black Walnut and Silky Oak (*Grevillea robusta*), and tend to occur following a sudden loss of leaf area due to fire, insects or pruning. The shoots arise from cells below the bark that can

left & middle: I took these photos during a heavy storm in 2016. Under the eucalypts the tunnels spewed out muddy water at the base of the slope. Under the Coast Redwood the water flowed clear over the soil surface.

right: We dug under the Coast Redwoods and found a mass of fine roots reaching deep into the subsoil.

opposite: I prune our Coast Redwoods to 8 m using ladders and a harness (left). Pruning does stimulate fine epicormic shoots (right). I remove these the following year.

differentiate into buds, either in anticipation of future canopy loss or in response to it. A common misconception is that the epicormic shoots arise in response to light reaching the stem when the branches are removed. Any stroll through a suburban park will provide plenty of examples of widely spaced trees with clear trunks fully exposed to the sun that have no epicormic shoots. Naturally, once initiated, shoots on the sunny side of the stem do tend to be longer and thicker than those that arise on the dark side, but light is not the cause.

In fact, to ask what initiates bud development is to miss the point. The real question is: what is it that holds epicormic shoots back, inhibiting their development on an unaffected tree? The bigger and healthier the canopy the less likely it is that any epicormic shoots will develop, suggesting that the suppressant agent must originate, or be derived, from the products of a healthy active canopy, including carbohydrates and hormones such as auxins.

In my experience, once the canopy has recovered from pruning the number and size of epicormic shoots drops off dramatically. In our Coast Redwoods this occurs two or three years after my final pruning lift. After that my focus shifts to growing an ever-enlarging canopy that can drive consistent diameter growth on the pruned stem.

The Mollongghip Coast Redwood plantation (planted in 1939) showing the large variability in tree diameter (left) and their relatively uniform height (right).

Back in the Mollongghip community hall we looked out through the frosted windowpanes for a sign. There seemed to be a gap in the snow flurries so we donned our wet weather gear and walked up to the plantation. Though less than a hectare in size, the reaction from the group on entering the forest was audible. Even an experienced bushman who has spent their life working with Australian eucalypts would never have seen such a sight. It is not so much the height of the trees but the sheer mass of wood. While the open canopy of a tall eucalypt forest lets much light through and allows a diverse range of understorey plants to flourish, the dense Coast Redwood canopy allows little natural light through and almost no undergrowth. The carpet of fine brown leaves, the high ceiling of dense foliage, the walls of heavily branched edge-trees, and the tall clean columns give the sense of being inside a large building. A Coast Redwood forest has a sacred ambiance, like being in a gothic cathedral. Or is it the other way around? Were the tall cathedrals of Europe designed to reflect the majestic nature of a towering forest?

We set up a rectangular plot in the 'nave', well away from the cathedral walls to avoid any edge effect. Our plot measured 29 by 30 metres, enclosing 0.087 hectares and the 33 live trees that would serve as our sample. By dividing the number of trees by the plot area we calculated that the stocking rate was 379 trees per hectare. The farmers then measured the diameter of each tree in the plot at 1.3 metres above the ground using a tape that converts the circumference to the diameter by dividing by π (3.142). Tree diameters ranged from 52.5 to 93.0 centimetres, although there was one tree within the plot that was just 37.0 centimetres.

To measure the height of the trees we stood outside the plantation, far enough back to get a clear view of the treetops. Using a clinometer and tape, and simple trigonometry, we estimated that the height of the tallest trees in that plantation was 40.8 metres. Irrespective of their diameter, all the dominant trees in the block were very similar in height except for a slight drop off on the exposed edge where the growing tips were being affected by exposure to damaging winds. Another burst of hail and snow had us scampering back into the cathedral for shelter.

The height growth of Coast Redwood, like all tree species, tends to follow a sigmoidal growth curve; starting out slowly then increasing, until the difficulty of maintaining the water supply to the growing tips slows growth. At some point the trees will approach a maximum height that reflects both their genetic makeup and, more importantly, critical site factors such as the severity of late-summer moisture stress. I went back to Mollongghip in 2015 and remeasured the height. I got the same result as we did eleven years earlier. The warming and drying climate may mean that the trees have already reached their limit.

Before we returned to the warmth of the hall we needed a measurement of bark thickness. Coast Redwood retains its bark for many years as protection against fire and disease. By pushing a penknife into the stem and feeling for the wood, we estimated that the trees had about 7 centimetres of bark at breast height, which would account for 14 centimetres of the measured diameter. If we ignored this when calculating the volume in a 70-centimetre-diameter tree, our result would be an overestimation of the solid wood volume by more than thirty percent.

Over lunch I crunched the data through a spreadsheet and presented the results back to the group: the average tree in our plot had a diameter of 71.2 centimetres, a height of 40.8 metres and a stem volume (assuming a conical form) of 5.4 cubic metres of which 3.5 cubic metres was solid wood and the rest bark. The total solid wood volume within our plot area was equivalent to 1378 cubic metres per hectare. This equates to an average of 25 cubic metres of wood produced per hectare per year over a 55-year period (and excludes any wood in the trees that either died or were removed).

To calculate how much CO_2 is stored in the woody trunks, we multiplied the wood volume (1378 m³/ha) by the bone-dry wood density of Coast Redwood (400 kg/m³) to give us the weight of wood (550 metric tons per hectare). Assuming, based on the chemical composition of wood, that half the molecular weight of wood is carbon we then calculated that the trunks held 275 tons of the carbon element. Carbon is traded in CO_2 equivalents so we needed to determine the weight of CO_2 that must have been sequestered to extract the 275 tons of carbon. The conversion is based on the proportion to which carbon contributes to the molecular weight of CO_2: C=12, O=16 so the molecular weight of CO_2 is 12+16+16 = 44. This means the weight of CO_2 that must be sequestered to store a metric ton of carbon in wood is 44 divided by 12 which equals 3.67 tons. Therefore, the 275 tons of carbon that was held in the woody stems of the Coast Redwood trees must have come from 275 x 3.67 = 1000 tons of atmospheric CO_2, and that doesn't include the carbon in the bark, branches, leaves or roots.

But then the amount of carbon we can store in a living forest has its limits and it can easily be lost back to the atmosphere if the trees are killed by fire or die. The only way we can increase the carbon storage of a forest that is approaching its maximum volume is to harvest some of the wood and allow the remaining trees to grow larger.

If half the trees in the Mollongghip plantation were removed and the logs milled for use in buildings and furniture, then (assuming a recovery rate for timber of 60 percent of log volume) 300 tons of CO_2 (1000÷2x0.6) could be locked up in timber immediately, while allowing the remaining trees to take up the growing space and lock up more carbon. Left as it is, a high proportion of the carbon in the forest will be lost back to the atmosphere, some of it in the form of the more destructive methane, as more trees die due to increasing competition.

Although most tree lovers are drawn to the Coast Redwood because of its height growth, as a sawlog grower, I've become more interested in its diameter growth. The trees in our Mollongghip plot averaged 71.0 centimetres in diameter at age sixty-five years, an average growth rate of just 1.1 centimetres per year. By comparison, my oldest Coast Redwoods, planted thirty years ago from cuttings derived from these very same trees, are only 28 metres tall but average 62 centimetres in diameter. If I can maintain these growth rates, then my trees will be approaching 50 metres tall and average over 115 centimetres in diameter when they reach the same age as the Mollongghip trees. But that won't happen of course, well not the height growth anyway.

Height and diameter growth are essentially independent of each other. You cannot extrapolate the early height growth rate of a tree into the future but you may be able to maintain diameter growth for decades to come if you control the competition between the trees. When I returned to the Mollongghip plantation with a new class in 2015 we set up a plot in the same general location as we had done back in 2004. The results suggested that the average diameter (74.4 centimetres) had increased by only 3.4 centimetres in eleven years, or just 0.3 centimetres per year. Clearly they had done better than that in the past or they would never have reached their current size. Was diameter growth going the same way as height growth?

I pointed to the edge trees to illustrate my point to the students: if diameter growth does slow down as a tree gets larger, how could the edge trees growing on the same site achieve more than twice the diameter of the trees inside the plantation? It must be competition, not climate, which was having an impact on diameter growth.

Repeated measurements of our own Coast Redwood show that their annual rate of diameter growth has been constant, and may even be increasing a little, over time (figure 1). At age ten the average diameter was 18.5 centimetres, an annual average increment of 1.9 centimetres per year. The average diameter is now 62 centimetres, which means that over the previous ten years they have been growing at an average of 2.3 centimetres a year.

To understand diameter growth in a living forest, whether natural or planted, we need to be able to measure competition. The simplest measure of *top:* In 1987, I planted rooted cuttings of Coast Redwood taken from the Mollongghip plantation. I used carpet as a mulch and protected the trees from sheep using electric wire rings. Shown here six months after planting.

middle & bottom: The same trees in 2001 (14-yrs-old) and again in 2017 (30-yrs-old). None of the original trees have been thinned.

crowding is the stocking rate; the number of trees per unit of area. But because big trees exert greater competition, stocking rate alone is not a very effective measure. Therefore, we need a measure that includes both tree size and stocking rate. Total wood volume would work but because height growth reflects site quality and is largely independent of competition, it would only be useful for comparing plantations of the same height. A more useful measure is the cross-sectional area of the stems at 1.3 metres above the ground, known to foresters as the 'basal area' (m^2/ha).

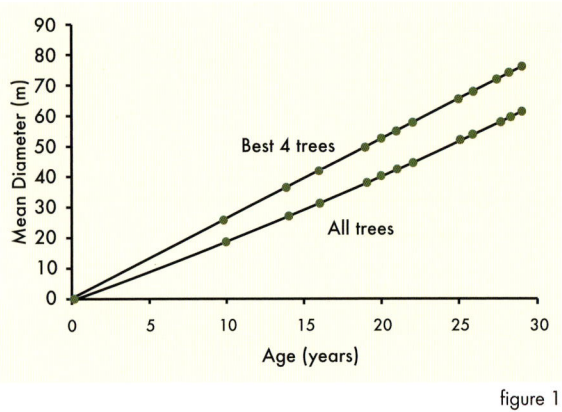
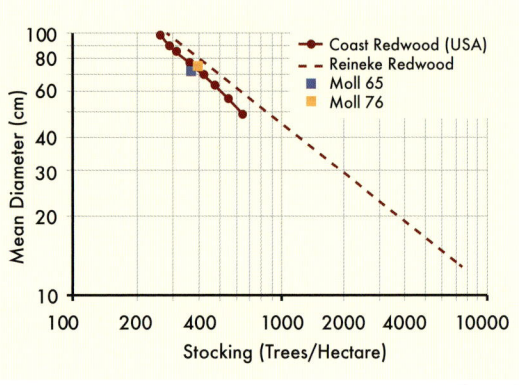

figure 1

figure 1: Diameter growth of our 1987 planting of Coast Redwood over 30 years.

figure 2: The self-thinning lines for Coast Redwood as suggested by Reineke[2] in 1933 shown against real data collected from the Fritz Wonder Plot in California[3]. I have added the measurements of the Mollongghip plantation at ages 65 and 76 years.

opposite: Grazing sheep under our young Coast Redwood helps control the fire risk (planted in 2005, photographed at age 12 years).

To visualise the basal area of a forest, imagine cutting all the trees at 1.3 metres above the ground—the basal area would be the surface area of the cut stumps per hectare. We calculated the total basal area in our sample plots by adding up the individual cross section area of each tree as calculated from their diameter at breast height: tree basal area in square metres = $(DBH/200)^2$ x π, where DBH is the diameter at breast height in centimetres and π =3.142. By dividing plot basal area by the plot area we can calculate the forest basal area (m²/ha). The basal area of the Mollongghip Coast Redwood plantation was 155 square metres per hectare at age sixty-five years and 173 square metres per hectare at seventy-six years. This is very high for any forest and reflects the ability of Coast Redwood to tolerate competition. I have collated data from hundreds of eucalypt plantations and none had a basal area of over 70 square metres per hectare.

To summarise: for each tree species there is a limit to the total leaf activity that is possible on a particular site—you might think of this as 'leaf carrying capacity'. In a fully stocked forest the available leaf area is shared between all the trees. The greater the stocking rate (trees per hectare) then the less leaf activity there will be on each tree and therefore the lower will be their rate of diameter growth.

In an earlier chapter I introduced the concept of there being a natural limit to the number of live trees of a given size that could survive on any site. To compare how the Mollongghip plantation was performing, I plotted our measurements against real data collected from repeated measurements in a high quality native regrowth forest in California (figure 2). This shows that the Australian plantation is growing very close to the natural limit of the species. If left unthinned, the plantation will behave like a native forest with the smaller trees dying in order for the largest to grow on. What is not shown is that at age 76 years the Australian plantation had a similar average diameter (approaching 75 cm) and stocking rate (about 380 stems per hectare) to the one-hundred-year-old native forest.

As a forest grows it approaches the self-thinning line by passing through several stages of increasing levels of competition, which correspond to reductions in annual diameter growth. If the aim is to produce large diameter

pruned trees in a healthy monoculture plantation, the stocking rate should be kept less than half the limit indicated by the self-thinning line. At this point the plantation will be close to fully-stocked so having more trees on the site would not necessarily increase wood yield. The growth would simply be distributed across more stems.

For example, if the average diameter of the trees in a Coast Redwood plantation was 60 centimetres, the maximum stocking rate suggested by the American research is about 500 trees per hectare. Aiming for about 250 trees per hectare would ensure a reasonable diameter increment without compromising volume production or tree health. To achieve a similar rate of diameter growth when the average diameter was 75 centimetres, the plantation would need to have a stocking rate of less than 200 trees per hectare. The secret to growing fat trees fast is simple; give them space so they can achieve their potential.

Southern Boobook (*Ninox novaeseelandiae*)

1   M. Qadir, J.D. Oster, S. Schubert, A.D. Noble and K.L. Sahrawa, 'Phytoremediation of Sodic and Saline-Sodic Soils,' *Advances in Agronomy*, 96 (2007): 197-247.

2   L.H. Reineke, 'Perfecting a stand-density index for even-aged forests,' *Journal of Agricultural Research* 46 (1933): 627-638.

3   Gregory A. Giusti, Daniel Porter and Mathew Gerhardt, 'The Fritz Wonder Plot--80 years of UC Forest Research.' Poster presented at: *A symposium for scientists and managers*. Pacific Southwest Research Station, Forest Services, United States Department of Agriculture. General Technical Report PSW-GTR-XX, 2011.

How much space does a tree need to grow?

Self-thinning lines for different species show how many trees of a certain size (as measured by trunk diameter) can fit on a hectare of land. This represents a biological threshold for each species irrespective of site quality or management. Adding fertiliser or water may make the trees grow faster and taller but there is nothing a tree grower can do to defy the natural diameter and stocking limits of a species.

When drawn on a logarithmic graph, the self-thinning lines are straight and parallel, their position differing depending on the relative tolerance of each species to competition. Drawing on others' research and my own measurements, I have estimated the position of the self-thinning lines for a few of the species I grow (figure 1). English Oak and Blackwood are less tolerant of competition than Mountain Ash which, in turn, needs more space than Radiata Pine. Coast Redwood can cope with very high stocking rates.

I use the self-thinning lines as a guide to determine how much space I need to provide my trees. Theoretically, there are four competition zones below the self-thinning line:

1. Isolation: where the trees are effectively growing on their own.
2. Mutually sheltered: where the trees benefit from the shelter provided by other trees but diameter growth is unaffected by competition.
3. Increasing competition: where individual tree diameter growth is being affected but total volume production per hectare is still increasing.
4. Full Stocking: where the plantation is producing the maximum volume growth and any increase in stocking simply distributes production across a greater number of trees.

Research suggests that the point of full stocking is at about half that indicated by the self-thinning line. To illustrate, figure 2 shows the average spacing between trees of 60-centimeter diameter, which would result in a fully stocked plantation. I often used this as a target when determining how many trees to leave after I complete my thinning and pruning to grow on into large sawlogs. Note, the spacing between trees does not need to be uniform although it is good practice to ensure there is at least half the average distance between any two trees to avoid canopy crowding.

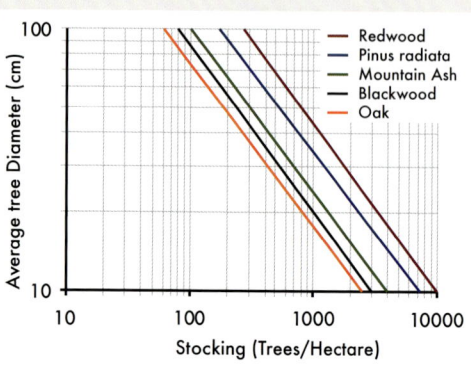

figure 1

English Oak: About 75 trees per hectare, average spacing of about 11.5 m

Blackwood: About 90 trees per hectare, average spacing of about 10.5 m

Mountain Ash: About 120 trees per hectare, average spacing of about 9 m

Radiata Pine: About 200 trees per hectare, average spacing of about 7 m

Coast Redwood: About 250 trees per hectare, average spacing of about 6 m

figure 2

figure 1: Self-thinning lines for some of the tree species I grow show their relative tolerance of competition. For details see my paper: 'Diameter–basal area ratio as a practical stand density measure for pruned plantations,' *Forest Ecology and Management* 233 (2006): 375–382.

figure 2: The stocking rate and average spacing of 60-centimetre-diameter trees that represents a fully stocked plantation. Increasing the stocking above this point will not result in a greater total volume yield per hectare.

Chapter 5

Australian Silky Oak
Grevillea robusta

At the conclusion of an international workshop on small-scale timber production at the World Agroforestry Centre in Nairobi we did a ceremonial planting of some of Kenya's more promising farm timbers in the grounds. It was 2004, seventeen years since that fated trip to Kenya that had led Claire and I to Bambra. I was now a father of three, a grower of thousands of trees and a senior lecturer at the University of Melbourne. As the only Australian presenter at the workshop I was invited to plant the Australian Silky Oak.

A few days earlier, the workshop field trip had taken us north, over the equator and into Kikuyu country, the heart of the East African coffee zone. From the back seat of the Hilux the countryside looked like an idyllic permaculture garden. Assorted tall tree species were integrated with maize, beans, coffee, potatoes, tea, fodder grasses, bananas, avocados, mangoes, pawpaw, macadamias and other farm crops. Chickens scratched through the understorey while dairy cows, pigs and goats in pens fed on cut foliage and food-garden waste. In this landscape, where it is the farmers who choose what to grow and all available ground is required for subsistence, the Australian Silky Oak is everywhere: amongst the food crops, around the homesteads and along the roadsides. I could also see it in the loads of fuel wood and fodder being carried on the heads of children, in the furniture being crafted in the village workshops and in the small private tree nurseries along the roadside. This species has become part of the Kikuyu landscape, embedded in the Kikuyu culture, and has been for so long that most Kenyans think of it as their own. One farmer noticed my interest in his trees and asked, 'Do you have Grevillea in Australia too?'

Silky Oak was introduced into Kenya more than 100 years ago by the British as a shade tree for their Tea (*Camellia sinensis*), Cacao (*Theobroma cacao*) and Coffee (*Coffea arabica*). All three cash crops were once rainforest shrubs and are particularly sensitive to frost, wind and direct sunlight. Having trees spread through the plantations ameliorates the climatic extremes, protecting the fresh shoots, flowers and fruit. But there are other, subtler advantages of growing Silky Oak that are well understood and appreciated by farmers. The abundant orange flowers, which fill the canopy each year, support a diverse range of insect pollinators, improving fruit set in both cacao and coffee plants. Silky Oak is partially deciduous. It drops its leaves during the dry season, providing a timely mulch that protects the bare soil from the breaking rains, and improving soil structure and fertility as they decay. They also regenerate freely on the red Kikuyu soils, can be easily transplanted, and recover well from pruning.

preceding page: High pruning our Silky Oak.

left: In 2004, I planted a Silky Oak in the grounds of the World Agroforestry Centre, Nairobi, Kenya.

right: Many farmers in the higher-rainfall areas of Kenya use Silky Oak as a productive shade tree in their food gardens.

bottom: A woman collects Silky Oak prunings from shade trees on a farm in Kenya.

The highland farmers continuously thin, prune and harvest their Silky Oak trees to control the extent of shade across the seasons and add new seedlings to fill gaps. As the dry season approaches, the farmers prune the trees to reduce moisture competition and expose the coffee or cacao plants to more sunlight as the fruit sets. Although the Silky Oak canopy naturally thins out in the dry season, many farmers will prune before this occurs to use the green foliage for animal fodder. Some climb the trees each year using rough ladders made of eucalypt or bamboo poles and cut the branches off close to the stem in a similar way to how I prune my own Silky Oak for sawlogs. It is far more

left: These Silky Oak on a farm in Kenya have been pruned to provide fodder and reduce shade.

opposite: Rows of Silky Oak planted to mark farm boundaries are now providing valuable timber.

common to see the lower branches hacked off with a panga (machete) about 30 centimetres out from the trunk, leaving a live ladder for the boys to climb each year. And, they don't stop pruning until they reach the top of the tree, leaving a tall spiky stump. Silky Oak tolerates this abuse and regrows hundreds of fresh lush shoots that can be cut for stock fodder in the next dry season.

My guide on our 2004 field trip into the highlands was Sammy Carsan, a Kenyan research scientist who was working on a project helping small farmers to manage and harvest their trees for timber. I was introduced to a farmer who still had a row of large straight Silky Oaks growing along his farm boundary. When he patted one of the largest in the row and smiled with pride I pulled out a tape and showed him how to measure the tree's diameter. We didn't share a

common language but it was clear that he understood that an objective measure of tree size might help him compare prices and negotiate a better outcome for his family.

Sammy's hope was that achieving a good price for their old Silky Oak trees might embolden them to plant more trees. He wanted them to trial some of the local indigenous timbers such as the Meru Oak (*Vitex keniensis*), which has a wood similar to Teak (*Tectona grandis*) but with the added attraction of

left: Local chief, Anthan Kiumbe, measures a 27-yr-old Silky Oak on a small farm in the Meru district of Kenya using the Master TreeGrower tape (59 cm).

opposite: In 2012, my 8-yr-old Silky Oak in the grounds of the World Agroforestry Centre was 26 cm in diameter.

an edible fruit, or African Cherry (*Prunus africana*), a recognised high value timber tree whose bark provides an extract used in both traditional and modern medicine to treat prostate related disorders. But none of the local species grow quite as fast as the Silky Oak.

I was back at the World Agroforestry Centre in 2012 and was pleased to see that my Silky Oak had grown well. I got out my tape; it was 26 centimetres in diameter in just eight years. A year later I was back in Kenya again to find it had grown another 4 centimetres in diameter! At this rate, it would be worth harvesting very soon. Back in Melbourne I'd taken down a similar sized garden Silky Oak and milled it into boards with good results.

The tree was growing hard up against a fence in a small suburban backyard. To get the log on the ground I had to begin at the top, removing branches and lowering them down with ropes, taking care to avoid the house, fence, pergola, barbecue and garden shed. The final cut dropped a three-metre-

long log across the back lawn with a thud. As it weighed more than half a ton there was no way I could move the log out to the roadside so I fitted a Swedish jig to my German Stihl 044 chainsaw and cut slabs off the log where it lay. The jig holds the chainsaw bar square as it runs along a straight edge. To get started on the round log I used a running board that I'd made from reclaimed hardwood flooring and fixed it to the side of the log with two large homemade wooden brackets and woodworking clamps. Using this guide, I opened the Silky Oak log with two right-angle cuts, providing a square edge on which I could then rest the jig for the rest of the job.

    Conventional chainsaw chains are designed to cut across the grain, not along it. For cross-cutting, each tooth is sharpened to an angle of about thirty degrees for speed and efficiency. But in this case, I used a specially prepared ripping chain that was sharpened to a ten-degree angle. It doesn't cut as fast but it leaves a much smoother surface. My ripping chain is also thinner and runs on a special narrow bar. A conventional chainsaw cuts a kerf more than 9 millimetres wide and, accounting for vibration, wastes nearly twice the wood of a regular circular saw blade on a portable sawmill (6 millimetres) and four times my band saw mill (3 millimetres). The narrow ripping chain has a kerf of just 5 millimetres and cuts more evenly.

The Silky Oak boards cut cleanly off the fresh log, like slices of ham off the bone, and within an hour I had a stack of 1½-inch boards that I stickered out to dry in the garage. Silky Oak is susceptible to *Lyctus* borer so I coated any sapwood with an insecticide and left the stack for a couple of years. It dried beautifully, without any warping or checking. I've since used the timber to make up a benchtop for the kitchen in our visitor centre, retaining the sapwood and bark to give it a natural edge.

The day after the job, Michael, the homeowner, who also happens to be a doctor, phoned to say he had developed a severe rash after cleaning up the branches. We each searched the literature in our respective disciplines with little success. A few years later I came across a scientific article from New Zealand published in the *Australasian Journal of Dermatology*[1] which reported on several case studies going way back to an explorer on an expedition to Queensland in 1847 who developed welts and blisters after carrying *Grevillea* pods near his skin. More recent cases involved arborists, one who developed recurrent episodes of itchy skin followed by oedema and formation of vesicles on his forearms, neck and face after working with Silky Oak.

The allergen was thought to be a phenolic compound that resembles the sensitising urushiols, an oily organic compound found in plants of the family Anacardiaceae, which includes Poison Oak and Poison Ivy (both American plants from the genus *Toxicodendron*). It seems I'm not allergic to Silky Oak so it was interesting to read that the reaction can develop after repeated exposure to related species, in particular, the ornamental grevilleas Robyn Gordon and Fuschia Grevillea. As it turns out, Michael has a Robyn Gordon growing beside his front path that I'm now very careful to avoid.

Chainsaw milling of a backyard Silky Oak in Melbourne using a Logosol Timberjig on my 044 Stihl chainsaw.

The common name of Silky Oak refers to the silky texture and prominent ray cells that the early European timber cutters noticed when they felled the unfamiliar tree in the dry rainforests of northern New South Wales and southeast Queensland. All trees have medullary ray cells. They run from the centre of the stem radially out to the cambium and have the role of transporting nutrients and sugars back and forth between the cambium and the sapwood. In most timbers the ray cells are too small to be seen with the naked eye, but in the English Oak the ray cells are very conspicuous and this led to the term 'oak' being used to describe the many species they found in the colonies that had a similar appearance. Ray cells are best seen on the face of a perfectly quartersawn board, where they appear as horizontal streaks. On a backsawn board the cross-section of the ends of the ray cells appear as narrow cat's eyes.

Despite being shaded on one side, the Silky Oak in Michael's backyard was growing straight. The leading shoot of any tree is programmed to grow either towards light (phototropic growth) or against gravity (negative geotropic growth). This directional growth is induced by the flow of hormones called auxins released in the meristem (the growing tip). In a phototropic species the auxins move to the shaded side of the stem, causing greater cell elongation thereby bending the stem towards the light. In the leading shoot of a geotropic species, the auxins are pulled by gravity to the lower side causing a horizontal stem to turn upwards. On a sheltered open site both types of growth will lead to a straight stem but if one side of a phototropic species is shaded, the leading shoot will bend towards the light, allowing it to explore for openings in a patchy canopy. Geotropic species tend to be more shade tolerant and simply push through any overhanging foliage. In seeking to avoid the many sawmilling problems inherent in leaning trees, I now search out geotropic species to plant in small gaps, or along the edge of existing belts of trees. I've found Silky Oak, Queensland Kauri, English Oak and Coast Redwood all work well.

Other than correcting the occasional double leader, the pruning of Silky Oak, like Coast Redwood, is easy because the branches are pre-programmed (by the same process as the main leader) to grow perfectly horizontal. This characteristic is often used in the horticultural sector to create ground-covering prostrate plants by taking cuttings from a branch of a geotropic species, including many of the flowering Grevilleas and even some conifers. Even so, growing Silky Oak for high quality timber has come with its own unique challenges.

I planted a few Silky Oak trees close to a large hollow-bearing Manna Gum. They grew well and I had pruned the stems up to about 4 metres before I noticed a problem. Something was chewing through the bark. Years before,

left: The locally endangered Sugar Gliders chew into the bark of our Silky Oak to stimulate the flow of sticky gum. The damage will affect growth and timber quality but that is a cost I'm happy to accept.

opposite: This dense monoculture plantation of pure Silky Oak at Thora in northern New South Wales shows no signs of any negative effects that might be attributed to some chemical toxicity.

I found a dead baby Sugar Glider under the old Manna Gum. In addition to eating insects and gathering nectar from flowers, Sugar Gliders feed on wattle gum to survive the winter. In our area, this would have been Black Wattle and I've included it in other plantings for this very reason.

It seems the Sugar Gliders prefer the gum of my Silky Oak. By chewing on the stem, they cause the sweet gum to bleed into large globules that they later harvest. One of the trees had been 'farmed' to the point that it lost its top due to being totally ringbarked. It survived by throwing out masses of epicormic shoots off the trunk. It won't be any good for timber now but I'm told Sugar Gliders tend to adopt preferential feed trees so I'm leaving it for them.

Sugar Gliders are a locally threatened species and an important predator of the large adult Christmas Beetles that menace our eucalypts. For now, I'm planting new Silky Oaks well away from any tree with hollows so they get a good start before the gliders find them, sometimes in mixtures and sometimes in monocultures.

A common criticism of conventional plantation forestry is that it involves growing even-aged monocultures, rather than mixtures of tree species

or age classes. Although there are native forests that tend to be natural even-aged monocultures—such as the Cypress Pine (*Callitris* species) forests of inland New South Wales, or fire-regenerated Mountain Ash—mixtures are perceived by many as being *more* natural. In the mid-1960s two eminent Australian rainforest scientists noted that native Silky Oak was only ever found in mixed species forests and hypothesised that one of the reasons for this was that it could not regenerate under its own canopy.[2] After some field and pot trials, Len Webb and Geoff Tracy concluded that the mature Silky Oak produced some type of water-transferable substance that inhibited its own kind while not affecting other tree species. They saw this as a process of self-exclusion that might explain the diversity of tree species found in many tropical rainforests. Unfortunately, their research has been used to argue that Silky Oak should never be grown in monoculture plantations.

Yet, I have seen many healthy and productive monoculture Silky Oak plantations around the world. There are also written reports from Hawaii, where Silky Oak was introduced almost 150 years ago, of extraordinary sawlog productivity in pure plantations.[3] One US Government Forest Service report that dates back to before the Australian research (1962) talks of a 44-year-old plantation that had a mean annual increment of 17.5 cubic metres per hectare per year, which suggests a total volume of 770 cubic metres per hectare! A later report (from 1982) provides measurements of another Silky Oak plantation that was carrying 490 cubic metres of sawlog per hectare at age forty-three years with an average tree diameter of 40 centimetres. These plantations are clearly very heavily stocked and not suffering any ill effects.

Just because a particular species tends to be found in mixtures in native forests does not mean it cannot, or should not, be grown in monocultures. I

left: A young Silky Oak growing straight up despite being under the canopy of a large eucalypt on our farm. I'll harvest the eucalypt for timber and allow the Silky Oak to spread its canopy.

opposite: The rich farmland on Mount Elgon, Uganda, is very susceptible to landslips.

plant Silky Oak in a number of configurations including in small monocultures and mixtures. From my own experience I have learnt that Silky Oak can grow reasonably well in dappled light under our tall widely-spaced eucalypts, despite the moisture competition. So, I am now under-planting some of these sites with Silky Oak seedlings, with a view to having a well-developed secondary timber option underway when I harvest the eucalypts.

    My argument is that there are many different ways to grow trees, and no right way. Farmers just need objective science and the opportunity to design, adapt and manage their tree plantings so that they best reflect their own needs and aspirations. It could save their lives.

In Uganda in 2010 more than 300 people were buried alive by a landslide on the slopes of Mount Elgon. While the scale of the event was unusual, landslides are a common occurrence on the deep fertile volcanic soils, particularly following heavy rain. Geomorphologists stress that it is wrong to attribute any landslide event to a single causal factor. Rather, they look for three requirements: firstly, an underlying susceptibility due to inherent factors such as the slope, soil

type and geology; secondly, preparatory factors that may increase the risk of failure such as clearing for agricultural development; and thirdly, a single event or sequence of events that actually trigger the landslide.

Mount Elgon experiences two distinct wet seasons. The wettest and most welcome rains mark the end of the big dry, and begin with uncanny regularity about 1 March every year—or at least they used to. I visited the area on 20 March 2012. The paddocks were ploughed but the rains were late, again. Farmers told me how the rains seemed to be starting later in recent years but once they did start they were as wet as ever. This meant it was harder to establish the crop and thereby hold the soil before it became waterlogged. Analysis of the data supports farmer perceptions: both seasonal variability and total rainfall has increased.[4] Some government officers, aid agencies and scientists have attributed the delay to climate change, but there may be another more local explanation: the clearing of forests around Lake Victoria.

The laws of physics suggest that a continuous cover of forest running inland from the ocean can increase the reach of coastal rains.[5] Sunlight and warmth drive the release of moisture from the forest, which increases the air pressure above the canopy and causes it to rise, drawing up moist air as it does.

Much of the interior of the African continent, including the area around Mt Elgon, was once covered in a dense forest that stretched westwards from the Ugandan/Kenyan border across to the Congo and over to the Atlantic Ocean. While the dry savannah plains of Kenya and Tanzania break the forest link with the Indian Ocean, Lake Victoria, just to the southwest of Mount Elgon, is effectively an inland sea. In the last few decades, clearing for farming has dramatically reduced the extent and spread of the moist forests across southern Uganda leaving isolated remnants concentrated in the more inaccessible areas.[6]

Changes in forest cover may also explain the twenty percent decline in rainfall that has occurred within my own lifetime across the agricultural belt of southwest Western Australia. Although climate change may be contributing, recent research demonstrates a link between land clearing and decreased rainfall resulting from southwest cold fronts.[7] Again, the vertical mixing of moist air above the forest was identified as a driver of rainfall. Just how much moisture the southwest eucalypt forest returns to the atmosphere was demonstrated by a clearing trial undertaken south of Perth that found the forest transpired ninety-seven percent of the annual rainfall compared with pastures that transpired just eighty-eight percent.[8] The difference in transpiration was 60 millimetres per year. Much of the extra water soaked down through the pastures and into the subsoils, causing the saline watertables to rise, further threatening farm productivity. Further inland the result was lower rainfall.

When the rains finally fall on the farmland of Mount Elgon, the ploughed fields quickly become waterlogged increasing the risk of landslides. Waterlogging induces a pore-water pressure differential between the surface layers and the less permeable sub-soils below, creating a frictionless layer between them. An explanation of pore-water pressure takes me back to the beach. When the tide was low we used to throw a plywood skiffle board onto the saturated sand then run and jump onto it. Our weight pushing down through the board against the saturated sand created a frictionless layer that allowed us to glide freely.

On the slopes of Mount Elgon the profiles are reversed but the result is the same. With no tree roots to bind the soil layers together, gravity takes over and the slope begins to move. Whether replanting trees in and around small farming communities can prevent future landslips depends on the degree to which the vegetation can alter the mechanical and hydrological processes that give rise to the problem. To anchor the slope, sufficient roots must grow across the boundary between the soil layers and bind them together. To prevent soil saturation, the trees need to be more effective than crops at drying out the profile at depth so that it takes longer to become saturated. Despite their fast growth rate and reputation for being aggressive water users, eucalypts were found to be less effective than Silky Oak at anchoring a slope because they tend to develop extensive shallow root systems rather than extend into the heavy clay subsoils.

But the farmers of Mt Elgon can't afford to plant trees just to reduce the risk of a landslide that may never happen. Unless they believe the trees can also assist in helping meet their immediate needs and aspirations they are unlikely to give up valuable land for the purpose. The World Agroforestry Centre and local partners realised this and introduced the Australian Landcare concept to local village groups around Mount Elgon. In its purest form, Landcare is about a community taking collective responsibility for land management with a view to protecting or improving soil, water and biodiversity, while also acknowledging the right of individuals to use their land for their own benefit.

For the farmers around Mount Elgon, Landcare is about food, housing and their children's education. Before Landcare was introduced, farmers acted alone and often in direct competition with one another. What they couldn't produce from their own land was gathered from the public forests that grew near the village. Government forest guards charged with the protection of the national park either failed in enforcing an impossible policy of total exclusion or, due to corruption or compassion, turned a blind eye to indiscretions. Either way the result was the same: a tragedy of the commons.

Grazing, firewood collection and hunting quickly degraded the park, undermining conservation values, reducing water quality and increasing the risk of landslides. Public land within the communities, including roadsides and creek lines, suffered an even worse fate, with individuals having as-of-right access to free graze their cattle and to collect fuel. Even on private land, the traditional land tenure system did not extend to protecting a farmer's right to their own trees unless they were food crops.

Allowing landless people or nomads to cut trees for fuel and fodder might have been justified in the past as a means of sharing natural resources and soothing social tensions, but, with increasing populations, greater freedom of movement, commercial markets and improved roads, these traditional rules erode any incentive a farmer might have to plant or retain trees for their own benefit.

Once the Mount Elgon community had agreed on local bylaws covering tree ownership, the Landcare group set about trialling a number of innovative land management practices including the pen feeding of cows, contour trenching and tree planting. They also worked collectively to support each other, particularly those families less able to act alone, including the landless who were most disenfranchised by the new property laws. I visited one community that had secured permission to set up collectively owned beehives within the national park, with the funds from the sale of honey and wax shared. They had also gained rights, under strict rules, to hunt game, collect bush food and allow landless families within their community to gather fuel wood and fodder from the park.

They told me how Landcare had changed their lives. In the past, many children would be held back from school to stay with the family cow as it searched out feed from roadsides and the native forest. With the stock moved into household stalls, the children were free to go to school while their parents fed Silky Oak prunings and farm waste to their cows. We visited a household who had installed a biogas plant that ran on cow dung with the methane being collected and piped into the house for cooking. The pressure in the biogas chamber pushed the spent dung out into channels that fertilised their food crops. This reduced the need for children to collect firewood from the forest and the risk of respiratory disease from wood smoke in the home. The gas could even provide light so the children could study after dark.

After meeting the villagers and walking through their homes, yards and gardens I found myself on the top of a hill overlooking the lower slopes

Landcare in action: collectively-dug contour trenches in a private garden, trap runoff and leaf litter while Silky Oak trees hold the soil. The trees are pruned for fodder and fuel and will one day provide timber for housing.

of Mount Elgon. There were Silky Oak trees on almost every farm but I found myself searching for some more tangible measure of how the widespread adoption of tree growing might have changed people's lives.

Suddenly the sun broke through the clouds and the landscape came alive with the twinkling of new corrugated iron roofs. If a family invested in a new roof it probably meant that they had enough to eat and were providing an education for their children. In essence, they had confidence in the future. Whether or not planting trees was the reason for this hardly mattered, trees were part of what they wanted for their future.

What I didn't understand was why they weren't also collecting rainwater from their new roofs to save the women and children having to cart it up from the creek, but maybe there is more to that issue than a bit of guttering, a downpipe and a plastic drum. As an outsider, I have learnt not to jump to judgement but to ask, look, listen and try to understand how and why farming families make land management decisions.

Agroforestry is not just about planting trees. There is always, just under the surface, a tangled web of physical, social and economic issues, mixed with technologies, past experience, prejudice and tradition. Though I couldn't articulate this when I first visited East Africa back in 1986, it was exactly this complexity that captured my imagination and set me on a journey into my chosen career. A journey that has taken me back to East Africa, again and again; each visit yielding more invaluable lessons.

Sugar Glider (*Petaurus breviceps*)

1   J.G. Derraik and M. Rademaker, 'Allergic contact dermatitis from exposure to *Grevillea robusta* in New Zealand,' *Australasian Journal of Dermatology* 50 (2009): 125–128.

2   Len J. Webb, J. Geoff Tracey and K.P. Haydock, 'A factor toxic to seedlings of the same species associated with living roots of the nongregarious subtropical rainforest tree *Grevillea robusta*,' *Journal of Applied Ecology* 4 (1967):13-25.

3   T.M. Resch, '*Grevillea robusta* A. Cunn.' In: Burna R.M., M.S. Mosquera and J.L. Whitmore, *Useful Trees of the Tropical region of North America*. North American Forestry Commission Publication Number 3 (Washington, DC: North American Forestry Commission,1998).

4   M.K. Kansiime, S.K. Wambugu and C.A. Shisanya, 'Perceived and Actual Rainfall Trends and Variability in Eastern Uganda: Implications for Community Preparedness and Response,' *Journal of Natural Sciences Research* 3(8) (2013): 179-194.

5   D. Sheil and D. Murdiyarso, 'How Forests Attract Rain: An Examination of a New Hypothesis,' *BioScience* 59(4) (2009): *341-347*.

6   J. Obua, J.G. Agea and J.J. Ogwal, 'Status of forests in Uganda,' *African Journal of Ecology*, 48(4) (2010): 853–859.

7   J. Kala, T.J. Lyons and U.S. Nair 'Numerical simulations of the impacts of land-cover change on cold fronts in South-West Western Australia,' *Boundary-Layer Meteorology* 138(1) (2011): 121–138.

8   A. Bell, 'Trees, water and salt – a new balance,' *Ecos* 58 (1988): 2-8.

Geotropic and phototropic growth in trees

The leading shoot of a healthy Australian Silky Oak tends to grow straight up, and its branches almost perfectly horizontal, resulting in an even pyramid shape. Coast Redwood does the same, even if one side of the tree is shaded. The reason for this is that the direction of growth of both the leading shoot and branches is guided by gravity. By contrast, the leading shoot and branches of an Australian Red Cedar and Blackwood will tend to grow towards the light.

Plants that grow in response to gravity are said to be gravitropic, whereas those that respond to directional light are phototropic. In both cases, the growth hormone auxin (essentially indole-3-acetic acid, IAA) moves to one side of the growing tip, resulting in greater elongation of the cells. For example, in a gravitropic species auxins will concentrate on the lower side of the leading shoot causing it to bend up straight. In the phototropic species they are moved to the shaded side of the shoot, causing it to bend towards the light.

Strongly gravitropic species are often very easy to prune because the branches are programmed to grow horizontally.

Geotropic growth explains why cuttings of *Grevillea* and *Sequoia* taken from branches tend to develop as ground covers rather than trees. I have also seen Coast Redwoods that have lost their top in a storm that never regrow a leading shoot and develop a 'weeping cherry' form.

For a shade tolerant species like Red Cedar and Australian Blackwood, being phototropic allows them to seek out a gap in a dense rainforest canopy. The result can be a crooked stem that has less value for timber. Fortunately, eucalypts don't cast a dense shade so both species can develop reasonably straight stems under the diffuse light of an even eucalypt canopy. The sun-loving phototropic species like eucalypts and Poplar are best grown in full sunlight.

The leading shoot of all trees exerts some degree of apical dominance over the lower branches, slowing their development or encouraging a more horizontal growth pattern. The agent of control is the ratio of two hormones; auxin (produced by a dominant terminal bud) and cytokinin produced by the roots. If the leading shoot is weakened or removed the ratio of auxin to cytokinin falls, allowing secondary buds to develop and compete for leadership. This can result in multiple leaders. If this occurs in any of our timber trees, I select the strongest and straightest leader and remove the others before they reach two centimetres in diameter. Acting early to correct a double leader allows the retained stem to grow straight, ensuring there is no kink left in the trunk.

Gravitropic Growth

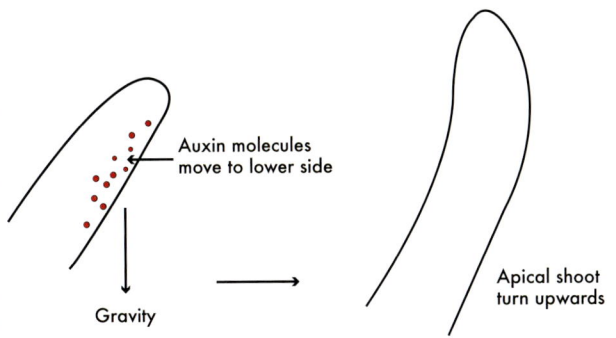

In gravitropic species the auxins move to the lower side of the stem increasing elongation of the cells, which causes the shoot to bend upwards. In phototropic species the auxins move to the shaded side of the stem causing it to bend towards the light.

Phototropic Growth

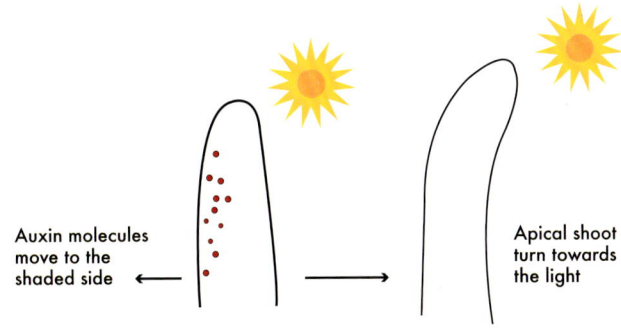

left: Blackwood is phototropic, allowing the leading shoots to bend in search of gaps in the canopy of this 35-yr-old plantation in New Zealand.

right: Norfolk Island Pine (*Araucaria heterophylla*) exhibits strongly gravitropic growth. The leading shoot always grows straight and the branches are close to horizontal.

Chapter 6

Manna Gum

Eucalyptus viminalis

Heartwood

On the evening of the 16 February 1983, I was on the south coast of New South Wales on my way home from a summer vacation job in the forests of Queensland. I was totally unaware of the devastation unfolding along the Great Ocean Road. Thirty-six hours later I was standing amongst the ashes of our beachside home. I could walk from room to room as it was laid out in the warm white ash. Everything was in its place: the free-standing brick fireplace, the remains of the fridge, stove and sink in a neat line, and the molten metal of the cutlery drawer beside a family-sized mound of powdered ceramic crockery. The house hadn't exploded; they rarely do in a wildfire. It just burnt down.

    The day before Ash Wednesday, and at the height of a severe drought, a blocking high pressure system stalled over the Tasman Sea as an impatient cold front pushed up behind it from The Great Australian Bight. The synoptic charts set the scene for a perfect storm. By midday the following day temperatures were over 40° Celsius, the humidity had dropped to less than ten percent, and a howling northerly wind was blowing down from central Australia. All that was needed to ignite a catastrophe was a spark. It happened in the dry grass not far from Bambra at about 2.45pm. Within minutes the fire had crossed the pastures and was into the foothill Manna Gum forests.

6 Manna Gum

preceding page: We have many large Manna Gum that I know are less than 80-yrs-old yet have hollows that are used by wildlife.

opposite: Our beachside house a couple of days after the Ash Wednesday fire (1983). You can see the pile of crockery beside the burnt cutlery which indicates that the house did not explode. The bikes were under the house.

right: Historic Chart Analysis at 11am EDT on 'Ash Wednesday', Wednesday 16th February 1983 showing areas with extreme fire weather. Image courtesy of the Bureau of Meteorology.

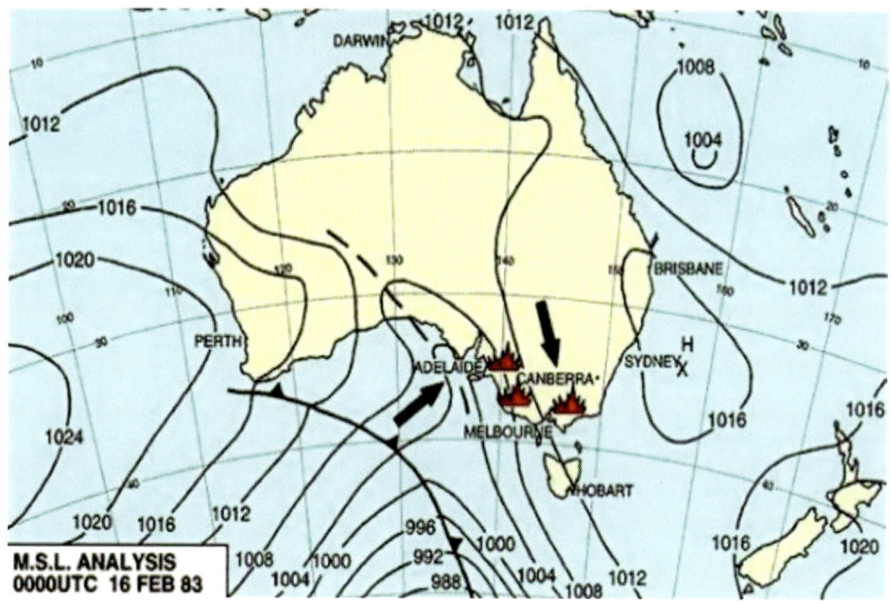

Supported by the heat of the running ground fire, the flames climbed up the Manna Gums' long ribbons of dry bark and leapt from canopy to canopy. Manna Gum leaves have a low ash and moisture content and a high energy and volatile oil content. This means they would have ignited quickly and generated a lot of heat, resulting in the rapid forward spread of the fire.

The updraft of hot air sucked up the burning bark and leaves into a rising convection column and rained them down on the drought-dried forest floor ahead, igniting hundreds of new spot fires. The radiant heat vaporised the oils in the eucalypt leaves well ahead of the fire front, releasing massive plumes of invisible vapours, which burst into flames high above the forest canopy. The wildfire would have now been generating its own wind, drawing oxygen back into the fire front from ahead and alongside itself. On the ground, the spot fires would have been burning backwards, against the northerly winds and towards the main fire, trapping confused wildlife and people as they tried to flee.

At 6.15pm, just as the spot fires took out a few houses on the outskirts of the coastal town of Lorne, the cool change arrived. But it brought no relief for the firefighters. As the one-kilometre-wide fire front hit the coast, the twenty-kilometre-long eastern flank, spanning all the burning forests from the northern slopes to the sea, became the new fire front. The increase in humidity, falling temperatures and setting sun had little influence on fire behaviour: all a mega-fire needs to maintain its rage is fuel and wind. The west coast frontal surge—a recognised phenomenon whereby the cold front stalls over the Otway Ranges whilst still moving further east over the ocean creating a type of barometric slingshot[1]—hurled the fire along the Great Ocean Road through the coastal forests of Manna Gum, Southern Blue Gum, Red Ironbark and Messmate and into our beachside house at about 7.30pm.

More land was burnt, and more houses lost, after the cool change than before, the fire only stopping when it ran out of the forest into droughted farmland, where it was finally contained at 10am the next day. In all, 41,000 hectares of forest and 782 houses were burnt—and three people lost their lives—in the Otway Ranges fire that day. Across south-eastern Australia, seventy-six people were killed, making Ash Wednesday the worst bushfire day in our nation's history, until Black Saturday 2009.

The Forest Fire Danger Index (FFDI) was developed by Australian bushfire researchers in the 1960s as a numerical rating of fire risk. It incorporates temperature, humidity, wind speed and the moisture content of the fine forest fuels (grass, leaves and twigs less than 6 mm thick). The variables are combined in a way that reflects their relative and compounding impact on fire behaviour to give a single fire danger rating. The benchmark was Black Friday, 1939, which was rated as having a FFDI of 100: the worst the researchers had ever experienced and felt they might expect in the future.

Over an average summer the FFDI typically ranges from 10 to 70 in our area. If it gets above 30 the authorities might call a total fire ban day. If it gets over 50 the consensus is that it is near impossible to fight a running forest fire at its front. In this case, suppression and containment work focuses on the flanks, particularly on the eastern edge, in preparation for a wind change. If the FFDI approaches 70 the focus must be on saving lives, not property. The FFDI on Ash Wednesday reached 120 before the change.[2]

On Black Saturday, 7 February 2009, I was once again out of the state, running a course for farmers in a paddock of deep green grass in south east Queensland. This time I knew the forecast for Victoria and was on edge all morning: the FFDI was going to be higher than Ash Wednesday! Between pruning and thinning demonstrations, I was getting data through my mobile phone from the closest weather station to Bambra. When I saw the 1pm readings—temperature 44.2° Celsius, relative humidity eight percent and average wind speed 91 kilometres per hour with gusts exceeding 110 kilometres per hour—I didn't need a smart phone app to know the FFDI was off the scale. I later read that the FFDI reached 172 that day.[2] It is not surprising that past experience of fire behaviour didn't apply.

When I got the 2.30pm weather data, I saw that the cool change had arrived. I immediately checked that there were no running fires, then, with relief, reported to the tree growers that the Otway Ranges had just survived the worst fire danger day in the modern era. I climbed back up the ladder and continued the class. What I didn't know was that further east, where the front was still a couple of hours away, fires had started to the north and east of Melbourne and were just about to enter the native eucalypt forests under the full force of the hot, dry northerly winds.

What followed was the same pattern of events that had occurred in the Otway Ranges on Ash Wednesday, but with even worse consequences for human life, wildlife and property.

Our family beach house was Mum's refuge from the church manse in Melbourne but it was never meant to be our refuge from a wildfire. Like a Mountain Ash, rather than withstand an inferno she always expected our house would be destroyed by a wildfire one day, it was just a matter of time. But Mum knew that fire could not destroy her country; it was an integral part of it. Her forest would grow back, her birds would return, and she would rebuild.

Claire and I flew home from a London winter four years after the Ash Wednesday fires. Mum had a new house overlooking my home surf break and the hills were clothed in a new forest. I borrowed my brother's car and drove up into the eastern foothills of the Otway Ranges. I was on a search for the land that I had dreamt about in Kenya.

Early European reports of the area create an image of easily-journeyed, open forests with sheltered clearings of native pastures. This was the traditional territory of the Gadubanud people. Like me, they spent their summers on the coast feasting on seafood and their winters in the bush, where they would have farmed the Southern Shortfin Eel in the marshes, collected their annual harvest of the starchy Water Ribbon tubers (*Triglochin procera*) from the wetlands, and tended their plots of the sweet milky Murnong Yam (*Microseris lanceolata*) and Bracken Fern (*Pteridium esculentum*) in open glades amongst the Manna Gum and Messmate.

But on that day, my graded gravel road cut a corridor through impenetrable regrowth. The heat of the wildfire had broken the wattle seed dormancy and created a seedbed for regeneration. Though blackened, the Manna Gum, Messmate, Southern Blue Gum and Red Ironbark had largely survived, with eucalypt seedlings coming up through a thicket of regenerating wattles. The forest in the days before the fire hit was very different to what it was 200 years before, and now it was something else again. There is no such thing as a 'natural' state in these forests.

As I emerged from the bush into the open farmland my focus changed. I spent the day visiting agents and inspecting all the promising blocks on their books, but nothing came close to the image I had in my mind. I began questioning my methodology. Surely, I should have started my search for land with a list of requirements: must-haves, like-to-haves and things-to-avoid. I should have defined my goals, set out strict soil type, climate, location, access, and amenity criteria. I should have been clear about what I was hoping to do so I could objectively assess or compare any options.

I decided to head back to the beach house and get out the soil and rainfall maps. I needed to do some homework. But rather than retrace my morning route back to the coast I took a parallel road over the ridge. As the road began to climb out of the valley I passed under the huge branches of two old Manna Gums that created a gateway to the hills. Then, as I changed down gears, I caught the view up the valley—it was the exact image from my African dream. I'd found my farm.

But there was no welcoming 'For Sale' sign at the entrance. I parked at the gate and looked into the valley. The north-facing slope was bare of trees other than a couple of pines on the hill and one old Manna Gum on a steep bank close to the creek. Judging from the boundary fence I could see that 'my' block crossed the valley and included the south-facing slope that had a patchy cover of degraded native forest.

It looked like dairy country, but there were no cows. Neither was there any obvious clue as to why this view had been my premonition. As I scanned the landscape the pieces of the puzzle started falling into place: I had been here before. Five years earlier I had been driving this same road on my way from the forestry school in central Victoria down to my spot on the coast when right there, under the big old Manna Gums, my path had been blocked by a herd of cows crossing out of the dairy and over the road into *my farm*. I turned around; it was late afternoon but there was no milking happening on this summer evening. I could see that the old herringbone dairy had been converted into a shearing shed. Stepping out of it, the owner was coming over to see what I was doing.

I can't recall how I introduced myself but I'm sure that all Ian saw was a young curly-headed kid in a city-type car acting suspiciously. I attempted to reassure him by asking if he knew who owned the block and whether he thought they might be interested in selling. It wasn't his. He'd bought part of *opposite: The view up our valley showing the eroded creek as it was in 1987.*

top: The view to the north across the valley in early 1987 showing the regrowth forest on the steep south-facing slope that is less than 80-yrs-old.

bottom: Imagining a future. Claire and I on the farm together for the first time. We were 25-yrs- old.

the old dairy farm, including the house and dairy, but not *my* bit. The rest had been divided in two and shared between the other neighbours. Following Ian's directions, I drove back down the valley and up the road on the opposite ridge and knocked on the door of the current owner of my farm.

What was the block he had down there? Would he be interested in selling? It was as if he'd been waiting for me. We jumped in his utility and entered my farm through the patchy native forest. The only structures were the hay shed and one internal fence. His family had just decided they wanted to expand their farm tourism business and yes, if the price was right, they would be interested in selling. Without knowing any more, I suggested a price; Neil said yes and we shook hands.

What had I done? This was no way to buy a farm! I was supposed to be a scientist, a professional; I had just spent my grandfather's gift on the back of a vision I'd had in an African dream.

As our solicitors drew up the contracts I tried to adopt a more considered approach. I walked the valley and climbed the hills. I dug holes and massaged the soil in my palms to gauge its texture. I identified the trees and matched species against soil type. And, I got Claire down to have a look. We sat under the old Messmate Stringybark and agreed we'd sign up as the future makers for this block of land. But I was kidding myself, this wasn't due diligence, there was no way I would renege on this deal just because the soils were a little too clayey or the slopes too steep. This block had been waiting for me, the fact that I'd found it and that the owners were prepared to sell was enough to know this was where I was meant to be; this was where I'd set up my 'agroforestry education centre'.

The block suited my purpose well, well almost. From the climate maps I'd estimated that the annual rainfall was about 750 millimetres, which, at the time, was considered marginal for commercial forestry. I was comfortable with that; my aim was to break with conventions. But, I should have known that being located on the northeast slopes of the ranges meant Bambra was in a rain shadow, so averages didn't mean much. Since we've been here, annual totals have varied from less than 500 to more than 1,100 millimetres. Had I read the native vegetation, rather than the maps, I might have got a better understanding of the local rainfall patterns. In the foothill forests of the Otway Ranges, Manna Gum competes with Southern Blue Gum for the most fertile acid clay soils. The faster growing, taller, but less drought tolerant, Southern Blue Gum dominates on the higher rainfall sites. In Victoria, the Southern Blue Gum might normally be expected to extend down to sites with average annual rainfall as low as 600 millimetres per year.[3] But the boundary between the species in our area is a kilometre or so up the valley from our farm where the average is more like 850 millimetres. When selecting tree species to plant, it is the extremes rather than the averages that will largely determine their suitability.

The soils held some surprises for me too. I could tell from the stunted growth of the native Narrow Leafed Peppermint (*Eucalyptus radiata*) that the grey sands were leached of nutrients and held little moisture through the summer months. But some of the remnant Manna Gums on the clays were over 30 metres tall. In Australian forestry, a mature tree height of 30 metres is used as a distinction between the classification of an 'open' (10–30 m tall) and a 'tall open' eucalypt forest, the latter being much more productive. But, you don't really know a soil until you have spent some time getting your hands dirty.

With our first autumn break I came to appreciate how the area got its name: Bambra is derived from the local Aboriginal word for mushroom. My first soil tests came back with an organic carbon content of more than four percent. Organic matter consists of carbon (about sixty percent), nitrogen (five percent), and hydrogen (35 percent) so, to convert the percentage of soil organic carbon to soil organic matter, you multiply by 1.7. This is often rounded up to two because the 'loss on ignition' test tends to underestimate organic carbon. By any measure, an organic matter content of eight percent is very high for farmland, making our paddocks ideal for fungi.

Our soils have a high organic matter content making them ideal for fungi. We identified this one as the native Amanita farinacea.

Like the wood in trees, the carbon in soil organic matter originates from atmospheric carbon dioxide. Assuming a conservative soil bulk density (soil mass per unit volume) of 1.0, the top 10 centimetres of our soils contain about eighty tons of organic matter per hectare. This is the equivalent of about 150 tons of sequestered atmospheric CO_2 per hectare.[4] Soil organic matter content declines with depth but it is still possible that the top 30 centimetres of our pasture soils contain the equivalent of 300 tons of CO_2 per hectare. The problem is that most of this carbon is not in a stable form and could easily be lost to the environment and contribute to global warming.

Soil organic matter can be present in one of four forms: living (such as plant roots, insects and worms), decomposing (dead plants and animals), relatively stable (humus) or inert (charcoal). The proportion of humus in any soil remains relatively constant, as long as the soil conditions, climate factors and land use does not change. Like peat, humus can hold many times its own weight in water. Also, the tiny humus particles are as much as thirty times more negatively charged than clay particles of the same size, thereby greatly increasing the ability of the soil to hold more of the important base nutrients like calcium, magnesium and potassium. But the organic matter in dead plant and animal material breaks down quickly, releasing the carbon as CO_2 or methane (CH_4) and its nitrogen as nitrites (NO_2^-) and nitrates (NO_3^-) that can feed plant growth or be converted into nitrous oxide (N_2O). Methane and nitrous oxide are powerful greenhouse gases.

The clearing of native forests for cropping can lead to a reduction in the organic matter content of our soils by more than forty percent.[5] The decline is rapid in the years immediately after clearing as the readily decomposable plant material breaks down. This is why newly cleared country tends to perform well at first but then productivity declines unless fertilisers or organic matter

are added. After forty or fifty years of cropping, a new low carbon equilibrium is reached where the rate of decomposition matches the rate of addition. By contrast, research shows that the conversion of native forest to pasture can lead to an increase in soil carbon and that planting trees on farmland is not necessarily a proven pathway to increasing soil carbon, especially if the site is cultivated or ripped prior to planting.[6]

The potential of new forests on farmland to sequester and hold carbon dioxide lies not in the soil but in their capacity to store large amounts of carbon in the living woody biomass and the undecomposed debris. But there is still a limit to how much live wood a forest can sustain and the carbon held in both the living and dead biomass is always at risk of being released by fire or decay.[6] Rather than a secure carbon store, I see our planted trees as a perpetual carbon sequestration *plant*. Repeatedly harvesting a proportion of the live wood and storing the carbon in timber, or using it as a source of renewable energy, allows me to free up the land to lock up more carbon. In this way, there is no limit to the amount of carbon our land can extract from the atmosphere.

above: Local nurseryman and tree grower Mike Robinson-Koss planted this Manna Gum for shelter and pruned it for timber. At age 25-yrs-old it was 95 cm in diameter. We milled the log into solid timber (a long-term carbon sink) and Mike used the waste for firewood (carbon-neutral energy).

opposite: All the stages of hollow formation on one of our Manna Gums: Mistletoe infection causes branch death or drop, leading to trunk growth over deadwood and branch decay back into the main stem. From old aerial photographs, I know that this tree is less than 80-yrs-old.

My next soil lesson came in our first winter. Our clays, even on the slopes, hold so much water that it is often impossible to drive over the paddocks. I tried to dig a long-drop but it just filled with water. I built tight fences in autumn but they went limp with the rains. And I got bogged, and bogged again. I should have seen the tell-tale signs that first summer: the pugging left by cattle from the previous winter and the deep cracks that had opened up for the Black Field Crickets. I should have also recognised the plants that indicate seasonally wet soils: Sea Barley Grass (*Hordeum marinum*), Dock (*Rumex* species), Strawberry Clover (*Trifolium fragiferum*) and the native rushes (*Juncus* species*)*.

Waterlogging is a critical issue when selecting tree species for planting.

If the water is well oxygenated and flowing freely through a permeable soil, such as occurs below a spring on a sandy bank, most tree species will survive and flourish as if being grown hydroponically. But, if the water is being held in a heavy sticky clay it can become stagnant, leading to a build-up of toxic gasses and suffocation of the roots. Many of the specialty timber species we grow, including the Chestnut (*Castanea sativa*), Black Walnut and even the Hybrid Poplars, don't survive on our waterlogged clays so I grow them on the creek flats. Other species survive, but never develop into large trees. Even some of the local natives like Messmate Stringybark don't like it. Manna Gum, at least our local provenance, appears well-adapted to growing in poorly oxygenated carbon-rich clays, but then they face other threats.

A few of our big native Manna Gums have died under my watch. It's the mistletoe that takes them out in the end. There are seventy or so species of mistletoe in Victoria. Our most aggressive is Drooping Mistletoe (*Amyema pendula*). Mistletoes are a hemiparasite, which means that they have leaves and are able to photosynthesise but tap into their host's sapwood stream to steal water and nutrients. But the mistletoe does not act alone. It can only spread and infect trees because of its association with the Mistletoebird.

In an example of coincident evolution, the Mistletoebird assists seed germination by breaking the chemical dormancy of the seedcoat as it passes quickly through the gut. Then, whereas most birds perch across a branch, the Mistletoebird has learnt to perch sideways and wipe its bum on the woody branch to release the tacky seed. The seed then sends out aerial roots that tap into the sapwood flow of their host. Drooping Mistletoe is so effective at plugging into the tree branch that it can totally intercept the flow of water, causing the branch to die back to the point of attack.

The long thin leaves of the Drooping Mistletoe look very much like those of their Manna Gum host but, physiologically, they are different in two critical ways. Their stomata do not close to control water loss and they do not have secondary buds. On a hot summer afternoon when the stomata on the host's own leaves are closed to conserve moisture, the parasite will continue to transpire, drawing on the available moisture and its cargo of dissolved nutrients for its own benefit. But the mistletoe's greedy strategy is prone to backfire when the soil dries out and the flow of water is jeopardised, increasing the risk of summer branch drop. After the last drought, the ground under our worst-affected Manna Gums was littered with discarded branches carrying mistletoe, giving them some reprieve.

The other natural control factor is fire. Because mistletoe don't have secondary buds in their leaf axils or the ability to sprout epicormic shoots like their host, a cool burn that scorches the canopy can be enough to kill the mistletoe while allowing the eucalypt to recover. But then removal of mistletoe is largely ineffective as the parasite can quickly re-infest vulnerable trees.[7] The only real control option, which is clearly unacceptable, would be the removal of the Mistletoebird. There are no Mistletoebirds in Tasmania and no mistletoe.

I'm happy to retain some mistletoe, even if it occasionally overruns an old Manna Gum or infects my young Blackwoods. Mistletoe plays an extraordinary role in supporting our native wildlife. The nutritious fruit and abundant nectar are consumed by many other native birds and may also help sustain populations of small native mammals like our Sugar Gliders. I've also come to appreciate the role that Drooping Mistletoe plays in the formation of nesting hollows for our native gliders, possums, bats and birds.

While we are often told it takes hundreds of years to create a hollow in eucalypts, this rarely challenged myth ignores the fact that hollow formation is simply a growth response to a chance event. All that is required to drive the natural process of hollow formation is a dead branch on a living tree—a natural outcome of a mistletoe infection.

When I prune for timber production I cut the small branches off close to the stem, being careful not to disturb the branch collar. This allows the callus growth, fed by sugars flowing down the main trunk, to develop evenly around the wound, completely encasing the small branch stub within a year. Hollow formation occurs when wind damage, summer branch drop or mistletoe result in a dead branch that extends well out from the trunk. In this case the callus grows out along the old branch. How far it extends seems to depend on the vigour of the tree but in many eucalypts the callus growth can reach more than 25 centimetres out along the branch.

Over time the dead branch will decay, creating a hollow down through the callus and into the trunk that is the same shape and diameter as the old branch. Wildlife hasten the hollow formation process by digging out grubs from the dead wood and depositing nitrogen-rich manures that encourage decay.

I'm sure that I have seen new hollows develop in our mistletoe-infected Manna Gums within the time I've been here on this farm. I am also experimenting with lopping branches off young Manna Gums to see if I can initiate the process and provide new hollows amongst our planted trees for our

Sugar Gliders. I'm thinking that the branch should be on the sheltered eastern side and about 10 centimetres in diameter. It will take some time, but not hundreds of years.

Actively stimulating the formation of hollows for endangered wildlife is not natural, but it is possible. Although many local populations of our flora and fauna, and in some cases entire species, have been lost or are under threat because of the changes we have made, most of the wildlife we do see in the agricultural landscape has learnt to live with us, even to depend on us.

This points to a new future for conservation management; rather than simply withdrawing all human activity and thinking Nature will look after herself, we could be using our knowledge and understanding of natural processes and risks, and our unique ability to actively manage land and vegetation, to create landscapes that not only support native wildlife but also sequester more carbon dioxide than they would have even under native forest.

Mistletoebird (*Dicaeum hirundinaceum*)

1.   G.A. Mills, 'A case of coastal interaction with a cool change, *Australian Meteorological Magazine* 51(4) (2002): 203-221.

2.   Kevin Tolhurst, *Report on the physical nature of the Victorian Fires occurring on 7th February 2009*. Department of Forest and Ecosystem Science (Melbourne: University of Melbourne, 2009).

3.   J.B. Kirkpatrick, Natural distribution of *Eucalyptus globulus* Labill, *Australian Geographer*, 13(1) (1975): 22-35.

4.   The molecular weight of CO^2 is 44 (O=16 and C=12). Therefore, each ton of carbon locked up in the soil requires the sequestration of 44/12 = 3.67 tons of CO^2.

5.   L.B. Gui and R.M. Gifford, Soil carbon stocks and land use change: a meta analysis, *Global Change Biology* 8 (2002): 345-360.

6.   R.J. Harper, A.E.A. Okom, A.T. Stilwell, M. Tibbett, C. Dean, S.J. George, S.J. Sochacki, C.D. Mitchell, S.S. Mann and K. Dods, Reforesting degraded agricultural landscapes with Eucalypts: Effects on carbon storage and soil fertility after 26 years, *Agriculture, Ecosystems and Environment* 163 (2012): 3-13.

7.   D.M. Watson, *Mistletoes of southern Australia* (Melbourne: CSIRO Publishing, 2011).

Attracting wildlife to your farm

The patches of remnant native vegetation, regrowth, plantations, shelterbelts, gardens and roadsides in our agricultural landscapes can, together, provide all the habitat needs to sustain viable ecological communities of many native bird and animal species. The problem is often the small size and isolation of the critical habitat elements required to maintain a viable population and allow them to spread across the region.

Just locking up native vegetation and planting indigenous species for conservation alone in our highly-modified farming landscapes is not necessarily the best way to support biodiversity, particularly in the face of climate change. We need to acknowledge that native wildlife can adapt to different habitat types and often prefer diversified landscapes that include non-native and actively managed trees and forests. Many farmers growing and managing a diverse range of forest types of different ages for different reasons are likely to achieve the greatest conservation benefits at the lowest cost.

Our own properties will be just a small part of the home range of most native wildlife populations. Nonetheless there are a few key design principles we can follow to make our farms more attractive to wildlife and enhance regional biodiversity.

Wildlife corridors: Shelterbelts, riparian plantings and even scattered trees can provide linkages and stepping stones for wildlife to move between patches of useful habitat. Try to link tree planting projects into a continuous web-of-trees that provide multiple pathways for wildlife to move across the landscape.

Patch size: Some native species of plants and animals prefer the edge of a forest and do well in a landscape of scattered trees or thin tree belts. Others require larger blocks with a complex vegetation structure. Consider planting blocks of trees or adding buffers around existing remnant vegetation to establish nodes embedded in your web-of-trees.

Mimic natural systems: The structure and diversity of the native vegetation can be used as a model for planting design. For example, in our riparian forest of tall eucalypts growing over rainforest species mimics the structure of the wet sclerophyll forest that was once there. Our parklands of wide spaced trees mimic a savannah woodland.

Understorey: An understorey increases the complexity of the forest structure and the diversity of habitat elements including flowers, bark, leaf and litter types. But, shrubs are just small trees so having a diversity of tree species and size can compensate for a lack of native understorey. There are also productive shrubs for specialty timbers, oils, flowers and bushfood that can be grown under a canopy of tall timber trees.

The diversity of patches and species: The original native vegetation on many farms may have been very similar across the property. There is no reason to follow this in our own tree planting. In fact, providing a diversity of species, even including exotics, can support a greater number and diversity of birds and animals than were there prior to clearing.

Disturbance can be good: Different plants and animals prefer different environments. Harvesting timber, burning and grazing, or the exclusion of these, can be used as tools to increase the patchiness of a plantation.

Decaying wood: Standing dead trees, tree hollows, logs on the ground, stumps and woody debris in waterways and dams can provide critical habitat elements. In young plantings, trees can be ringbarked, pruned or thinned to create these elements that might otherwise take years to develop.

Age matters: Allow time to create greater complexity in your forests. I do this by selectively harvesting our timbers and underplanting shade tolerant timber species so that I never need to return a site to a cleared paddock.

S.J. Platt, *How to Plan Wildlife Landscapes: a guide for community organisations* (Melbourne: Department of Natural Resources and Environment, Melbourne, 2002).

right: Some of the wildlife we have on our farm.

Chapter 7

Shining Gum
Eucalyptus nitens

A few days after my fortieth birthday, I arrived at the 2001 Australian Stream Management Conference in Brisbane carrying a deconstructed hall table packed inside a surfboard cover. I'd made the piece from timber milled from ten-year-old Shining Gum trees we'd harvested from our mixed species riparian buffer strip. Josquin Tibbits, an arborist before becoming a student of mine and going on to do his PhD in gene technology, felled the trees. Russell Washusen, a farmer before becoming a student of mine and going on to do his PhD in wood technology, supervised the sawing and drying trial. I made the table myself, under the guidance of Hamish Hill, who ran the timber workshop at the University of Melbourne. Hamish became my 'supervisor' and guided me to the completion of my academic goal: to make a piece of furniture before I turned forty, from a tree that I'd planted myself.

Our conference paper was titled, 'Sawn timber from 10-year-old pruned *Eucalyptus nitens* grown in an agricultural riparian buffer'.[1] Given that, I wasn't surprised I had been allocated to a small side room rather than the main auditorium. But as I was setting up my table in front of the lectern the seats were filling up. Dr Peter Hairsine was there; he nodded at me as he took his seat, a gesture I took as acknowledgment of the challenge I had set myself. In part, it was his research that had given me the confidence to challenge mainstream thinking about the role of trees in rehabilitating degraded watercourses on farms.

Years before, I'd watched Peter wade out into the middle of the Tarago River in Gippsland and stand where the east and the west branches came together. It was easy to pick the point of confluence. The west branch flowed out of the native forest and had the colour and smell of strong black tea, while the east branch, draining the farmland, was more like weak white coffee. Built to supply Melbourne, the dam downstream of this 'cafe' junction lay uncommissioned because of the unacceptable sediment and nutrient loads coming off the catchment.

Peter's research pointed the finger directly at the farmland. The tannins that gave the forest water its tea colour were not a problem. They would break *preceding page: Felling a 28-yr-old Shining Gum in our riparian buffer strip.*

left: Josquin Tibbits felling our 10-yr-old Shining Gum for our first sawing trial.

right: I used some of the backsawn timber to make my first home-grown table.

bottom: Peter Hairsine points out the difference in water quality coming from a forested catchment (to his right) and farmland (where he is standing).

down naturally as the water slowly moved through the dam. But the sediments and nutrients flowing off the farmland risked undermining Melbourne's reputation as having one of the cleanest natural water supplies in the world.

The fine clay particles held in suspension carried a cocktail of pollutants, including phosphorous. What we couldn't see were the dissolved nutrients, the most significant being nitrogen. In 1991 there had been a toxic blue-green algal bloom in the Tarago Reservoir that was thought to be a result of excess nutrients in the runoff. Peter explained that the nutrients originated from both point and diffuse sources.[2] The point sources were easy to identify: septic tanks, dairies and road crossings. These could be tackled with improved engineering, better design, more regular maintenance and regulation. Peter's interest was the more elusive diffuse sources: the run-off from farm paddocks in particular. His research was testing whether vegetated buffer strips could trap and store the sediments and nutrients before they reached the waterways.

We moved to a site where Peter had compared the effectiveness of six-metre-wide buffer strips of different vegetation types. Grass trapped ninety-eight percent of the sediments but only fifty-nine percent of the phosphorus. Peter explained that the finest sediments, the charged clay particles, carried most of the nutrients but were the hardest to capture. Nonetheless, grass was more effective than native forest, which captured ninety-five percent of the sediment and only fifty-three percent of the phosphorous (figure 1). What interested me most was that a combination of both—3 metres of grass and 3 metres of trees—was significantly better than either, trapping ninety-eight percent of the sediment and seventy percent of the phosphorous. The grasses and trees played different roles: grass was more effective at trapping sediments in overland flow but trees could dry out the soil profile to a depth, which increased water infiltration, thus helping absorb more of the fine sediments.

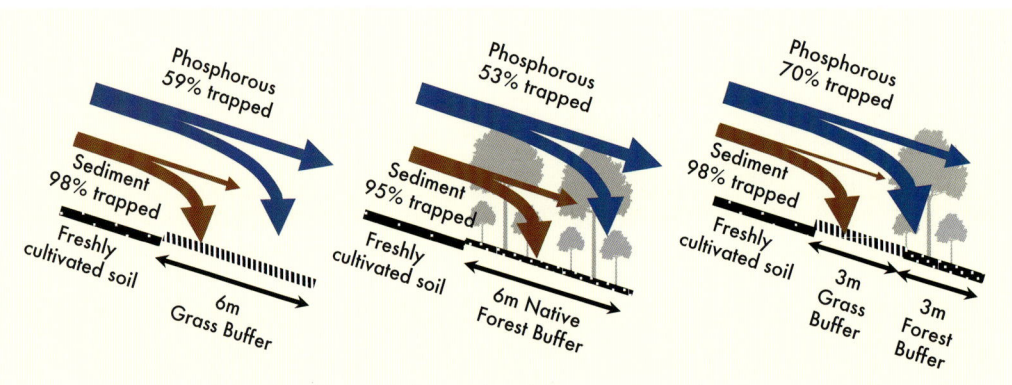

figure 1

Our discussion turned to the design of an effective riparian buffer strip for farmland. Fast growing trees would help dry out the banks and deplete soil nutrient reserves between rainfall events and under the trees, a dense sward of grass would be better than a natural leaf litter layer. Buffer strips should also be located close to the source and wider at points where drainage entered the stream. By working through the underlying processes and the possible role of vegetation we'd exposed the absurdity of specifying minimum widths for buffer strips, dense planting of indigenous trees and shrubs, and focusing works on the larger waterways.

As we walked across the paddocks, I asked Peter for his thoughts on harvesting timber from the buffer strip. He acknowledged that extracting a whole tree, leaves and all, would be an effective means of removing nutrients

figure 1: Buffer zone performance on a granite-derived loam in the Tarago Reservoir catchment (Vic.) showing how, in this case, a riparian buffer containing both trees and grass was more effective than either alone.[2]

top: In 1987, our creek was like many others on farmland: unfenced and tree-less.

bottom: During a flood, the debris along our creek pile up creating natural 'beaver dams'.

from the site. Harvesting might also ensure that there was sufficient light to maintain a healthy sward of grass to trap surface sediments. But he did add a note of caution about the use of heavy machinery close to the watercourse because of the risk of soil disturbance.

    I returned to our farm confident that there was a sound scientific basis underpinning the environmental integrity of my own research into the practical and economic viability of selectively harvesting timber from a riparian buffer strip.

We are now selectively harvesting eucalypts from our creek to encourage the high-quality rainforest timber species to develop and shade the water. One day, these will also be harvested on a sustainable basis.

I began my conference presentation with photos of the bare and eroded creek running through our farm as it was in 1987. I then described how we'd fenced it out and planted a range of indigenous and native tree species, pruned the best for timber and culled others to maintain the understorey and promote diameter growth. I explained how I killed some trees by ringbarking and left them standing to enhance biodiversity and felled others into the drainage line itself. I used photos to show how the logs are pushed up into heaps during high flow creating a series of natural 'beaver dams' which slow the waterflow. These provide aquatic habitat elements (deep pools and organic matter) that have been largely missing since our farm creeks were cleared, desnagged and turned into open drains.

Then I spoke about the harvest and milling of the ten-year-old Shining Gums. The nine trees had an average diameter of 40 centimetres (breast height over bark) and were cut into eighteen pruned mill logs. These produced a total of 1.9 cubic metres of backsawn timber, a recovery of forty-one percent (the logs were not large enough to quartersaw). I pointed to my table to show off the timber.

There was polite applause. But then question time confirmed I had provoked the reaction I expected after all: 'You can't do that, or if you can you shouldn't be allowed to,' and 'You certainly shouldn't be using our conference to sanction timber harvesting from riparian buffers'. Peter let the room mock me before he spoke: 'This,' he told his peers, 'was an example of how research could inform the design of practical land management options that were attractive to farmers' (or something to that effect).

During a plenary session, Dr Ian Rutherfurd told the gathering that there are more than 17,000 kilometres of degraded waterways running through farmland in Victoria alone—maybe over 100,000 across Australia. He stressed that revegetation should focus on the smaller creeks and unnamed tributaries on private land in the upper reaches.[3] Once the flow reaches the lower reaches of the big rivers, like the Hunter, the Blackwood, the Goulburn, the Mary or the Johnstone, planting trees along the banks will do little to improve the quality of the water before it flows, or floods, through Maitland, Nannup, Shepparton, Gympie or Innisfail on its way to estuaries, sea grass beds, coral reefs and fishing grounds.

The public purse cannot pay for every fence along every creek, let alone the ongoing cost of maintenance. Unless farmers believe that it is in their interest to fence, plant and manage trees along their drainage lines it just won't happen. Regulating land management is tricky and can lead to perverse outcomes. Banning the harvesting of trees from riparian land just encourages farmers to leave their drainage lines open for grazing. You cannot legislate against neglect.

At the start of our farm tours I stand on the stump of the twenty-five-year-old Mountain Ash I harvested for timber. It had grown just a few metres from the creek. Beside me, a young Australian Red Cedar is now filling the space. I explain my plan to slowly harvest all the eucalypts and transition our riparian forest from a eucalypt-dominated plantation into a rainforest of specialty timbers. The reaction has been fascinating. Many commercial foresters say my example is too complicated, too expensive and lacking the efficiencies of scale and uniformity that they strive for in their own plantation models. Many of those working in the conservation sector view any form of timber harvesting from Landcare plantings as an anathema and my attempts to mix the two, abhorrent. But for the farmers who visit, it's just common-sense to manage waterways on farms for both conservation and profit.

What single-interest observers don't appreciate is that a forest that is neither the best for production or conservation might actually be better for both. Economists use the concept of joint production to determine the most attractive combination of multiple products that might be produced from a single enterprise.

Imagine a factory that has the equipment and staff capable of producing leather boots and leather belts. Clearly, the business can focus all their time, equipment and skills on producing just boots or just belts, or they can choose to produce any combination of the two. Now, let's assume that if our hypothetical boot and belt firm concentrates all their resources on the production of only one product, it can produce *either* 500 pairs of leather boots *or* 5,000 belts per week. A joint production function is the line on the graph linking these two extremes that indicates the maximum number of each product

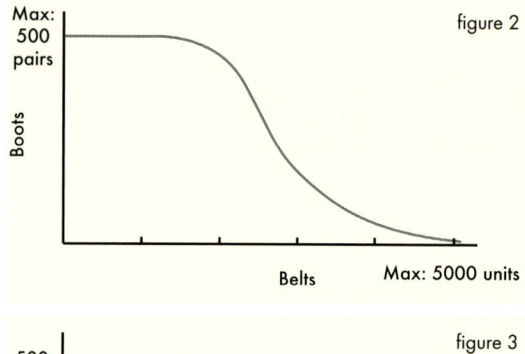

Joint production functions illustrate the various possible combinations of different products that can be produced using the same resources (land, time, capital and skills). Our hypothetical example is for a company that can produce belts (at a profit of $1 each) and boots (at a profit of $10 per pair). The most profitable option may be a combination of both (in this case 450 pairs of boots and 2000 belts).

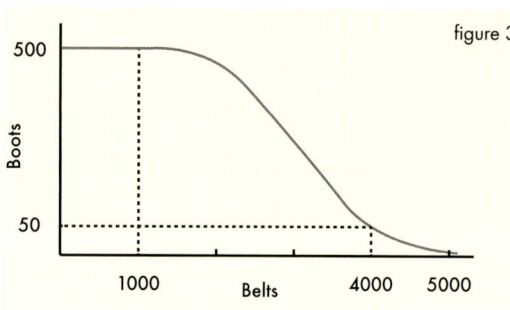

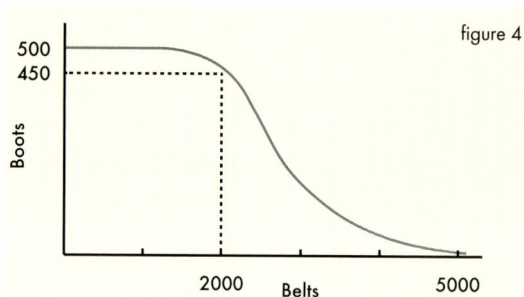

the firm can produce for the same cost (figure 2).

In the example, when the company is producing 500 pairs of boots (the maximum possible) it is also able to produce 1,000 belts at no additional cost; maybe by using waste from the boot production process (figure 3). Whatever profit they can generate from selling belts is a bonus. However, if they wanted to increase the number of belts above 1,000 then this would require a sharp fall in the number of boots produced per week. At the other end of the curve the relationship is very competitive: if the company produces just belts they can make 5,000 units, but if they wanted to produce 50 pairs of boots per week then the production of belts would need to be reduced to 4,000 units per week.

If the profit from each pair of boots was $10 and each belt was $1 then the profit from producing 500 pairs of boots or 5,000 belts, would be $5,000 per week. Working along the curve there is a point at which our hypothetical firm could, for the same cost, produce a combination of 450 pairs of boots and 2,000 belts which would provide a profit of $4,500 + $2,000 = $6,500 per week (figure 4). So, the best option is not to maximise the production of either but to produce a mix of products.

Of course, it would require years of research and a very complex data set to develop a joint production function for a multipurpose tree planting project along a degraded creek. But there is much that is intuitive: close to the conservation-only end of the joint production function there might be the opportunity to harvest some firewood without having any negative impact on the biodiversity or water quality. In our case, I may have compromised the conservation values a little by planting non-indigenous eucalypts but I believe that our tree management and harvesting has enhanced biodiversity and water quality. More importantly, the prospect of a commercial return, however small,

The milling of our 16-yr-old Shining Gum logs at the Black Forest Sawmill in central Victoria (2004).

has encouraged many other farmers in our district to fence out their creeks and plant trees, thereby amplifying the conservation benefits across the landscape.

When our Shining Gum trees were sixteen years old, Russell contacted me about a second trial. He had secured some Shining Gum logs from a 65-year-old native forest and was keen to do a comparative quartersawing trial. Josquin and I harvested a sample of 50-centimetre diameter trees from the creek and sent them to the mill. A few weeks later I watched as the logs were broken down by a 12-inch bandsaw then sawn into boards. It was a great learning experience. As I expected, the sapwood band in our logs was wider than in the native forest logs (about 50 mm compared to 25 mm); faster growth requires more leaves and more water. I was also able to see that my pruning wounds had recovered well and there was plenty of clear knot-free timber around the core. But it wasn't all good news: some of our trees had been infected by borers!

The culprit was a longicorn bull's-eye borer, so named because it leaves a fist-sized circular wound on the trunk. The beetles lay their eggs in cracks in the bark and the larvae tunnel into the stem to feast on the sapwood. A full two years after the egg is laid, the adults emerge through a hole in the centre of the bull's-eye. The damage is made worse by the introduction of fungi into the tree, which spread up and down the stem, discolouring the wood. From the depth of the wound, I estimated that the trees were attacked during the 1997/8 El Nino drought. That made sense: longicorns target trees under stress by recognising a drop in the moisture content of the wood.

A year later I returned to the mill to help Russell grade the kiln-dried timber. Factors that can cause a piece to be downgraded include discolouration, rot, knots, insect attack, kino veins, unrecovered collapse, warping and cracks. The batch of 65-year-old native logs yielded a twenty percent recovery of the clean select-grade timber, whereas our plantation grown logs produced about half that. Part of the problem was insect attack but the main issue was log size. If young plantations are to replace native forests as a source of high quality quartersawn timber then not only do the trees need to be artificially pruned, they also need to be grown to a larger size to compensate for the wider sapwood band and the larger knotty core. I have now increased my target tree size for eucalypts to 75 centimetres, which means longer rotations and a wider final spacing (about 12 m between trees). But then, I still think I can achieve the same quality of log in less than half the time it takes in a native forest.

I came away from the trial with four cubic metres of home-grown, kiln-dried, quartersawn Shining Gum timber. I also had a few of the 65-year-old native forest boards for comparison. The two looked very different: the growth rings in the native timber were less than 2 millimetres apart whereas in mine the spacing was more than 1 centimetre. The obvious question was: how good was my wood for furniture and would it be a viable substitute for native forest timber?

Density is one measure of wood quality. It affects strength and, to a lesser extent, the lustre and depth of the finish you can achieve. I tested some samples and found that, by age ten years, our fast-grown trees were laying down timber that had a density equal or higher than that from the 65-year-old native forest timber. Our harvest might have been a little premature, but the signs were good for the future.

With an eye on its fine furniture potential, I was more interested in what our timber looked like. Its grain patterns, colour, feature and lustre. The real surprise for me was the high proportion of fiddleback grain: twelve

left: A growing stack of clear-grade quartersawn Shining Gum from our 16-yr-old pruned trees at the Black Forest Sawmill in central Victoria.

right: The two sides of fiddleback: On the left I split the wood along the grain to show the wavy pattern of the fibres. When sanded (right) the angle of the grain reflects the light in different ways, giving the fiddleback appearance. Image courtesy of Luke Popovic.

of the eighteen trees produced some fiddleback and nine percent of all the sawn timber boards had a prominent wavy grain along their full length. This attractive 'tiger-stripe' pattern is only evident on the quartersawn face of a board and is due to a wavy grain running up and down the stem on the radial plane. When polished, the fiddleback grain gives a smooth flat surface an uncanny three-dimensional appearance.

If a log is split on the radial plane, like a split hardwood fencepost, fiddleback grain will appear as a corrugated surface that can be seen and felt. It is often called 'curly' grain when the waves can be measured in terms of numbers per foot, and 'fiddleback' when the waves are measured in numbers per inch. The fact that fiddleback is seen across the face of a quartersawn board tells us that the wavy pattern is laid down over many years and is not a one-off event in the life of the tree. If it is genetic, the opportunity to select and clonally propagate plants with a propensity to produce fiddleback grain is appealing. If it is largely environmental—triggered by soil conditions, weather events, disease or damage—there may be something we can do to a standing tree, or the environment in which it is growing, to induce the cambium to produce a wavy grain.

I could reject any theory that implied that fiddleback could only be found in slow growing, old, heavily branched or bent trees; our Shining Gum were fat, straight, fast growing and pruned. But that left me with no idea what might have caused our trees to produce fiddleback. Then I met Adam.

Adam Newnham was a student of furniture design and construction when he called to talk about sourcing sustainable timber for his student project. When I told him about my Shining Gum timber he was immediately taken by the idea that producing furniture from farm-grown timber could help drive landscape restoration. His brief was to produce a piece of furniture in response to the needs of a client. I agreed to provide the timber and pay for the hardware if I could keep the piece as a demonstration. Adam came over for dinner to discuss design ideas with the family and left with a concept-plan for an entertainment unit.

Adam's teachers were initially sceptical about the suitability of young, fast-grown eucalypt wood for fine furniture, so the exercise became as much a challenge for the wood as it was for him. When I asked what exactly they thought the problems might be, Adam suggested that how it behaved when machined and its stability in use would be the most critical measures, but that it would hardly matter because they expected the wood to be featureless and boring. I picked out the best fiddleback boards for the project. Adam used the fiddleback feature in all the drawers and cupboard fronts to contrast with the plain timber of the carcass. It looked fantastic and his supervisors must have agreed as they selected the piece for a public exhibition. The cabinet now sits in our lounge room and I often find myself staring at the grain rather than the television screen.

The following year Adam decided to switch careers and enrolled in our forest science degree. When he had the opportunity to do some research,

we designed a project focusing on fiddleback. He began with a review of the literature and presented his findings to me. Firstly, wavy grain occurs across a range of tree species but there were no reports of it having been prominent in plantation grown timber. That's interesting. Secondly, detailed analysis of the phenomenon in North America suggested that the waves have a regular frequency and amplitude within the tree and that the lines we can see on the radial axis are not horizontal but either rise or fall at a regular angle. I looked at our samples. Yes, the stripe did seem to fall towards the bark.

Adam explained that this implies that, rather than being constant, there is a continuous change in the orientation of the new cells produced at each point in the cambium, and that, down the length of the stem, the change is consistent over time ensuring a regular pattern is produced over several years. He could see I was lost. 'Think of the wave pattern as the "trace" of the continuous and regular changes occurring over time in the cambium zone where the wood cells were produced,' he said, 'like drawing a wave pattern in the sand with a stick, it is the position of the stick that is moving through time, not the groove it leaves in the sand.'

But what causes it? The best Adam could find was some research on wound responses in trees which suggested that interrupting the flow of carbohydrates and hormones running from a branch into the stem could cause the wood-forming cells in the cambium to reorient themselves. He hypothesized that my pruning might have triggered the wavy grain.

Wow! We inspected the boards to see if there was any evidence to support this idea and were stunned to find that the fiddleback only appeared after pruning and often started just below the point at which a live branch was removed. Maybe this explains the observation that fiddleback is more commonly found in trees growing on exposed ridges; storm damage might be like pruning.

left: Adam beside the cabinet he made from our fiddleback Shining Gum (16-yr-old).

right: Within a few years the timber darkened highlighting the fiddleback grain.

opposite: Alistair with the hall table he made from our 16-yr-old Shining Gum. The tree beside him is a 22-yr-old Shining Gum growing along the same creek from where we harvested the trees. Also in the photo are a couple of small Shining Gum logs growing Shiitake mushrooms.

Alistair McKendrick graduated from the same furniture design course as Adam and took up a position as furniture maker in residence in a fully equipped workshop set up to help young graduates get started. His idea was to establish a business around the use of recycled or reclaimed native timbers and imported Bamboo (*Phyllostachys* species). When he heard about our timber, he was interested in adding a third line to his custom-made furniture business. Ever keen to get more feedback, I delivered some of our Shining Gum timber to his workshop. I wanted to present the case that timber harvested from multipurpose plantings on farms was a better environmental choice than either Bamboo or recycled timber.

A few weeks later, he sent me photos of a Shining Gum hall table with fine inlays of dark red reclaimed Jarrah. He added some notes:

> *Having never used young plantation eucalypt timber before I had no idea how it would perform. The first thing that caught my eye was the heavy fiddleback feature to the boards. It has an aesthetic that is very hard to source in the more common eucalypts, making it a unique and appealing timber to use in one-off furniture pieces. It is paler than the Vic Ash and, being fast grown, the quartersawn boards didn't have the numerous close growth rings you see in ash. As I began working it, I soon realised that the timber was relatively soft, making it easy to work, but stable enough for fine joinery. There was some 'chipping out' in the thicknesser but it sanded and finished well, showing the characteristic shimmering grain under the light. I'm certainly keen on using more farm-grown timber and believe that its green credentials and scarcity of supply will mean that we can ensure it has a place, and value, alongside Jarrah or other Australian timbers.*

Will James works for Fethers Veneers in Melbourne. He showed me around their warehouse; millions of dollars' worth of the most valuable raw timber product, sourced from all around the world; Walnut burl, quilted Mahogany, bird's-eye Maple, fiddleback Sycamore and the like. I was there to explore whether my timber could find a home here. Will was looking for something different, a timber that was both beautiful and sustainable. He opened a stack of pommele figured Southern Blue Gum veneer that was grown in Spain. The term refers to the 'quilted' or 'copper-beaten' grain that looks like masses of tiny round apples. 'This comes from a plantation,' he said, 'Is there anything like this in Australia?' I told him about a young Southern Blue Gum tree that my friend David Jenkins had milled up on his farm in Western Australia that was full of bird's-eye, but it was only one tree.

Sliced veneer is a specialty market. Less than one millimetre thick, each piece of veneer is sliced off a sawn green board, then dried and repacked in the same sequence, which allows the buyers to lay the veneers to match the colour and grain. It is a high value, low volume product that is traded internationally. It could be grown in South America, sliced in China, traded in Milan and sold in Melbourne. Prices can vary enormously. Nondescript Asian-grown hardwoods like Albizia (*Paraserianthes falcataria*) from Java might sell for as little as $1 per square metre whereas pommele Sugar Maple fetches as much as $50 per square metre. Will showed me the full set of veneer from one Maple log that totalled 762 square metres. He expected to get $37,000 for the lot ($48.55 per square metre), though was quick to add that he was yet to find a buyer!

Will came to the farm to see what we had to offer. He was impressed by the Shining Gum growing along the creek and committed to running a trial. He returned with Anthony who would oversee the transportation and processing. Although his family had a long history in the veneer business in Queensland, Anthony's plan was to send a container of our logs to China for milling and slicing. The back-loading cost of freighting containers meant it was cheaper than carting the log up to the mill in Brisbane, but price wasn't his only concern. He explained that modern veneer production requires very expensive, precision equipment and that labour costs weren't really a consideration when siting a new machine. With the world's largest furniture manufacturers setting up in China, the veneer companies followed.

Within a day I'd harvested ten 22-year-old trees that had an average diameter at breast height of 67 centimetres, from which we extracted 17.4 cubic metres of pruned log in 5.8-metre lengths that would fit neatly into a six-metre container. The logs left the farm in November 2010 and, although they paid me handsomely for the trees and the work, I was left waiting anxiously to hear the results.

A year later, Will contacted me to say the veneers were back in Melbourne; but the results weren't so good. When I got to the warehouse he broke open the pack and he gave me a lesson in veneer grading. Ideally veneers would be laid out on panels in the order they came off the sawn board, thus

Our harvest of 22-yr-old Shining Gum for veneer logs. I felled the trees with a chainsaw and used our tractor logging winch to extract the pruned logs (top). The ten logs ready for their trip to the veneer factory in China (bottom).

matching colour and grain. But this means that any flaw in the log would show up in a succession of sheets. Of course, I understood that branch stubs, rot and insect holes were unacceptable, but what Will was pointing to now—small grain deviations that looked like fingerprints—weren't defects to me. Will called them *ghost knots*. He laid the sheets out side by side across the table. The sequence of identical patterns immediately caught my eye.

The ghost knots were only evident on the backsawn face. They appeared to come from a point just below the pruned branch stubs and extend right out through the clearwood zone. I think what we were seeing were radial strands of cells left behind by a cluster of dormant epicormic bud-producing cells as they moved outwards with the expanding cambium. The markings have no impact on timber strength or performance and would most likely be seen as adding character to a solid timber table, but that's not how Will saw it. He

left: Will James inspects the best of our Shining Gum sliced veneer back in Melbourne.

right: The product of our multipurpose riparian buffer on the walls of the Australian Tax Office in Dandenong.

added that this 'unfortunate outcome' could be partially amended by randomly matching the sheets to mix up the pattern on the panels, but this would significantly reduce the value of the veneer. I left disappointed and more than a little embarrassed having not been able to explain why my clearwood was not absolutely clear.

Over the next year Will sent me a few encouraging reports:

> The Nitens veneer is slowly exiting the building. We sold all the quarter-cut face veneer and we have had a couple of bites on the feature grade. As I said, this is not a production failure, it is a marketing challenge…

> We laid up fifty-eight 2400 x 1200 sheets of plywood for a house in Gippsland. We have random matched the material to prevent the 'feature' from repeating and emphasizing itself. This natural earthy rustic look is sought after with the right marketing. So much for clear wood ay!

Thinking we'd turned the 'marketing corner', I sent an enthusiastic reply. But Will soon set me straight:

> This represents about three percent of the parcel we sliced so we have a long way to go to make a return on our investment.

However, the price we have achieved for this sale represents a good gross profit.

As the bulk of our veneer languished in Will's warehouse, the market was slowly changing. Buyers were beginning to warm to the natural defects in timber as being proof of its, and possibly their own, environmental credentials. I just had to wait. Then, a full four years after the logs had gone to China, Will texted me:

Hi Rowan. We are currently supplying 3,000 square metres of your Nitens into a fit-out of a new office for the Australian Tax Office in Dandenong. The interior designer thought your veneer had the exact amount of feature she was hoping for!

Six years after the logs went to China I approached the security desk of the ATO office. I'm not sure they believed my story but they called the building officer down and I got my chance to see my timber in service. We had planted out an eroded creek to control soil erosion, improve water quality and enhance biodiversity. Within a few years our sheep were enjoying the shade and shelter and we were enjoying the view. Our regular harvests have not reduced any of these values, but they have produced an alternative source of Australian native timber that is neither from native forests or industrial plantations. A third wave.

Grey Fantail (*Rhipidura fuliginosa*)

1. Rowan Reid and Russell Washusen, 'Sawn timber from 10-year-old pruned *Eucalyptus nitens* (Deane & Maiden) grown in an agricultural riparian buffer,' Paper presented at the Third Australian Stream Management Conference, Brisbane, 27–29 August 2001.
2. Peter B. Hairsine, *Controlling sediment and nutrient movement within catchments*. (Cooperative Research Centre for Catchment Hydrology, 1997).
3. Ian Prosser, Ian D. Rutherfurd, J.M. Olley, W.J. Young, P.J. Wallbrink and C.J. Moran, 'Large-scale patterns of erosion and sediment transport in river networks, with examples from Australia,' *Marine and Freshwater Research* 52(1) (2001): 81–99.

Measuring moisture content and wood density

Whether for firewood or furniture, the moisture content of wood can be critical to its performance. Wood density will be important if selling or buying firewood by volume. Density can also affect the strength of timber and its bushfire rating.

I use an electronic meter, which determines the moisture content based on the electrical conductivity of the timber between two pins. Electronic moisture meters vary in cost, and presumably accuracy. Growers who plan to regularly sell firewood should consider purchasing a basic moisture meter to test each load of wood they sell. It is important to always test a freshly cut surface. In most states, it is illegal to sell firewood as 'dry' or 'seasoned' unless the moisture content is 25 percent or less. Wood less than 20 percent burns well and produces little smoke. For furniture timber the moisture content should be between 8 and 12 percent. A meter with pins that reach deep into the timber should be used to ensure the moisture content is even to the core (see photo on page 67).

Both the moisture content and density of wood can be measured in a home kitchen:

- Cut a sample of the wood. Remove the bark.
- Weigh the sample on suitable scales.
- Fill a large bowl with water and set it on the scales.
- Using tongs or a pin, carefully lower the wood into the water until it is fully submerged (being sure not to touch the bottom or sides) and note the increase in weight of the water.
- The increase in weight (in grams) will equal the volume of the wood sample (in cm^2) (displacement theory).
- Put the disc in the oven at about 100–110 °C for few hours or until the weight doesn't change.
- Weigh the bone-dry sample.

Then you can do the following calculations:

- Basic Density (kg/m^3) = Bone Dry Weight (kg)/Original Volume (m^3)
- Original moisture content (%) = (Original Weight – Oven Dry Weight)/Oven Dry Weight x 100
- 'Air-dried' wood density (at 12 % m.c.) (kg/m^3) = Basic Density (kg/m^3) x 1.12

Wood density and tree age

Although the average wood density across each new growth ring in eucalypts tends to increase with the age of the tree, wood density per se is not an age-related factor. Young trees produce wood of lower density because the cells laid down near active healthy leaves tend to be larger than those produced further away from the canopy. Therefore, it is the size and shape of the tree, and when and where the wood is formed, that matters, rather than how old or how quickly it is growing. As the trees grow taller, and their branches grow longer, the distance from the lower stem to the active canopy increases, leading to an increase in the wood density in the new wood formed over the inner core. Evidence for this comes from research that shows that pruning, which lifts the canopy, can hasten the transition from juvenile to mature wood on the lower stem.[1]

To compare the wood density of timber sawn from our 16-year-old Shining Gum and 65-year-old native forest Shining Gum, I cut sample blocks from the sawn timber that corresponded to different locations in the tree: an inner sample close to the pith that would have been produced when the tree was young, a middle sample, and an outer sample from near the sapwood boundary. I found that the wood density in both the plantation and native forest timber did tend to increase from the centre out to the edge of the log. This trend was more pronounced in the plantation wood suggesting that the inner section was picking up some of the low-density juvenile wood. However, by about age 14 years, our fast-grown trees were laying down timber that had a density equal or higher than that from the 65-year-old native forest timber.

1   B.J. Zobel and J.P. van Buijtenen, *Wood Variation: Its Causes and Control* (Berlin: Springer Verlag, 1989).

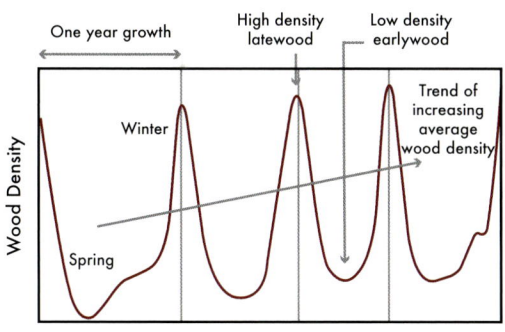

figure 1

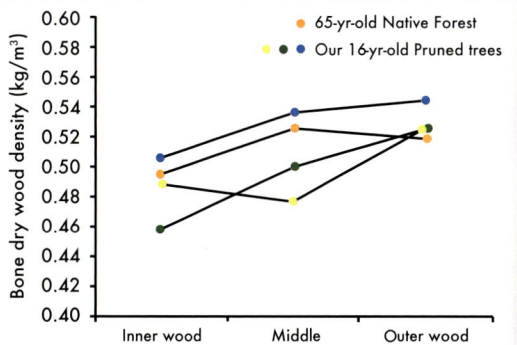

figure 2

opposite: Measuring the moisture content of our firewood with an electronic moisture meter. For-sale firewood should be 25 % or less.

figure 1: In eucalypts and Radiata Pine, wood density varies dramatically within each growth ring between the earlywood and the latewood and the average wood density of all the wood within each growth ring tends to increase further out from the pith (centre of the tree).

figure 2: The wood density (dry weight/air dry volume) across the width of three 135-mm-wide quartersawn boards from our 16-yr-old Shining Gum and one board of 65-yr-old native forest Shining Gum.

Chapter 8

River Sheoak

Casuarina cunninghamiana

Premier Slate in Sydney usually deals in roofing slate, but Vic McKay contacted me when they had an order for timber shakes for a heritage restoration project. The plans specified 'sheoak' but Vic had heard that it was a protected species in New South Wales. When he'd searched out possible suppliers they seemed very guarded. One even told him, 'It's illegal but I can get you some'. All Vic knew was that he needed sheoak for the job and that the prices being quoted were high enough to suggest there was indeed an illicit trade. 'Was Forest Oak the same as sheoak?' he asked. And, 'what did it mean to be protected?'

Sheoaks have a special conservation status in eastern Australia because they provide feed for some of our most threatened species of Black Cockatoo. Unlike the Yellow-tailed Black Cockatoos, the Glossy Blacks have not adapted to the introduced pines and remain almost totally dependent on casuarina seed, principally from Forest Oak (*Allocasuarina torulosa*) and Black Sheoak (*Allocasuarina littoralis*). Though less important as a source of food for Cockatoos, the River Sheoak, the largest of the sheoaks, has additional conservation value due to its natural habit of forming dense forests along inland waterways where it plays a critical role in controlling bank erosion. Further south, the Red-tailed Black Cockatoo, found in western Victoria and South Australia, has a similarly perilous relationship with another sheoak: the Buloke (*Allocasuarina luehmannii*).

This dependence of wildlife on the sheoak suggest they must have been more common than they are today. Ecologist Ian Lunt believes so. He has studied the records and notes that the word 'oak' was often inscribed across the original survey maps of Victoria in areas that are now dominated by eucalypts.[1] The European settlers certainly found the timber useful.

Like English Oak, many of the sheoaks have large radial ray cells which make them easy to split into thin weatherboards and shingles using just an axe and wedge. Being familiar with preparing oak shingles, the early settlers in Sydney immediately took to the Black Sheoak and Forest Oak. Just six months into the settlement of Sydney Cove, Governor Phillip wrote: '*The barracks and all the buildings will be covered with shingles which we now make from a tree like the pine-tree in appearance, the wood resembling the English Oak.*'[2]

Strictly speaking, shingles are sawn (always on the quarter) whereas true shakes, which are usually thicker and longer (60 cm) than shingles, are hand split along the rays to produce wide wedge-shaped flaps. Although more wasteful, splitting ensures a perfectly quartercut board, which guarantees the shake will

preceding: Running a piece of our 17-yr-old River Sheoak through the thicknesser.

right: The ray cells can be clearly seen in the end grain of this piece of sheoak.

be waterproof (because the hollow ray cells do not run from face to face) and remain flat (because it will shrink evenly as it dries); both critical aspects to ensuring shakes can be overlapped to create a flat, durable and waterproof roof.

But, it wasn't just the value of sheoaks for shingles that led to their demise; it was the need for bread.

While the railways and factories preferred to burn dense eucalypts in their furnaces, sheoaks were known as 'bakers' fuel'. They were prized because they burnt fast and hot and produced coals that kept their heat, which allowed the early risers to get their ovens up and running quickly and maintain an even temperature during baking. Regeneration might have followed the harvest but the sheoak seedlings were very palatable to the settlers' sheep, and later the rabbit. In most areas sheoaks have now been missing from our landscapes for so long that no one can remember they were ever there.

The qualities for which sheoaks were destroyed, the usefulness of their wood and the palatability of their foliage, are the same qualities that could bring about their revival.

In 1995, near the end of the Indonesian occupation of Timor Leste, Justino Monteiro Menezes judged it was safe enough to take his family back to his ancestral lands in the hills. I visited his farm in 2014 with a group of Timorese farmers to see how he was managing the indigenous sheoak (*Casuarina junghuhniana*), which they know as Ai-Kakeu. On the way up into the hills I had seen neat stacks of dark red sawn Ai-Kakeu timber for sale beside the road and noticed how it coppices strongly, allowing it to survive fire, occasional grazing and harvesting.

left: Justino Monteiro Menezes beside his native sheoak in the highlands of Timor Leste.

opposite: Our 38-cm-diameter River Sheoak (17-yr-old) just before and after I felled it to examine the timber.

    Justino rebuilt the family home using local timber. He told me that the Ai-Kakeu was traditionally split to use for building timbers and roof shingles but if there was a chainsaw operator in town the logs could be sawn into boards. He had also sold trees. A good sized sheoak could be worth more than US$100 standing, a relatively large amount in local terms.

    Seeing how his crops performed better under the trees, Justino had transplanted naturally regenerating Ai-Kakeu seedlings into his food gardens. The trees provided shelter from the elements but it was what was happening in the soil that made them so valuable. Casuarinas develop a symbiotic relationship with *Frankia* (a bacteria) that allows them to form root nodules—similar to those created by *Rhizobium* in the legumes—that capture nitrogen gases out of the air and fix them into organic compounds that can be transported through the tree to where they are required for growth. Some nitrogen is made available to the food crops through natural leaf fall and the decay of fine roots but this can be enhanced by lopping the live branches or even felling the trees and using the foliage as fodder or mulch.

    Across the Arafura Sea in Papua New Guinea the highlanders have been planting their native sheoak (*Casuarina oligodon*), which they call Yar, amongst their vegetables for hundreds of years. Johnny Wemin collected soil samples from a range of food garden sites close to where his own ancestors once farmed the hills. He analysed the samples then flew back to the University of

Melbourne to work with us on the data. His results showed that as much as seventy percent of the nitrogen in the soil was derived from the atmosphere.[3] However, the trees store most of the nitrogen in their above-ground biomass, extracting what they can from the leaves before they drop. Johnny's results supported the local practice of using pigs, rather than fire, to clear up the foliage and incorporate the nitrogen into the soil prior to planting the food garden. The wood itself contains very little nutrients so its removal from the site for fuel or building material had no impact on soil fertility.

Justino then showed us how he had been trying to extend his Ai-Kakeu plantings into his grazing lands to provide shade and fodder for stock and to promote grass growth—with little success. The transplanted seedlings were not surviving the first dry season. The problem here was the grass itself. The trees he had planted amongst his food crops benefited from the regular cultivation but those in the grasslands were struggling because of the competition. It is the same in Australia. Many farmers believe that if the grass is kept short by grazing or mowing it will not compete with the trees. That's not the case. At least a metre of bare soil or mulch may be required around the seedling to control moisture competition.

One of our own River Sheoak was just seventeen years old and 38 centimetres in diameter when I chose to harvest the timber. It had grown well but I needed to learn more about the wood quality of the species before I decided whether to plant more. River Sheoak is not native to our area but it can grow tall and is very easy to prune. There is some Black Sheoak growing nearby and Drooping

left & middle: I used the chainsaw mill to cut the River Shoeak into boards so I could examine the wood. My pruning wounds had healed over well.

right: The radial splitting of this eucalypt log is due to the release of growth stresses.

Sheoak (*Allocasuarina verticillata*) to the north, but neither grows very large or straight so I never considered them as a sawlog option.

A harvest of one tree hardly constitutes a statistically representative sample but I wasn't so much seeking answers as looking for questions. My lesson started as soon as the tree hit the ground; I was stunned by the lack of colour in the stump. Except for a 5-centimetre circle of reddish colour around the pith, the exposed stem was white. Surely it was not all sapwood! I quickly clamped the sawmilling jig onto my chainsaw and started it up.

I cut a sequence of 1-inch boards that exposed the tree's pruning and growth history. The news from inside the log was better. The stubs had healed well and there was an even growth of clean clearwood outside a narrow knotty core. The growth rings were all clearly evident and I could see how diameter growth had slowed during the years of pruning then responded as the canopy redeveloped.

One thing that did surprise me was that there was no evidence of growth stresses; no splitting, no 'banana' boards, no pinching of the saw. I'd heard it said by both researchers and sawmillers that the natural growth stresses in River Sheoak can make it almost impossible to mill. While acknowledging their experience, I'd always felt that this might be due to the shape and form of the trees they were harvesting. River Sheoak is phototropic, meaning it bends towards the light. It doesn't self-thin well either. Taken together, these factors explain why it is common to see dense clumps of tall thin River Sheoak along rivers that bend out over the water or into the open paddocks. I suspect that these are the trees that were ending up on the mill bench.

Despite their pine-like appearance—needle leaves and woody cones—sheoaks are hardwoods. The leaves have been reduced to tiny bracts that form a ring around the green stems. Being a hardwood, leaning sheoaks hold themselves up by laying down tension wood along the top side of the stem which, when released by milling, causes the sawn boards to bend away from the pith. In contrast, softwoods, such as pine and spruce, develop compression wood on the lower side of a leaning stem or underneath a branch to hold it up.

The development of tension wood is complicated—Russell Washusen did his PhD on it—but there is a simple metaphor that illustrates the concept: imagine a cardboard box wrapped in shrink-wrap plastic. The plastic is in tension and the box is in compression. The whole is in balance. Now, let's say a second, then a third layer of shrink wrap is put over the first, each layer adding further tension. The same happens in the tree. As new growth rings are laid down around the woody stem, a longitudinal (up and down the tree) tensile stress is imposed as these cells mature. The result is that the surface of the log can be in tension (like the outer layers of plastic around the box) and balanced by compression stresses in the central core (the cardboard box resisting being crushed).

As successive layers of shrink wrap are added, the compression forces within the box increase. Eventually, the box will collapse. The same thing happens in the tree: the active tension creates a passive compression in the centre of the log. The forces can reach a critical level, causing the failure of the wood cells. This is described as 'brittle-heart'; the cells have literally been crushed.

Cutting down a tree with severe tension wood can be dangerous. As the chainsaw releases the tension on the outside of the tree a split can suddenly run up the trunk, releasing a backstrap that flicks out towards the operator. Fallers have died in the tall Mountain Ash forests because of tension wood splits, even in trees that are growing straight.

Tension wood forms in straight trees to allow them to flex in the wind without breaking. Russell assessed a dense plantation of Southern Blue Gum and found that there was pronounced formation of tension wood on the windward side in the lower trunk of straight trees.[4] The extent and severity of the tension seemed to relate to what he called the aspect ratio: the ratio between the height of the tree and its diameter. He now advises growers and sawmillers to avoid harvesting and processing eucalypt logs from trees that have an aspect ratio of more than 80.

Our Shining Gum sawing trials seemed to confirm this. We saw no evidence of severe tension wood formation in either the ten-year-old trees (40 cm in diameter and 20 m tall) or in the sixteen-year-old trees (50 cm in diameter and 25 m tall), an aspect ratio of 50 in each case. By contrast, Russell found long bands of tension wood in the sawn timber that came from the 65-year-old native Shining Gum logs. Though these logs were also about 50 centimetres in diameter they came from trees growing in a wet native forest more than 50 metres tall, an aspect ratio of 100!

There are ways of relaxing the growth stresses in a log prior to sawing. I visited a mill in New Zealand where the sawyer told me it was their standard practice to throw any English Oak logs into the millpond and leave them submerged for a year to 'relax'. I have done the same with our Hybrid Poplar, a species that is notorious for developing growth stresses in tall straight trees. It worked well. I tried the same with our planted eucalypt logs, but they sank to the bottom of the dam! An easier option might be to store the logs under water spray for a few months. Water also reduces the risk of end splitting and Longicorn beetles attacking the sapwood.

I believe the reason why my River Sheoak showed no signs of tension wood was because it was a straight tree with a reasonable diameter for its height (38 cm diameter and less than 20 m tall). It was also growing in a sheltered area surrounded by taller eucalypts. It had no reason to form tension wood to maintain stability.

I stacked the freshly sawn River Sheoak boards with stickers between the layers to allow airflow. As I handled each board I carefully inspected them, searching for anything that might help me better understand the species and my management and processing options. I was certainly disappointed about the wood colour. At least the ray cells on the quartersawn boards were clearly evident—even without colour it would still be a beautiful timber. I returned to the books to see what else I could learn. I confirmed that the sapwood of most casuarinas is not *Lyctus* susceptible so it doesn't need treating against the Powder Post Borer. That was my first concern—if the sapwood band was really that wide, being resistant to *Lyctus* meant that it would still be useful without treatment with boron. Surprisingly, all the references talked about the chocolate-purple heartwood of River Sheoak. Maybe I could stain it. But, there had to be more to it. If the stem was indeed all sapwood this single tree was threatening to undermine my whole understanding of tree physiology.

I returned to the farm a week later to a greater surprise. The offcuts that I had left in the paddock had changed colour! Well, at least the parts exposed to the light. What was clearly heartwood was now a dark orange colour, plainly contrasting with a narrow ring of sapwood that was only about one centimetre wide. This was now better than I might have expected. I milled the second log and compared the white freshly sawn boards with the dark offcuts from the previous week. I now had more questions than answers: Why was the heartwood initially white and what changed its colour?

I found a book in The Botany Library at the University of Melbourne from 1919 titled *The hardwoods of Australia and their economics* by Richard T Baker.[5] Baker had held the position of 'economic botanist' with the New South Wales government and was responsible for researching the commercial potential of hundreds of native species. It is the sort of practical information we have lost during the industrial forestry age. Baker begins his section on casuarinas with the note that: 'Shee Oaks' (not Sheoaks or She-oak) were so named 'on account of the peculiar sound produced by wind when passing through the branches'.

A full-page colour plate shows a dark brown-red timber with a strong 'oak' figure. He listed the uses for River Sheoak timber as shingles, panelling, furniture and bakers' fuel and notes that the wood is the 'palest of all the Casuarinas', 'requires careful seasoning', is 'beautifully figured', has rays that are

A board of freshly-sawn River Sheoak on top of a board I milled a week earlier, showing the colour change in the heartwood.

'particularly large', and heartwood that is 'pale chocolate in colour and the outer portion almost white'. What's that? I'd never seen a description that implies the outer 'younger' heartwood is lighter than the inner heartwood, if anything the opposite is more likely the case.

I continued my research. I knew that once the extractives are deposited at the sapwood-heartwood boundary it is not possible for the tree to add any further chemicals to the cells that might change their colour. So, the most likely cause is oxidisation of some of the chemicals in the heartwood on exposure to air. Within the young healthy tree this process would be slowed by the high moisture content. With time the heartwood would dry, allowing some air into the cells. Fortunately, the resulting colour, whether it forms before or after milling, will be the same.

I added the freshly sawn timber to the stack in the shed and waited. As it dried, any board containing backsawn timber cupped. Baker was right about something: this species requires very careful seasoning or, at least, careful milling. The tangential shrinkage rate for the sheoaks can be as much as three times the radial shrinkage rate so there is nothing you can do, and no weight you can pile on the stack, that will stop a board that contains backsawn timber from warping. I'd learnt another lesson: to produce flat boards from any sheoak I would need to quartersaw it, which offers the bonus of showing off the ray cells. But it would require a large log.

I planted more River Sheoak but I've also started trialling some other species. John Carr, a member of our farmer group, walked us through a patch of Drooping Sheoak on his family block on the plains just north of the Otways. He estimated the trees were over 100 years old, probably regeneration from an early clearing for fuelwood. Saved from the plough and sheep by his grandparents, John's current management involves occasional grazing and light burning to control the wattle regrowth and stimulate sheoak regeneration. It seemed to be working well. But the older trees were starting to break apart. I suggested he bring a few of the fallen logs over to see what we could recover from them on the mill.

There was no question about what was heartwood in the freshly sawn Drooping Sheoak; the dark red colour in the old logs extended almost to the bark. I splashed water on the freshly cut surface to wash off the sawdust and reveal the wide ray cells. Drooping Sheoak, once also known as Shingle Oak, is Victoria's match for the beauty and utility of the Forest Oak in New South Wales and the Western Australian Sheoak (*Allocasuarina fraseriana*).

Starting in the early 1980s, Dr Rod Bird set up trials across Western Victoria testing tree species performance, provenance variability, direct seeding methods, weed control options, agricultural yield behind shelterbelts and the impact of widely spaced trees on pasture production. With a view to supporting wildlife, his focus was primarily native timbers, including the local River Red Gum and the Drooping Sheoak. He also planted River Sheoak; it grew tall and straight, and didn't seem to compete much with pasture, making it an ideal shelterbelt tree.

At the time, many local graziers were interested in his work. Rod was doing good local on-farm research that they could rely on as being relevant to their own properties. Also, the 1982 drought had just broken and the iconic River Red Gum, an emblem of the western district, had suffered and was in decline. The Red Gum country had been a gift to the first European settlers.

opposite: The backsawn section of this River Sheoak board cupped during drying due to the high tangential shrinkage. The quartersawn part of the board stayed straight.

left: John Carr's forest of Dropping Sheoak originated from regrowth that was protected from grazing.

right: Freshly cut Drooping Sheoak on our sawmill. Image courtesy of Tom Fairman.

Occasional indigenous burning had created a gentleman's parkland of Red Gums with an understorey of sheoak and wattle and the occasional clumps of regenerating Red Gum that would have come up in the low-lying areas after floods. The settlers cut the small trees for fuel and fenceposts and any straight Red Gums for sawn timber. But, the sheep prevented any regeneration so all that remained one hundred years later were the large old Red Gums that were too crooked to warrant felling for timber.

The farmers liked their old Red Gums. They provided shelter for their stock and defined their landscape. When the trees started dying they wanted to know why. Research suggested it may have been the drought, repeated insect attack, soil compaction and excess nutrient loading by stock, or soil erosion and dryland salinity. Whatever the reason, the trees were old and would need to be replaced. When the rain returned, planting trees emerged as a symbol of a family's heritage and their determination to stay on the land for generations to come.

Rod's research provided the technical know-how about species selection and tree establishment but it was a philanthropic initiative, the Potter Farmland Plan Project, that started in the mid-1980s that provided the vision. Andrew Campbell, born of a western district sheep farming family and a graduate in my forestry class of '83, was given the task of leading the project. His team immediately set about transforming a number of carefully selected family farms into real life examples of sustainable development.

It was literally ground-breaking stuff that confronted the conventional paradigms of both farming and conservation. Working with the farmers, the project developed multipurpose plantings that were designed to simultaneously address the productivity and environmental needs on each farm. Corridors of vegetation along drainage lines and ridgelines linked patches of remnant native vegetation and small block plantings located on unproductive land. The

left: The attractive mature River Red Gums of Western Victoria.

opposite: View over one of the Potter Farmland Plan project farms (in 2016) that later became part of Mark Wootton and Eve Kantor's Jigsaw Farms. It shows how Mark and Eve have expanded on the original plantings by filling in between the older narrow treebelts. Image courtesy of Eve Kantor.

plantings formed a complex web that enclosed irregularly shaped paddocks defined by soil type boundaries and agricultural productivity. They weren't trying to restore a colonial landscape; they were trying to create the vision of a new one that would encourage other farmers to act. As the project wound down, the enthusiasm amongst the farming community for planting trees increased.

But, a total farm makeover is expensive. For a while it looked like the high prices being paid for wool might be able to pay for repairing the country. In just five years from 1983 to 1987 the national woolclip increased by twenty percent and the wool price had more than doubled. The demand was real, the wool was leaving the country, but when the wool floor price was ratcheted up it sent a message of unwarranted confidence to growers. As we watched the tanks rolling into Tiananmen Square and the cracks appearing in the Berlin Wall, few woolgrowers could see that there would be far-reaching consequences. Within months both Russia and China—two of Australia's major wool customers—began pulling out of the market, triggering the floor price mechanism into play.

Talk of dropping the floor price encouraged farmers to flood the market with their private stores. Within a year warehouses across the country were bursting with more than four-and-a-half-million bales of unsold wool. Something had to give. The floor price was first reduced, then suddenly abandoned in 1991, releasing millions of bales onto a depressed market and sending shockwaves throughout the industry that would affect the confidence, commitment and the pride of woolgrowers for more than a decade.

Not surprisingly, farmers lost interest in planting trees. They were focused on surviving. Some jumped while others were pushed off the land as debts mounted and asset values fell. For those who hung on long enough for the dust to settle, it was actually trees that would cause property values to rebound, eventually surpassing pre-crash levels. But the trees being planted, or more particularly the style of planting, was not what Rod or Andrew had envisaged.

The boom in tax-effective managed investment schemes that began in the mid 1990s pushed up land prices and led to the purchase of hundreds of family farms for conversion to wall-to-wall Southern Blue Gum chipwood plantations. From the start, it seemed clear to me that the investments were not a true reflection of the relative profitability of wood and wool. Neither, despite the rhetoric, did they have anything to do with environmental reclamation, carbon sequestration or the development of a new industry that might provide an alternative future for the next generation of farmers.

The trees that were now changing the landscape were being funded by a bizarre tax ruling that allowed investors to deduct, upfront, all future growing costs. It was as absurd as the wool floor price. In effect, the tax gain pocketed by wealthy city investors was a government subsidy that supported an unsustainable plantation investment boom that changed family farms into corporate forests. There is no pride in selling the family farm, but getting a price two or three times what your neighbours thought it was worth certainly made it easier to pack up the house and lock the gate without looking back.

While working for a university did allow me to speak out, Rod Bird, being a government employee, was gagged. For him it was personal. Some of his trials, including several that were just starting to yield some useful growth data, and patches of remnant trees that he'd identified as critical habitat for the Red-tailed Black Cockatoo, were being bulldozed for Blue Gums. For him the plantation industry represented a form of government-supported land degradation, caused by planting trees rather than clearing them. Andrew shared our frustrations. He was managing Land & Water Australia (a national Research and Development corporation) at the time, which supported research into the joint production of farmland for conservation and profit. Rather than follow some of his neighbours and sell out to the plantation companies, Andrew was

also planting trees on his own farm for, amongst other things, high-quality sawlogs. There were a few other farmers in the district that were prepared to stay, and continue to plant trees in ways that supported, rather than replaced family farming.

left: Pruned Spotted Gum on Jigsaw Farms provide shelter for stock and help ensure their farm production is carbon neutral.

right: The parkland of 25-yr-old River Sheoak on Jigsaw Farms that was established to assess pasture production under wide-spaced trees.

Mark Wootton and Eve Kantor's farm is not far from Andrew's place. The beautiful Red Gum floor in their renovated homestead—cut from a few dead paddock trees—is a perfect complement to the million or so trees they have planted. With an eye on underpinning agricultural productivity in the face of a changing climate, they planted for shade, shelter and biodiversity. They are also interested in the carbon, both in the live trees and the timber, and are pruning many of their young eucalypts for sawlogs.

The couple saved part of Rod and Andrew's legacy when they bought two of the old Potter Farmland Plan Project farms. One included a spacing trial of River Sheoak that Rod had planted in 1985. He had established several trials in the district that used a systematic parallel-row design in which the spacing between the trees and between the rows varied across the paddock. This provided a range of tree stockings from plantation to parkland (625 to 25 trees per hectare) across which he could monitor tree growth and pasture production. Of all the eucalypts Rod tested, only young River Red Gum grown at a wide spacing showed any sign of promoting pasture production. In every other case, the more eucalypts there were, or the greater their size, the less pasture there was and the lower its quality. Radiata Pine was the same. River Sheoak was the other exception.

Rod found that pasture production under seven-year-old widely spaced River Sheoak (175 trees per hectare) was significantly higher than under open pastures. The impact of trees on agricultural production is the result of the balance of positive influences—like nitrogen fixation, nutrient cycling and shelter—and the negative effects of shading and moisture competition. Although there may be a sweet spot where a particular number of trees of a particular size actually enhance pasture productivity, it is really just a moment in time. For the farmer, the increasing prospects of a return from timber and the opportunity to use the trees as a shelter haven for stock might offset any concerns about a decline in pasture productivity as the trees grow past that point.

It was close to sunset on a late winter's day when I walked amongst Mark and Eve's 25-year-old River Sheoak spacing trial. The diameter growth of the River Sheoak was definitely better at wider spacings. Some were almost large enough to quartersaw on my bandsaw. I did a couple of quick basal area sweeps and measured the diameter of some of the better trees. It all made sense. I felt confident that my plan for growing high-pruned River Sheoak to 60 centimetres in diameter at a final spacing of about 10 to 12 metres was about right, for me.

As the light faded I sat down to take a moment to enjoy the view. The sheep seemed content; grazing under the parkland of widely spaced trees that seemed to mimic the River Red Gum that were once scattered across the landscape. It was a beautiful picture, one that hinted that the future of the Western Districts of Victoria might not lie with the restoration of an ancient Red Gum woodland but with the creation of something new. A landscape that included lesser grown native species integrated with farming in ways that support biodiversity and agricultural productivity. Besides, a parkland of trees on a family farm is much more attractive, to me and to the sheep, than a dense corporate plantation of any species.

Superb Fairy-wren (*Malurus cyaneus*)

1. Ian Lunt, 'Forgotten woodlands, future landscapes,' *Ecology for Australia – one blog at a time – Ian Lunt's Ecological Research Site*. Posted on 13/10/2103, https:// ianluntecology.com/2013/10/13/forgotten-woodlands-future-landscapes/

2. Frederick Watson (ed.) *Historical Records of Australia: series 1, Governor's despatches to and from England. Volume 1.* 1788-1796 (Sydney: Government Printer, 1971).

3. Johnny Wemin, Rowan Reid and Robert Edis, 'Nitrogen fixation by *Casuarina ologodon* L. Johnson agroforestry in the Papua New Guinea highlands,' *Journal of South Pacific Agriculture*, Volume 14 (2010): 38-52.

4. Russell Washusen, Jugo Ilic and Gary Waugh, 'The relationship between longitudinal growth strain, tree form and tension wood at the stem periphery of ten- to eleven-year-old *Eucalyptus globulus* Labill.' *Holzforschung*. 57 (3) (2003): 308–316.

5. Richard T. Baker, *The hardwoods of Australia and their economics* (Sydney: Government Printer, 1919).

Reaction wood: tension wood and compression wood

The term *reaction wood* refers to the development of abnormal cells by the cambium in response to movement forces such as gravity or wind. The nature and location of reaction wood in trees differs between hardwoods (the flowering plants) and softwoods (conifers). In a hardwood, like my sheoaks, English Oak, eucalypts and Hybrid Poplar, tension wood will form on the top side of a leaning stem or branch, which creates a tensile stress that holds, or even pulls, the stem up straight. In softwoods, like my Coast Redwood or Radiata Pine, compression wood forms on the lower side of a leaning tree or the underside of a branch, and acts like a spring to hold the stem up. In both cases the reaction wood adds diameter to the stem on one side, leaving the pith off-centre (figure 1).

The development of tension wood in tall, straight, skinny hardwood trees is a response to wind inducing a bending stress and is common in plantations of closely spaced eucalypts or poplars growing on productive sites. In this case, bands of tension wood tend to form on the outer part of the lower stem, which helps it resist and absorb movement (figure 2).

Whilst the standing tree is held in balance, when felled or milled the tension or compression forces are released causing the log to split or boards to bend as sawn. Reaction wood also affects how the timber behaves as it dries. Tension wood has a much higher tangential shrinkage than normal wood, which can result in large cracks or bands of collapsed wood cells developing as the timber dries.

In softwoods, the compression wood cells have very thick walls and a high lignin content resulting in an increase in wood density. Also, the tiny cellulose fibres that make up the cell wall are not orientated along the grain as in normal cells (their micofibril angle is greater than 40 percent). Both factors make the wood more effective in holding up the living tree but the advantage does not extend to the usefulness of the sawn timber. When dried, the zones of compression wood shrink more in the longitudinal direction than the normal wood, which causes the sawn board to bend and twist.

To avoid the formation of reaction wood, growers should aim to ensure their trees are straight and spaced sufficiently apart to encourage diameter growth. In hardwoods, larger diameter trees have two advantages with respect to avoiding and managing tension wood (figure 3):

- The trees are more resistant to wind sway so they are less likely to develop reaction wood; and

- Any tension stress added to the outside of the tree is spread across a larger diameter therefore reducing the difference in tension across a sawn board.

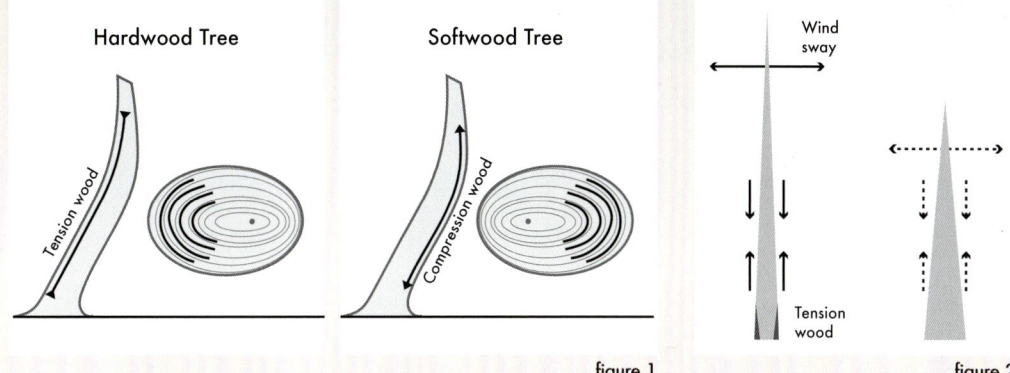

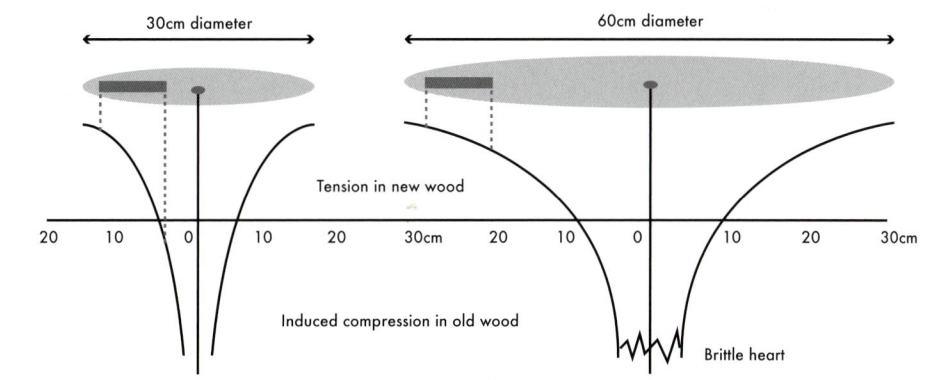

figure 1: Hardwoods form tension wood on the upper side of a bent stem or branch whereas softwoods form compression wood on the lower side.

figure 2: Tall straight trees can develop tension wood in the lower stem in response to wind sway. Short, fat trees with a large canopy are more stable.

figure 3: Boards sawn from larger logs will bend less during milling because the difference in tension across a board is lower. In some cases, the induced compression in the centre of the log can cause collapse of the wood cells in the centre of the tree. Brittle heart is rarely a problem (the centre of the log is usually waste wood) and may be an advantage (as it releases some of the stress).

left: Reaction wood adds growth to one side of the stem resulting in the pith becoming off-centre. As it dries, tension wood tends to shrink more than normal wood causing cracking and distortion.

right: Straight eucalypt logs can still contain some tension wood as shown by this five-metre-long log on our sawmill.

Chapter 9

Sydney Blue Gum

Eucalyptus saligna

In early spring 2004, I drove south from Perth to Bridgetown then turned up the road that ran out past the showgrounds and into the native Jarrah (*Eucalyptus marginata*) and Marri (*Corymbia calophylla*) forest. I was heading to David and Di Jenkins' valley farm, just as I had done many times before, prior to the December 2003 wildfire. The native bush told the story. It had been a very hot fire. There were epicormic shoots sprouting out from the lower trunks of some of the Jarrah trees, but the absence of shoots on the upper branches and the death of some of the biggest trees was a measure of the intensity of the fire. Given time—only a few years—the native forest would grow back. Nothing natural would be lost and some might even argue that much has been gained, ecologically, from such a *good* burn.

With time David might be able to say the same about his farm. Maybe that was why I needed to be there. Why he needed to show me his trees. But, I was also there to learn. Across southern Australia fire is the greatest threat we face as tree growers. I needed to understand what it felt like to be *burnt-out* and which species performed best.

David had written: '*This was the third fire we've experienced in the 'twenty-seven years of living here. The first two were much less damaging. In those fires any eucalypt over about four years old escaped any damage that might cause degrade in their sawlog value. The wide-spaced pruned trees actually acted as firebreaks, slowing the wind and retarding the rate of spread of the fire.*' This fire was very different.

As the local fire-control officer, David had been listening to the radio as the first crews in the next district adopted a direct-attack strategy on a small fire. The firefighters were quickly overwhelmed and the order came to concentrate on saving life and property. As the fire entered David's region he was organising crews, monitoring the radio, watching the weather readings and studying the maps. Together, it all added up to the same story: the fire was heading directly towards his own farm. It's the dilemma that has faced every rural volunteer firefighter: heeding the call meant they mightn't be at home to protect their own house, sheds, fences, stock or family.

Late that night, after the fire was contained and the major threat to property had passed, David drove down that same dirt road I'd come in on through the Jarrah forest. Like me, he didn't know what he would find. Unlike me, his stakes were unbearable. I tried to imagine. As the forest gave way to the farmland he would have seen that the neighbour's house had survived. At first *preceding: I regularly burn off the leaf litter under our Sydney Blue Gum to reduce the fire hazard.*

top: A native Jarrah forest in Western Australia recovering from wildfire.

bottom: David Jenkins with his favourite Sydney Blue Gum tree 9 months after the fire in 2004 (left) and 10 years later in 2014 (right).

glance, his seventeen-year-old parkland of high-pruned east-coast eucalypts opposite might have looked okay; the fire hadn't run from crown to crown. I remembered how Phil Cheney, the eminent bushfire researcher, had said that a crown fire couldn't run without a supporting ground fire. David's pruning had lifted the canopy up and his stock had kept the grass down so there was no fuel to sustain a canopy fire.

Hopefully David only gave the trees a passing glance—his focus would have been further down the road. When he did venture up there the next morning the shock of the dead was only surpassed by the horror of the living. Just as they would have when any other storm came up the Blackwood Valley, his sheep had sought refuge under the trees. He would need to do the triage, decide which sheep might survive and which would need to be put down. Just as he was working up the courage to get started, a group of farmers drove down the road, stopped, and approached him in the paddock. They didn't know David but they knew what had to be done. They sent him back to the house: 'Leave it to us, we'll take care of this.' Only fifty of their 400 ewes survived.

David's wife Di described her experience of being in the house that day to me. The fire split in two and then came together in the government-owned Radiata Pine plantation just across the valley. The pines were almost 30 metres tall, and she judged that the flames reached 60 metres, maybe more. The roar was deafening. The sudden increase in fire intensity sucked all the air out of the valley and threw an ember storm up and over the house.

David had told me some of this on the phone a few days after the fire but it was still a shock to be there on the farm. It was more than just the loss of sheep, trees, pastures, machinery and fences. And it certainly wasn't about the money. With the timber salvage that followed, David and Di were better off than many of the other farmers who'd been burnt out, and many that hadn't. But something else was clearly bothering him. As we walked and talked I began to understand. The fire had taken something more.

David had written: '*At times my feelings of loss have been overwhelming. Pastures, fences and even livestock can be replaced relatively quickly after such dreadful losses. A plantation cannot be regrown or repurchased in one growing season. The loss of many years of timber growth on a highly-managed saw log rotation is immense.*'

What David taught me that day changed forever the criteria I use for selecting eucalypts for wood production. Fast growth is good but being able to survive a wildfire is better.

David and Di had planted four east-coast eucalypt species for sawlogs: Southern Blue Gum, Sydney Blue Gum, Spotted Gum (*Corymbia maculata*) and Red Ironbark. By the time I arrived most of the Southern Blue Gum had been salvaged. To be saleable, badly burnt trees need to be felled well before the next summer when deep cracks would begin to form and the Longicorn beetles would begin attacking the drying sapwood. Any large pruned butt logs were sold at a reasonable price as sawlogs. Selling the smaller stems for pulpwood was more difficult. Even using an industrial harvester, the dry bark on the burnt trunks was hard to get off the stem and any charcoal left in the wood reduced its value.

They were lucky that there was a good demand for Southern Blue Gum chipwood at the time and, on hearing about their loss, harvesting contractors and wood buyers were keen to help. Two machine harvesters began salvaging his Southern Blue Gums while David manually felled any that were too large for the machines. In all, about 1,000 tons of log were salvaged, of which 800 tons went to a local sawmill and the rest for export woodchips. The sale netted valuable income at a time of great need. The harvest and onsite milling, using a borrowed portable mill, of a small block of burnt Radiata Pine even paid for a new portable sawmill to replace the one that was sitting under the trees when the fire came through.

Now that the worst of the Southern Blue Gum had been harvested, David was asking me to help with the triage of what remained. The Sydney Blue Gum looked reasonable and the Spotted Gum seemed fine. Over the winter both species had shed their damaged outer bark to reveal a clean trunk. But I couldn't see through the bark to see if the critical cambium layer had been damaged.

If you examine a cross-section of fresh bark on the end of a log, it is easy to see that there are two distinct zones: the inner and outer bark. The inner bark is moist. Most of the cells in this zone are formed by the cambium and play an active role in transporting food down the stem. The outer bark is made up of dead inner-bark and specially produced cork cells that originate from secondary cambium layers in the transition zone between the inner and outer bark. As new growth pushes the bark cells further out they are impregnated with tannins, waxes or resins to provide a protective air, fire and waterproof coating over the stem.

Eucalypts that have evolved to survive fire tend to hold on to their outer bark for longer, allowing it to get thicker with age. In species that retain their bark, such as Red Ironbark, deep vertical grooves or furrows form in the outer bark as the tree expands in diameter. Sydney Blue Gum and Spotted Gum adopt a different strategy. Both species have evolved in a landscape prone to more regular, though less intense, fires than experienced by the Southern Blue Gum in its natural habitat of the wet forests of southern Victoria and Tasmania. Although they shed their outer bark as they grow larger, secondary growth ensures they retain a thick corky sock covering the cambium right up to the higher branches.

We started by examining the few Southern Blue Gums, which David had initially judged as worth saving. They were certainly alive and would recover but their value for timber would be compromised in two ways. The death of the upper branches had allowed epicormic shoots to develop right down the pruned log. These would need to be removed immediately to prevent new knots forming in the stem. Then there was the damage to the trunk itself. We could see that the bark was beginning to pop off the wood in areas where the cambium had been killed. David pointed out how the scars occurred on the same side of every stem; the lee or sheltered side to the approaching fire. Fanned by very strong winds, flames wrapped around the trunk to the back of the stem where they generated the most heat for the longest time.

With the death of the cambium, the sapwood would begin to dry out, allowing insects and fungi to invade the unprotected wood. Then, following

the orientation of the wood fibres and ray cells, the decay would spread rapidly up the stem and in towards the centre of the tree, infecting the sound wood. Fortunately, trees are quite effective at preventing rot travelling around the stem or outwards into new wood.

We discussed David's options: he could bring the harvesters back and continue cutting out the Southern Blue Gum logs while the wood was still good or prune off the epicormic shoots and let them grow on, accepting that one side of the tree would probably be useless. David had lost enough trees. He'd leave them for now and gradually harvest and mill what he could himself.

The seventeen-year-old Sydney Blue Gum and Spotted Gum were a different story. There were a few with patches of dry bark on the lee side close to the ground but it didn't seem to extend far, either into or up the tree. I couldn't see any damage on the Spotted Gum. We then walked over the ridge to a younger planting of Spotted Gum and Red Ironbark on a dry bank. Being close to the top of the hill, the fire had run through the area as hot as anywhere on the farm. The fire had scorched the canopies, causing all the leaves to fall, but the thick bark on the upper branches had protected the epicormic buds, allowing the trees to sprout a new canopy. Nine months after the fire it was as if there was no fire at all.

Bridgetown and Bambra are on opposite sides of the Australian continent but both are located in, or just beside, one of four identified areas of extreme bushfire potential in the country.[1] The others are around Hobart in southeast Tasmania (Black Tuesday 1967 and the 2013 Tasmanian Bushfires) and northeast of Melbourne (Black Saturday 2009). I'd been lucky, and it is only luck that has saved us. I knew the risks, I'd lost a house in Ash Wednesday (1983) and had built one on the farm to survive the worst. But, I'd been enticed by fast growth and had planted too many fire-sensitive eucalypts. No more. That's when I made the decision that I was only going to plant eucalypts that could survive an inferno. Species like Sydney Blue Gum, Spotted Gum and Red Ironbark.

left: David Jenkins milling 24-yr-old Sydney Blue Gum (his left) and Southern Blue Gum (his right) harvested from trees that survived the fire.

right: David Jenkins measuring the depth of the watertable under his trees. Before he planted, dryland salinity was killing pastures and salting up dams. The trees have lowered the watertable allowing the rain to flush the salt out of the topsoil. Image courtesy of Adam Jenkins.

Richard Davies-Colley and his wife Wilma began life as sheep and beef farmers north of Auckland but retired as tree growers and sawmillers. Sydney Blue Gum was their preferred timber species. They sold timber direct to furniture makers and, like selling coal to Newcastle, they had even made sales of stair treads into Sydney itself. This was at a time when the Australian timber industry, concerned about losing access to public native forests, was arguing that it was impossible to grow high quality eucalypt timber in plantations. It's ironic to think that, over the years, I've learnt as much about how to grow and mill our Australian native timbers from travelling overseas as I have in Australia, and often from farmers rather than foresters.

In 1993 Richard and Wilma led a tour of New Zealand farmers to Bambra. I began my farm tour just as I would with a group of Australian farmers but soon found myself outsmarted by their forestry knowledge and practical experience. I listened as they debated the finer points of eucalypt species selection, pruning and wood quality. They were using my profession's jargon—basal area, knotty core, tension wood etc.—to argue why my profession had got it so wrong about growing eucalypts for sawlogs. It's not unusual to hear farmers challenging conventional forestry wisdom, but this wasn't criticism borne of a lack of understanding, or of suspicion and cynicism. These farmers grew trees, they loved forestry and they knew the language, and enough of the science, to demand being treated as equals.

The visit left me stunned. No longer could I think of myself as the expert amongst farmers. My peers had told me farmers wouldn't be able to grasp the science and practice of forestry: 'Keep it simple, stupid' they would say, asserting that our job was to show farmers what to do and train them how to do it, rather than try to explain why. The New Zealand farmers got me thinking. If tree growing was to become attractive to the farming community, they needed to decide for themselves how forestry could be adapted and integrated into their lives and livelihoods. To do this they needed our language and our science but not our models. I knew what I needed to do.

I would hand over the tools and the language of tree growing, and encourage farmers to make it their own. I would take them to the sawmills, show them the production process and introduce them to the log buyers so they could hear directly from them about what they wanted and were prepared to pay for. I would give each farmer a diameter tape and instruct them in tree measurement and the science of how trees grow. I would then encourage them to design and manage their own forests for the reasons that were important to them. I set out my plan for how the University of Melbourne could run a farmer education program and went looking for funding, without success. I was told that the technical-training sector already provided courses in conservation, revegetation and forestry. Universities should stick to tertiary education. They couldn't see that there might be a third way.

Philip Myer, the son of Melbourne businessman and philanthropist Kenneth Myer, has a passion for wooden boats and trees. One night he rang

David Jenkins (left) and Richard Moore (centre) with a new group of Western Australian Master TreeGrowers.

me: 'I'm the chair of the scientific committee for The Myer Foundation and was wondering if you thought we could invest in a demonstration agroforestry plot to show farmers what they should do.' My response could have backfired: 'No, no demonstrations. That's exactly what we don't want. But I do have another idea.'

Within a few weeks, I was on the forty-fifth floor of a Collins Street skyscraper describing my plans for an Australian Master TreeGrower program. The scientific committee got it straight away. Within a month they provided $100,000 to get me started. I ran the first course in 1996 with my own community in the Otways. David Jenkins then helped me run a second in Western Australia, after which I headed to the Murray Valley region, then further north to the Sunshine Coast.

The farmers understood what I was trying to do and what I meant by being a 'master tree grower'. They were keen to learn, excited about taking control of their own projects, and were willing to share their experience with other landholders. I could see we were doing something new, but I didn't really know what it was. That's when I met Dr Tim O'Meara, an American anthropologist who was working in another faculty at the university. I knew he was the right person to help me understand what I was doing when he told me about his research in Western Samoa where he'd lived with farmers and got involved in helping them to fell, mill and export Mahogany timber from their over-mature shelterbelts. Practical academics are few and far between.

Tim was keen to help and we started by taking a long drive around the coast to Eden in southeast New South Wales where Simon Greenaway, a local extension agent, and I were about to start a new course. The area was the epicentre of a bitter debate over woodchipping in the 1980s and, even ten years later, the community was still deeply divided over the issue of native-forest logging. Many of the traditional farming families had repeatedly harvested their native forests over generations. While they certainly had concerns about the scale of the industry, most were comfortable with logging native forest and saw trees as a renewable resource. For them, the greater threat was the newcomers.

Deregulation of the dairy industry led to family farms being subdivided and sold off. Many blocks were bought by people seeking an alternative rural lifestyle. Simon was an outsider who had married into a local farming family and was comfortable in both camps. When Tim and I walked into the old schoolhouse on the first day of the course it was clear from their respective 'uniforms' that Simon had been successful in gathering participants from both communities. When they took their seats, the crowd divided into their natural clans: bushies to the right and greenies to the left.

Anthropologists, at least the few I've worked with, are comfortable being active participants in the research process. Tim just talked to them. He spoke of his own background and interest in trees and asked them about theirs. And, he watched me. Later I took Tim over to Western Australia and he did the same with a group of farmers in the southern sheep belt. All the while Tim and I talked about the landholders, their aspirations, how they learn from each other, why they might mistrust experts and how they come to make their land management decisions. We also talked about my teaching style, the role of our regional partners, the importance of peer learning, and the structure of the course.

Our Australian Master TreeGrower courses involve seven or eight days, each with a mix of classroom, field activities and farm walks, delivered over a period of six to eight weeks. By the end of the Eden course I'd seen how the partisan divisions that initially divided the group had broken down and were replaced by mutual respect and friendships. The same thing has happened in other courses. Participants find they are learning as much from each other as from any expert. By the time Tim submitted his report I had a good sense of what we were doing and knew what aspects of the program I needed to defend. I also had a new friend and mentor.

A year later Tim and I were working together in Kerala, in southern India. We were there to help plan a community forestry research project. Again, like at David's, I probably learnt more than I might have contributed. One day our driver dropped us beside a river and we were taken across by a local boat owner. With our guide, a young forest researcher, Tim and I followed the rough walking track up the river and into the dense forest. We passed a pile of manure that could only have been produced by a wild elephant, one of the deadliest animals in India, and crossed deep creeks on rickety rope bridges patched together with forest twine and plastic string. Everything—products out and supplies in—had to be carried.

It was on that walk that Tim said something very simple that has stayed with me ever since. It was both a warning about what we would see that day and a request as to how he expected me to behave, and it has become a guiding principle for my work ever since. 'When we get there,' he said, 'rather than judge what people do, I want you to think about why it is rational for them to do it.'

Heartwood

We emerged from the forest into a clearing containing a simple wooden building made of rough sawn timber. There was no garden or chickens. It wasn't a family's home. A young European man stood in the doorway; he was the teacher and this was his school. No students were there but he expected they would be coming tomorrow, depending on their workload. The school serviced several villages that were spread through the forest. He told us that the people survived on their simple gardens, farm animals, fish from the river and plants and animals harvested from the native forest. Any excess was sold for cash. To survive, everyone in the family had to help so sending a child to school increased the burden on others. Providing school breakfasts had helped although there were no funds so the teacher was buying the food and carrying it in himself.

Tim asked what else might help. 'Uniforms,' said the teacher, 'the poorest children are too embarrassed to come.' Tim's lesson had already changed my way of thinking: there were perfectly rational reasons why parents didn't send their children to school and why children didn't want to go.

Further along the track we reached the village, observed the lives of the villagers and talked, only with the men, about their dependence on the products and services of the surrounding forest. One man proudly showed me the fish trap he'd made from forest canes. I wondered if the women that were watching us from the shaded doorways of their huts, might have a different perspective. I was white, rich and male. Even if they could tell me, I could never really understand their lives. It wasn't so different to working with farmers back in Australia. I can't presume to know or understand the factors that influence a farmer's decision, but I can help them access the knowledge and networks required to make a better one, for them.

Back in the city that night I followed Tim from draper to tailor. We purchased cloth and ordered a class set of uniforms. I had to leave but he

left: Tim O'Meara with me in a native forest in Kerala, India.

right: An Indian forest farmer shows me his fish trap made of bush cane, a non-timber forest product.

opposite left: Peter Davies-Colley explains the sawing pattern he uses to produce quartersawn timber from Sydney Blue Gum on a horizontal bandsaw.

opposite right: Ugandan workers pit-sawing pine logs.

stayed on to ensure our donation made it out to the forest school. As I boarded the plane my mind was already back in Australia. The reason why there were so few trees on Australian farms was not because farmers didn't want them. Given what they knew, and the regulatory and commercial environment in which they made their farm management decisions, they had made a rational determination that it wasn't worth planting trees. They could just as easily come to a different decision.

Twenty years after Richard and Wilma visited our farm, I was back in New Zealand taking notes as their son Peter drew chalk lines on the end of a large Sydney Blue Gum log. He was explaining, cut by cut, the sawing pattern that he was about to demonstrate on his horizontal bandsaw mill. There are two types of small portable sawmills commonly used on Australian and New Zealand farms: the horizontal bandsaw and the circular swing-blade. David Jenkins' mill uses a circular swing-blade that can cut both vertically and horizontally as it runs along tracks allowing a series of boards to be cut off the top of a log that is lying on the ground under the mill. It is a robust machine that works well for large diameter logs, even those too heavy to lift. Peter's horizontal bandsaw also runs along a track but the log rests on a sturdy frame and can be rotated during the milling process.

Over the years of running courses for farmers I've visited hundreds of sawmills around Australia, from the old bush mills that were once on the outskirts of every country town, to the enormous 'sausage factories' that can process hundreds of thousands of cubic metres of Radiata Pine each year for house framing. I've also watched itinerant labourers pit-saw logs in the forests of Uganda, the free-sawing of coconut trees with chainsaws in Timor Leste, and teams of Javanese workers pushing tiny logs through unguarded vertical bandsaws to recover every last splinter of saleable Teak. There is always something

left: David Jenkins' Sydney Blue Gum lining boards showing a mix of backsawn (growth rings appear as wavy lines) and quartersawn boards (growth rings appear as straight vertical lines).

opposite left: David Jenkins amongst his 22-yr-old Sydney Blue Gums five years after the fire. He has cleared the seedling regrowth to reduce the fire hazard and increase pasture production. Image courtesy of Adam Jenkins.

opposite right: Forest researcher Richard Moore beside a high-pruned, wide-spaced Sydney Blue Gum on another farm in Western Australia. Richard's work on growing high quality eucalypt sawlogs has guided farmers around Australia, including myself.

to learn in the many and varied ways people use the technology, skills and labour available to them to cut the logs they have into something they can sell.

Peter Davies-Colley shares my obsession with quartersawing eucalypts. He showed us how he starts by squaring up the log to remove some of the tension wood off the outside. Then, rather than divide the log into quarters as I'd seen done in the commercial sawmills, he cuts around the central core producing large flitches that are pulled off to the side for re-sawing later. This breaking down process releases the growth stresses so each flitch needs to be restraightened before being sawn into boards (see technical note at the end of this chapter). Peter explained how log diameter affects the length he can mill without wasting too much wood when straightening the flitches: If a Sydney Blue Gum log is 40 centimetres in diameter he will cut it down to three metre lengths. If it is over 80 centimetres, he's comfortable milling six-metre-long logs.

David Jenkins is not so concerned about quartersawing his large Sydney Blue Gum. He cuts one inch boards with his circular swing-blade sawmill and sends them off to be dried and dressed into flooring and lining. The cathedral grain on the backsawn face looks good and he doesn't seem to have any drying or performance problems. Two farmers, one to my east and one to my west, growing and milling farm-grown Sydney Blue Gum, a species that naturally grows to my north. I'm the one in the middle, trying to work out how they can both be right and what might be right for me and my trees.

Whenever I am in the west, I make a point of driving up through the Jarrah trees to revisit David and Di so I can walk amongst their planted forest. It's spectacular. The Sydney Blue Gum have recovered well and many are now well over Peter's target of 80 centimetres in diameter. But rather than bringing in the harvesters and the log trucks and carting them all away, David prefers to manage his forest as a kind of perpetual cash cow. When he receives an order

for his Sydney Blue Gum flooring or lining boards, he walks amongst his trees and selects the ones he is willing to give up. He never picks the best. Small-scale selective harvesting provides an opportunity to leave the forest in a better state; healthier, straighter and more evenly spaced trees. His eldest son fells the trees—David says he's become too attached to them to do it. But he's happy to do the milling. His younger son then helps turn the branches into firewood.

When David and Di planted their first Sydney Blue Gum back in 1987, you could buy clean red, native Karri and Jarrah timber for next to nothing. When David started pruning, a government forest economist did a financial analysis of growing eucalypts for sawn timber. Based on the current prices they couldn't make the numbers stack up. Western Australian silvicultural researchers like Richard Moore had proved it was possible. Locals like David Jenkins had proved farmers could do it. But, that didn't make it a rational investment of a farmer's land, time or cash. David didn't care much for conventional economic theory, he was making decisions based on a more complex investment model that involved family, risk, diversification, land degradation control, shade and shelter for stock, future market uncertainty, aesthetics and personal satisfaction. Even with hindsight David can't prove that their decision to plant Sydney Blue Gum 30 years ago was economically rational, but he's pleased they did.

Grey Shrike-thrush (*Colluricincla harmonica*)

1   R. Blong, D. Sinai and C. Packham, *Natural perils in Australia and New Zealand* (Sydney: Swiss Re Australia Ltd, 2000).

Hardwood sawing patterns for a horizontal bandsaw

There are many ways to mill a log. The possible sawing patterns will depend on the species, the size and shape of the log, the products you are hoping to produce and the sawmilling equipment being used. The best option might not be the one that produces the highest recovery (the percentage of sawn timber per cubic metre of log). My preference is for the method that produces the greatest value given the time and equipment I have available.

I use a simple horizontal band saw that is pushed over a log, which is held tight on a log trailer using chocks. The mill allows me to make a cut 75 cm wide and 20 cm deep. The log can be rotated between saw cuts and any piece can be reloaded onto the bench for re-sawing.

Using this equipment there are essentially three sawing patterns I can use:

1 Through-and-through pattern

This is the simplest option. It involves starting at the top and cutting a series of slabs off the log. I can use this method to mill a log about 70 cm in diameter. If the log is too large, I'll square it by removing some of the sapwood to reduce the width of the slabs.

Through-and-through sawing will produce wide backsawn boards off the top and bottom of the log and quartersawn boards close to the centre. The pith will be included in one or two of the centre slabs. If the pith and corewood need to be excluded, the centre slabs can be resawn into perfectly quartersawn boards.

I often use this method for Blackwood and Black Walnut. Neither species have severe tension wood and the timber will dry without too much distortion as there is little difference between their tangential and radial shrinkage rates. I have used the method with a large English Oak (photo) but wouldn't recommend it because the backsawn boards do not show off the ray cells and are more prone to developing radial cracks and cupping during drying.

2 All-backsawn pattern

If the preference is for backsawn boards it may be worth varying the through-and-through method a little to avoid producing any quartersawn boards at all. The pattern shown in figure 2 requires the log to be rotated as the cuts approach the corewood. The corewood contains the knots, pith and juvenile wood and is often discarded. Of all the hardwood species I grow, I would only mill Blackwood and Black Walnut this way.

3 Quartersawing pattern

For most hardwood species, particularly eucalypts and those that have prominent ray cells (e.g. English Oak, Australian Silky Oak and the sheoaks) my preferred sawing pattern is the method I was taught by Peter Davies-Colley in New Zealand. The first step involves squaring up of the log. This removes some of the outer tension wood and much of the sapwood. If the sapwood is useful (as in Mountain Ash) I often skip this step to produce live-edge quartersawn boards. In species that have durable or coloured heartwood the sapwood is usually considered waste.

The next sequence of cuts divides the log into four flitches and extracts the corewood. This releases all the growth stresses resulting in the flitches coming off curved. The flitches are straightened before being sawn into boards. The amount of curvature in the flitches, and therefore the amount of wastage during straightening, depends on the length of the log and the severity of the growth stresses in the standing tree. Small-diameter logs from tall skinny trees need to be milled as short logs.

On our manual sawmill the continual turning of the log and the offloading and reloading of the flitches is laborious. But, it is worth the effort as it produces the widest possible quartersawn boards.

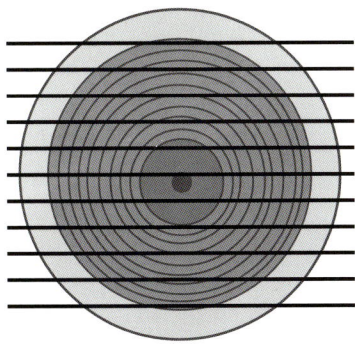

figure 1

figure 1: The through-and-through sawing pattern using a horizontal band saw.

Logs of Black Walnut (top) and English Oak (bottom) that I have sawn using the through-and-through method then re-assembled for air drying.

Science and Practice

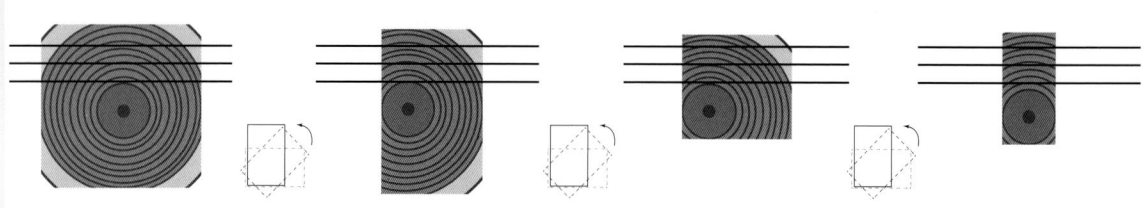

figure 2

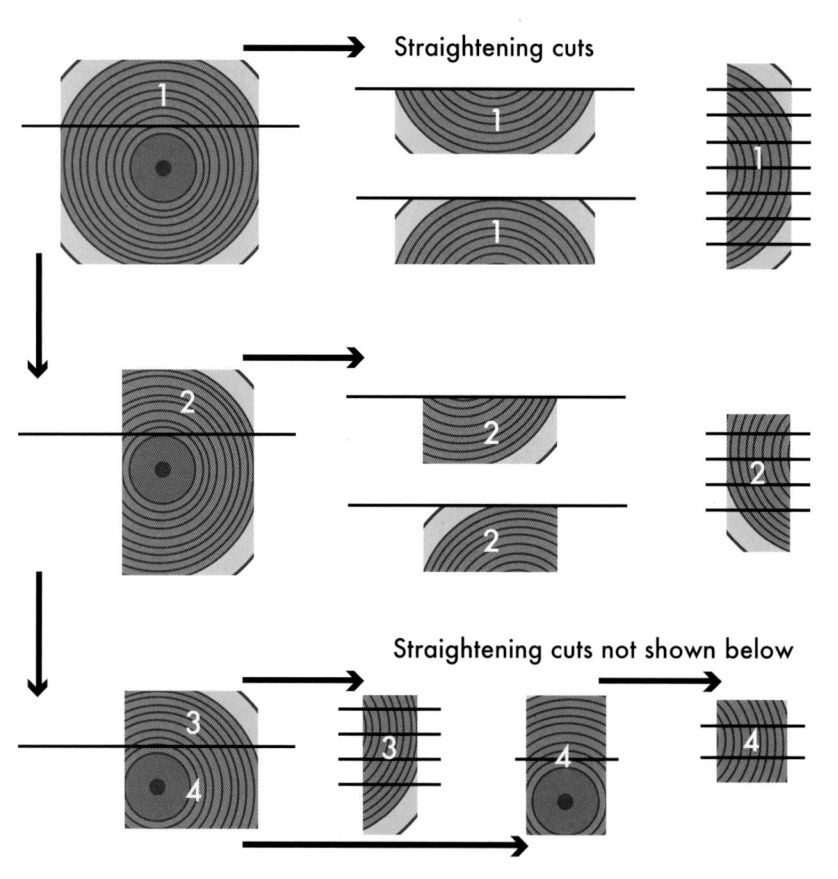

figure 3

figure 2: The all-backsawn sawing pattern requires the log to be rotated. The central core is usually waste.

figure 3: My preferred quartersawing pattern for use on a horizontal bandsaw. The log must first be broken down into four flitches to release the growth stresses and extract the corewood. The flitches are then reloaded onto the mill and straightened to remove any distortion before being sawn into boards.

top: Breaking down a 25-yr-old Manna Gum log zwith a horizontal bandsaw (removing flitch number 2 in figure 3).

bottom: After straightening this flitch of English Oak (flitch number 3 in figure 3) I am now cutting a series of quartersawn boards. Note how the boards show no signs of bending because the growth stresses have already been released.

Chapter 10

Poplars and Willows

Populus and *Salix*

When I was a young teenager, the American Cottonwood (*Populus deltoides*) in our front yard in Melbourne was taller than our family's two-storey 1930's Californian bungalow, and probably as old. It sucked the shallow soil dry in summer, destroying the lawn, and then smothered what was left of the grass in a blanket of leaves every autumn. The leaves also filled the gutters and clogged the drains. It was my job to clear the leaves off the roof, which was fine; I was the climber in the family and was happy to do whatever it took to keep the tree. When I felt trapped in the city, the poplar was my natural escape. I would climb up into the canopy to my well-worn seat on a branch as high as the house.

Poplars came to Australia as a welcome immigrant. The broad-canopied American Cottonwood contributed to the making of the leafy eastern suburbs of Melbourne, whereas the more drought and frost tolerant Lombardy Poplar (*Populus nigra* var. *italica*) found its natural place along the rivers and creeks further inland. Like their close relatives the willows, poplars are easy to grow from cuttings, allowing anyone to become a propagator just by pushing a stick into wet ground.

Every Lombardy Poplar is derived from a single natural genetic mutant of the Black Poplar (*Populus nigra*) that was found on the banks of the Po Valley in northeast Italy in the early eighteenth century. Most mutations in nature lack vigour and amount to nothing. Some share their genes back into the general population, adding genetic diversity. The Lombardy Poplar might have been lost had man not made it his own. The tree's tall slender form made it a favourite for city avenues and farm shelterbelts. Nurserymen, gardeners and farmers spread the cuttings through Europe (to France in 1749 and England in 1758) and on to North America (1784).

Lombardy Poplars arrived in Australia in about 1830, well in advance of the Italian immigrants who became the tobacco growers in the Ovens Valley and the orchardists of Griffith, for whom the tree became a badge of honour that marked their farms and their allegiance. The American Cottonwood in our front yard carried no such nationalistic connotation for my Mum, and might not have survived the Vietnam War if it had. For her it was just a shade tree, shielding her house from the summer sun, and herself from the neighbours.

The first of the transatlantic hybrids—between the Italian Black Poplar, *Populus nigra,* and American Cottonwood, *Populus deltoides*—were a natural occurrence that followed the first introductions of Cottonwoods into Europe in the seventeenth century. Gardeners and farmers soon recognised the hybrid vigour

preceding page: Amongst our 29-yr-old Poplar trees.

right: The autumn colour of the Lombardy Poplars in the Ovens Valley, Victoria. Image courtesy of the University of Melbourne.

in the cross and cuttings were taken from selected seedlings for wider distribution. The hybrids became collectively known as *Populus x euramericana* but it wasn't until the beginning of the twentieth century, with the development of commercial markets for poplar timber in Italy, that any formalised breeding and clonal selection process began. This included the formal registration of superior clones, many of which were given numbers that identified their origin and pedigree.

When the Poplar Fungal Rust (*Melampsora medusa*) arrived in Melbourne in 1972 our Cottonwood went from bright green to yellow and never regained its vigour. The disease was first detected in January 1972 just north of Sydney. By April, driven by a wet cyclonic summer weather system, the rust had spread north to the Queensland border and south to Melbourne. The initial outbreak was confined to the Cottonwoods but a year later a similar disease was found on Lombardy Poplars (*Melampsora larici-populina*). At the time, plantations of Hybrid Poplars were being grown in Australia to supply match maker Bryant and May Ltd with timber to produce their iconic Australian Redhead brand. The plantations were based on a handful of clones of the American Cottonwood and the hybrid, all of which proved to be susceptible to the Poplar Rust.

It is true that clonal plantations—in which all the individuals are derived from the same parent tree—are at greater risk of being wiped out by disease or insects. However, the epidemiology of tree diseases is not that simple. In a natural forest or seedling plantation, diseases can adapt over time, eventually infecting all the closely related individuals. By growing a range of unrelated clones, either in a mixture or as small blocks, growers can reduce the risk of a disease taking out all their trees.

    The first wave of infection dropped plantation growth rates dramatically, particularly for growers in the milder coastal areas of New South Wales. Over time, the disease became less damaging as an indigenous Australian fungus began to parasitise the spores of the introduced fungi. But this was little consolation for growers.

    About ten years after the rust first arrived, Keith Lober showed me how the disease had affected his plantations beside the Hawkesbury River. We stood between his pre- and post-rust plantings. The younger trees, a disease-tolerant clone developed by tree breeders in Canberra, were growing well; full of healthy green leaves and almost as tall as their older infected siblings with their thin yellow canopies. Years of wood production had been lost. Yet, Keith remained enthusiastic about the prospects for poplar timber.

Australians tend to associate quality in timber with in-ground durability, dark colours and high wood density. Poplar is none of these things, and that may be its market advantage. The wood is very light—almost white—and contains no oils, tannins or resin. These qualities have meant poplar has found special markets over the centuries: Leonardo Da Vinci painted the Mona Lisa on poplar wood in the early sixteenth century and the Dutch used it for clogs.

opposite left: I saw these Hybrid Poplars growing on a small farm in the Po Valley, Northern Italy.

opposite right: Poplar clones susceptible to the Poplar Rust on the left and the resistant clones on the right. Keith Lober's farm in the Hawkesbury Valley in about 1984.

right: A simple hall table I made from our Hybrid Poplar. Image courtesy of Luke Popovic.

Poplar wood has long been used for matches: it is light, ignites easily, burns well and doesn't splinter. The pruned logs are peeled on a lathe to produce a sheet of veneer the thickness of a matchstick which is then slivered into the tiny sticks. When Bryant and May pulled out of Australia we all got the chance to compare the structural strength, and the taste, of poplar against the tropical rainforest matches imported from south-east Asia. The latter often shattered when struck and splintered when chewed.

With the loss of the match industry, growers searched out new markets. Keith was supplying timber for Australian-made boat oars; Poplar is light but very strong, and floats. Another high value market was in the production of concrete formwork. Formply, as it is known, is a high-value product; it must be strong, tough and light and, most importantly, the surface must be smooth. Poplar is used for the outer layer of the plywood because it absorbs the thick black coating used to give a flat surface and avoids the risk of leaving an impression of wood grain in the dry concrete.

When our own trees were about ten years old, I got a call from a plywood factory 400 kilometres away. They wanted to know if my trees were ready to harvest. Not quite, I told them. I then asked how they could afford to truck logs so far and still pay me a three-figure sum for each cubic metre. They told me that was no problem, the wood was worth the cost. That was reassuring. However, by the time our trees reached the 45-centimetre diameter specification for peeler logs, the company had changed to using resin-impregnated paper on their pine plywood to give a smooth non-stick finish. That's the nature of timber growing. Markets will come and go while you wait for your trees to mature. Tree growers need to be open to new market opportunities that reflect the qualities of their timber that make it special.

Poplar wood has no taste and will not leach any chemicals when soaked in hot water or saliva, making it suitable for use with food. Think packaging for gourmet cheeses, fashionable kitchen utensils or even ice cream sticks. It also absorbs stains and colours well, allowing it to be matched to look like much more highly valued hardwood timbers. A Western Australian woodworker showed me how he stained poplar with black boot polish and used it as a fine 'Ebony' infill. He sandwiched a thin strip of soft blackened poplar between Jarrah timbers to absorb the unavoidable movement that occurs with fluctuations in humidity and so maintain a tight join. Not even Ebony (*Diospyros crassiflora*) itself could do that job as well as poplar.

Mum waited 'til I'd left home before signing my Cottonwood's euthanasia order. Removing the tree let the north sun bathe the front lawn and the nature strip for Dad's vegetable garden. The house soon looked like the set of the popular British comedy series *The Good Life*, although Dad had more than just the conservative neighbours to worry about. He was fighting back the poplar suckers for years. A propensity to sucker, particularly when the main canopy is under stress or removed, is a common survival trait of the poplars. Once seen as an asset when selecting tree species for soil erosion control, suckering has made many species, including the White Poplar (*Populus alba*), almost impossible to eradicate.

In timber plantations suckers compete with the main crop trees so, in addition to disease resistance, wood quality and branching habit, the tree breeders tested their Hybrid Poplar clones for any signs of suckering. Much of the breeding work undertaken in Europe and North America produced clones suited to high latitudes where the winters are cold. The clones that performed best were responsive to the hours of daylight thus ensuring they stayed dormant through winter. When grown at lower latitudes or in milder climates, such as on Keith's farm on the Hawkesbury, this adaptive strategy meant that the trees missed an opportunity for continued growth through the milder winter months. Geneticists then discovered that the Texan provenances of the American Cottonwood did not respond to day length in the same way as those from the northern states. In their case, bud burst and leaf drop were triggered by temperature, allowing them to grow for longer if the weather was favourable.

As the Australian tree breeders were exploring ways of incorporating the Texan genes into their poplar breeding program, a male mutant of the *Populus nigra* that had been widely planted in Chile was recognised as being

top left: Our 6-yr-old Hybrid Poplars in 1993 growing on the alluvial creek flats.

top right: Our 14-yr-old S.E. A65/31 Hybrid Poplar clones interplanted with Black Walnut.

bottom: I harvested this Hybrid Poplar during one of my university classes.

entirely 'day-length neutral'; staying green as long as the weather would allow. Better still, the Chilean clone, appropriately known as 'Persistente', seemed to be able to transmit this trait in a dominant fashion to half of its progeny when crossed with a recognised timber-producing female hybrid clone. As a result, we now have a range of Hybrid Poplar clones that include genes from the 'semi-evergreen' (S.E.) Chilean Black Poplar clone and the temperature dependent Texan selections of the American Cottonwood which stay green for much of the year.[1]

I grow three of these clones:

1. The female semi-evergreen S.E. I-488 is a manipulated hybrid of the well-regarded Italian hybrid (I-488) and the semi-evergreen

Chilean clone. It has the fastest diameter growth of the three, but this is offset a little by its propensity to throw large branches, which makes pruning more difficult.

2. S.E. A65/31 is a female clone. It was the result of a cross between a promising 1960 American Cottonwood (60/124) and the Chilean clone. It has a slender form with small branches, making it easy to prune.

3. Clone 67/1 is a female deciduous clone, with none of the semi-evergreen genes, that was created from a cross of two recognised seedlings of the Texan Cottonwood (G3 and 60/124). It is relatively day-length neutral and tends to have a long growing season in mild climates.

We are now harvesting and milling poplar timber and exploring our own market opportunities, particularly in the food sector and for children's toys.

I prune our Hybrid Poplars in late summer when the pastures are dry and the leaves are green, to provide supplementary stock fodder. Although our sheep nibble on all our fresh prunings, the leaves of most species probably take more energy to digest than they provide. While the oils in the eucalypt leaves and resin in pine needles don't help, the main problem with using tree leaves for fodder is their high tannin content. Some tannin in fodder is good for stock but levels higher than about three percent can cause the proteins in the feed to be bound up and pass through the ruminant without being fully digested. Mature tree leaves often have a tannin content of more than ten percent. Fed on their own, the foliage of most trees cannot maintain stock live weight, let alone fatten them up.

The green leaves of our Hybrid Poplar, and the related Crack Willow (*Salix fragilis*) that has spread in our area, are the notable exceptions. The poplars (*Populus* genus, with less than 50 species) and willows (*Salix* genus, with over 400 species) make up the two genera in the family Salicaceae. *In vitro* (test tube) assessments suggest that the fresh leaves of many species of poplar and willow have a digestibility of close to seventy percent, which is similar to fresh spring pasture and sufficient to drive moderate growth and production. *In vivo* studies involving pen-feeding trials with cattle have shown that the real feed value tends to be a little less because stock also eat the lower quality twigs. Sheep are more selective.

During the 1982–3 drought, Paul Dann noticed mobs of hungry sheep sheltering in the shade of healthy Crack Willows along the dry creek beds around Canberra. He fed both lambs and hoggets a sole diet of freshly cut *top: Our wethers amongst the 4-yr-old Hybrid Poplars in late summer. I prune our poplars in summer when the pasture is dry to provide supplementary fodder.*

bottom: Crack Willow being removed from our neighbour's creek by the local catchment authority. I killed the Crack Willow along our creek by injecting herbicide into the stem in summer.

willow leaves and twigs (up to three millimetres in diameter) for a continuous period of six weeks starting in January 1983.[2] The sheep ate an average of 0.94 kilograms of dry matter per day and gained an average of just under two kilograms in six weeks. Paul found that a 15-metre-tall tree produced about 200 kilograms of fresh feed, which he judged would provide a weight-gaining drought-saving ration of eighty sheep days per tree. They recovered well and would have been available to harvest again within a few years, when the next drought might be expected.

But, willows are a serious weed in waterways and wetlands in south-eastern Australia. The species that causes problems along the creeks in our area is Crack Willow. The name 'crack' comes from the ease with which the branches snap off. The cuttings get lodged in the loose alluvial soil within the creek bed and can take hold before the next flood. Unlike our natives, Crack Willow can survive long periods of inundation and over time develop into large multi-stemmed trees that block the flow and force the water into the banks, undermining their stability and widening the channel. The impact of the Crack Willow on aquatic life is more insidious. Being deciduous, the willows drop all their soft thin leaves in autumn, causing a sudden influx of organic matter and nutrients. This changes the oxygen concentration and the balance of invertebrates in the shallow late-summer pools, ultimately affecting the survival of native fish and amphibians.

Fortunately, the Crack Willow spreads slowly and only downstream. Most summers I take a walk up the dry creek bed with my stem injector to keep them under control. In Gippsland, Tasmania and New South Wales, willows spreading by seed have caused enormous damage to waterways and wetlands. That's something I don't want to see in our area and why I don't grow any willows. Well, I did once, but not anymore.

Back in 2005 I'd just finished a late-spring farm tour and was going around picking up the equipment I'd left out in the paddocks—the ladder, pruning tools and chainsaw—when I took the opportunity to inspect one of the plantings that I didn't show my guests, a species for which I had mixed feelings; the Cricket Bat Willow (*Salix alba* var. *caerulea*).

More than 10 years earlier Lachlan Fisher, the best known and most highly regarded cricket bat maker in Melbourne, came to our farm with a bag of very special cuttings. The story goes that during a break in play in the test match at the Melbourne Cricket Ground back in 1902, Archie MacLaren, the then captain of the English team, was chatting to the Australian test umpire. If his aim was to win over Bob Crockett it didn't amount to much; although MacLaren won the toss he had a forgettable test as opener (15 and 1) and as captain (Australia won in four days by 229 runs). Apparently, their conversation wasn't so much about the game as about the bats or, more particularly, the willow the bats were made of. Hearing that the most highly regarded clone of *Salix alba* var. *caerulea* was not yet in Australia, MacLaren agreed to send some cuttings back to Crockett on his return.

The cuttings arrived in a steel tube and were taken to the Crockett family farm in central Victoria. Only one of the original cuttings survived the journey from England, but fortunately one is enough to start a clonal cricket bat plantation. Within a few years the Crockett family had more than a thousand trees and, by the 1920s, were making bats under their family name. When the business was bought out by a multinational sporting goods company in the

left: A well-spaced and pruned Cricket Bat Willow plantation in central Victoria.

right: A rooted cutting of Hybrid Poplar. I will bury the roots just below the depth of the pasture roots, then cut the stems off just above ground level.

1960s the planting stopped, although the harvesting continued. Fortunately, a few trees survived and were used to re-establish the plantation by new owners. Lachlan sourced cuttings from the farm and wanted me to grow them and share my experience with other farmers.

I planted the cuttings in a small nursery bed by the creek. Over the first summer, with occasional watering, the cuttings took root and sent up new shoots taller than me. To establish my cricket bat plantation, I followed the same planting technique I'd used for our Hybrid Poplars: I dug a deep hole in the well-drained loam on our creek flats and planted the rooted cuttings, or what poplar growers call 'barbatelles', much deeper than they grew in the nursery plot. The method, which is only possible in deep well-structured soils, ensures that the established roots are well below the depth of the competing pasture, where there is more likely to be a store of soil moisture through the summer months. New roots would then form along the buried stem that could access the more fertile soils close to the surface. By spring, two or three new shoots would have emerged from the exposed buds so, before Christmas, I would identify the strongest and straightest shoot and cut back the others to leave a single stem to grow into the trunk.

While my Cricket Bat Willow cuttings were taking root, I visited Lachlan's factory in Melbourne to learn more. I needed to know his product specifications. He showed me a wide range of imported raw blank bat clefts and explained where in the tree the bat wood came from and what he was looking for in a perfect log: a two-foot-six-inch-long log greater than 15 inches (36 cm) in diameter that could be split into four or six clefts. The face of a cricket bat shows the radial plane of the timber with the growth rings running down its length. Lachlan said that the aim was to have five to seven growth rings evenly spaced across the 4.25-inch (10.8-cm) wide face of the bat. Sapwood is better than heartwood but he acknowledged that it was rare to find a bat that didn't contain both. Knots or grain deviations were considered a serious defect.

above: Cricket Bat Willow clefts drying (left) and the final product in Lachlan Fisher's workshop (right).

opposite: The fluffy catkins (seed heads) on our Cricket Bat Willow. The fluff can carry seed many kilometres on the wind.

From this I was able to design my target tree: the tree trunk had to be straight, with the pith running right up the very centre. Pruning was essential, but it needed to be done earlier than on my sawlog trees so I planned to prune to a 5-centimetre stem diameter rather than to 8 centimetres. Accounting for the stump, a pruned height of about 13 feet (4 m) would provide four logs per tree, more than sixteen clefts in total. The most critical consideration was spacing; I needed to ensure that the trees had plenty of room to develop in order to maintain an even growth rate of between 3 and 4 centimetres per year up to when the tree diameter, over bark, was approaching 40 centimetres.

Our early growth rates were promising. By the Boxing Day Test I had cut each barbatelle back to a single leader. My initial focus was then on ensuring the main stem was growing as straight as possible, then I started the pruning. Every winter I made a point of cutting off any branch that was over 2 centimetres in size to be sure it would not affect the shape and dominance of the main leader. Then, as planned, I removed every branch up the stem to where the trunk was 5 centimetres in diameter. This did stimulate the development of epicormic shoots so I had to return regularly during the growing season to cut them off before they could have any effect on wood quality. I pruned all the trees up to 4 metres before letting the upper canopy spread out to provide the 'factory' that would drive wood growth.

As the stem gets larger, the volume of wood required to achieve the same diameter increment increases. This means that to maintain an even diameter growth rate a tree must be able to spread its canopy wider each year: more leaves exposed to more sunlight to grow more wood. If anything limits the ability of the canopy to spread, including competition from other trees in the plantation, then diameter growth will slow down. It is a fundamental truth about tree growth that is so often misunderstood.

The highest recorded basal area that I could find for any planted willow species was measured in a twenty-year-old Black Willow (*Salix nigra*)

plantation growing on fertile alluvial soils beside the Mississippi River. The basal area was 184 square feet per acre, or just 42 square metres per hectare.[3] Even unthinned, irrigated poplar plantations don't achieve much more than about 40 square metres per hectare. From this, I knew that to avoid a dramatic drop in the diameter growth the final basal area of my Cricket Bat Willow plantation (averaging 40 cm in diameter) would need to be less than 20 square metres per hectare. This corresponds to a stocking of 160 trees per hectare, or an average spacing of about 8 metres. In England, many of the Cricket Bat Willow plantations are set out at even wider spacings to ensure an even diameter growth rate and the widest possible sapwood band.

Although I was enjoying learning about how to grow Cricket Bat Willow, I was never really comfortable having the trees on the farm. Our local Crack Willow is a male clone and the Cricket Bat Willow is a female. I'd been told the two species wouldn't normally hybridise, and even if they could their flowering times were quite different so it was very unlikely. I was willing to believe it all until that day in the spring of 2005 when I stopped to check my trees. I suddenly noticed the white woolly tuffs on the ripe female catkins. I couldn't see if there was any seed, but I still panicked; I didn't have time to research this one. If there were any viable seed it would be gone with the next dry wind. If just one single hybrid developed the genie could be out of the bottle.

Within a few days I had all my Cricket Bat Willow trees on the ground, the pruned logs in a pile to the side and the leafy heads pushed together and crushed down low. I then let the sheep in to clean up what we'd missed and trample any seed into the dry soil. At least it wouldn't travel far. I didn't sleep well that night: on one hand, I worried that I'd allowed the trees to seed and on the other I worried that I'd overreacted and undermined my chance to grow my own cricket bats. The next day I collected some of the fluff and set it under lights in a germination cupboard at the university. Then I rang Kurt Cremer in Canberra—he'd know whether Cricket Bat Willow could hybridise with the Crack Willow.

Although Kurt had long since retired from his forestry research role, he had continued to lobby anyone who'd listen about the weed risks of introduced willows. His wife answered; Kurt had died in the winter just past. I conveyed my sympathy. I didn't know Kurt well but I did know we shared an interest in trees on farms, so I thought he'd be happy if I asked his wife the question that was on my mind: 'Did Kurt ever mention that he was worried about the promotion of the Cricket Bat Willow and the risk of it hybridising with other willow species?' She didn't hesitate: 'Yes, of course, he spoke about it often.' That was enough for me, even if there was no viable seed that year I'd be fretting every spring thereafter if I didn't get rid of them. It could only take one unusual season, and we're having more of them than ever, for the flowering of the two species to synchronise.

I later found an article Kurt had written in 1999: 'Cricket Bat Willow – Environmental threat to streams?' I couldn't help jumping ahead through his words, scanning for clues to the answer. I picked up the threads where I saw any reference to hybridisation: 'this tree is likely to produce viable seeds', 'the most widespread sources of suitable pollen are the Crack Willow and Basket Willow, if these flower at the right time, and they probably do.' I took a deep breath and read it slowly from the start. Kurt's point was that if it was legal to grow the Cricket Bat Willow then the only way to ensure there was no risk of fertilisation from a suitable male was to ensure that the trees were out of range of any pollinating bees. He suggested that this might require a buffer of about two kilometres to any other willow species. There was Crack Willow growing less than 50 metres from where I'd had my little cricket bat plantation and my beehive was right there, between the two.

A few days after my premature harvest I returned to the pile of logs. I had a chainsaw, axe and wood splitter, and only a rough idea of what I needed to do to prepare the clefts for Lachlan. Cricket bat clefts are best split, not sawn. This guarantees the face of the bat closely follows the grain.

I cut two-foot six-inch sections out of the trunks then stood them on their end for splitting. Rather than wield the axe wildly, I placed it carefully across the pith and hit it with the back of the wood splitter. The wood separated easily along the grain, exposing the clean white timber. I immediately noticed

top: I cut the Cricket Bat Willow into two-foot six-inch logs then split them with an axe.

bottom: One of our split Cricket Bat Willow logs showing the pith, pruning stubs, heartwood and sapwood.

that my pruning wounds had healed well and were neatly confined to a central core less than about 7 centimetres wide. I was going to enjoy my work today; I was learning as I was harvesting. My main concern was log diameter. You really do need a 40-centimetre-diameter tree to cut six or more clear clefts out of each round log section. I settled on cutting four or five clefts, with the odd large log yielding six. The trailer quickly filled. I parked my harvest under cover and

picked out a few of the best clefts to take to Melbourne. I was a little nervous about what Lachlan would say.

'You cut the trees too early,' he said. But then added, 'These look okay, I can do something with them.' We made an arrangement whereby I would trade a number of clefts in exchange for each finished bat. Like an anxious parent I waited the full nine months. Lachlan dried, milled, planed, pressed and carved my clefts into bats. Then he gave me his feedback: the weight of the wood was good, it was light, and some of the grain lifted when sawn leaving a furry surface. 'That's not good,' I presumed aloud. 'No, that is good,' he said. Lachlan explained that the best willow did not cut clean on the bench. The face of the cricket bat is compressed, reducing about 10 millimetres of wood down to 6 millimetres to absorb the shock. Wood that cuts cleanly loses its reactivity if pressed too much whereas the fluffy wood performs better. 'It's a sign that the cells have more density,' he said. That sounded like tension wood to me: thick-walled cells that develop in response to movement in the stem and cut fluffy on the saw. I'd never thought of tension wood as being a good thing.

A year after I had harvested and split my own Cricket Bat Willow I was watching my teenage son play with his 'home-grown' bat. I was proud enough when I heard he had brushed off the hecklers from within his own team who mocked him about having a home-made bat. But, I was even prouder when Tristan scored a half century, held up the bat, and called out to me: 'Hey Dad, it works!'

above: Our son Tristan playing with his home-grown cricket bat.

opposite: Feeding tree prunings to stock—I pruned these 4-yr-old trees in winter. Our sheep consumed all the Blackwood foliage and even some of the fresh shoots on the eucalypts. But they are not as nutritious as Hybrid Poplar prunings in summer.

Kurt and I might be wrong to worry about Cricket Bat Willows hybridising with other species. But I can't take that risk. Until the tree breeders can produce Cricket Bat Willow clones that are sterile, I won't be planting them again. For those who are, maybe now is a good time to harvest, relax, and enjoy the game.

Tawny Frogmouth (*Podargus strigoides*)

1   L.D. Pryor and R.R. Willing, *Growing & breeding poplar in Australia* (Canberra: L.D. Pryor and R.R. Willing, 1982).

2   Paul R. Dann and A. Axelsen, 'Willow (*Salix spp.*) as drought feed for sheep,' *Proceedings of the Australian Society of Animal Production* 16 (1986): 408.

3   E.R. Toole, *Rot cull in Black Willow* (New Orleans: Southern Forest Experiment Station, Forest Service, U.S. Dept. of Agriculture, 1964).

Tree foliage for supplementary stock fodder

On a pastured grazing farm in temperate Australia the availability and quality of green feed tends to peak in spring and, to a lesser extent, in autumn. This results in feed shortages in late summer and winter. In response, farmers manage their stock numbers, cut and feed out hay or silage, grow summer feed crops or buy in feed for their stock. Trees can provide supplementary fodder to fill these seasonal feed shortages.

Trees can also provide a green fodder reserve, a living haystack, that can be accessed for emergency feed during drought. There is a long history of farmers lopping native trees and shrubs such as Kurrajong (*Brachychiton populneus*), sheoaks and wattles during droughts to maintain their stock. The most important introduced tree species for stock fodder in the temperate regions is Tagasaste (*Chamaecytisus proliferus*), a leguminous shrub that performs well on deep infertile sandy soils.

In practical terms, the value of tree fodder depends on the cost of alternatives, the quality of the fodder the trees provide and the cost of making it available to stock. Stock may be able to access the feed by directly grazing the foliage. If the feed is inaccessible, the farmer might need to lop the branches or even carry the foliage to the stock. Unless the work is part of the usual management of the trees, such as pruning or harvesting for timber, the need for intervention will increase the cost of providing the fodder.

The feed quality of tree foliage depends on its palatability (whether the stock will eat it), its nutritional value (protein content and digestibility), the presence of any toxic compounds such as oils, alkaloids or salt, the concentration of tannins and, to a lesser extent when used as a supplement, any mineral deficiencies.

The protein content of quality feed can be as high as 30 %. If it is less than 8 % the feed will be of very little value. A protein content greater than 13 % is recommended for growing stock. Assuming all the nitrogen in the feed is held as protein then the protein content is calculated from the nitrogen content by multiplying by 6.25.

The digestibility of fodder refers to the proportion of the feed that is absorbed by the animal. For example, if pasture has a digestible dry matter content of 70 % it means that for every 10 kgs of dry feed consumed seven kilograms will be used by the animal and only three kgs will pass through as manure. Because digestibility is related to the speed of digestion, the higher the quality of the feed the more an animal can consume and the greater their growth and production. If stock only have access to fodder with a digestibility of less than about 65 % they will find it difficult to consume enough feed to gain weight. If the digestibility is less than 55 % they can lose weight despite having access to feed.

A high tannin content is the most common cause of the low feed value of tree foliage. Condensed tannins can form strong bonds with the proteins in plant material thereby preventing their digestion. Hydrolysable tannins can break down during digestion releasing phenolic acids that can be toxic to the animal. Although a tannin content within the range of 2–4 % improves feed value by increasing the absorption of essential amino acids, mature tree leaves and stems commonly have a combined tannin content of greater than 10 %, making it very poor stock fodder.

Young fresh tree foliage has a much lower tannin content than mature leaves. However, the tree is unlikely to produce fresh shoots during the annual feed shortages or drought. Dosing of sheep with polyethylene glycol (PEG, a detannification agent) can increase the digestibility of foliage, although the costs involved may make this impractical.

Many trials have shown that providing free access to tree foliage, even a low-quality feed such as pine needles or wattle, can extend the value of a higher-quality feed supplements such as grain. This suggests that pruning trees for timber may help fill the winter feed gap. The consumption and trampling of the prunings by stock also help break them down, reducing the smothering of spring pastures and the fire hazard in the following summer.

Species	Relative Fodder value Protein (P) Digestibility (D)	Comments
Poplar and Willows	High P: 15-20 % D: 65–70 %	Fresh foliage provides high quality summer supplementary feed. Trees may drop leaves during drought. No winter feed value.
Wattles (*Acacia* spp.)	Medium–High P: 10–25 % D: 30–65 %	Fresh prunings are suitable as a summer or winter feed to maintain weight. Young shoots are very palatable and high in protein. High tannin content in mature leaves is likely to reduce feed value. Best fed as a supplement with high quality feed.
Sheoaks	Medium P: 10 % D: 30 %	Fresh foliage is very palatable with a reasonable protein content. Widely used as a stock fodder.
Silky Oak	Medium–High	Fresh foliage is very palatable. Widely used as cattle fodder in East Africa. Tendency to be semi-deciduous in some climates. No feed value data.
Radiata Pine	Low P: 6 % D: 53 %	Some potential as a supplementary feed in summer and winter, especially if provided in combination with a high-quality feed such as grain or summer crops.
Black Walnut	Very Low	Foliage tends to be unpalatable to stock.
Eucalypts	Very Low	Unlikely to provide any feed value other than possible mineral supplements.

Information from various sources, values provided as a guide only.
Useful fodder references:
- R.A. Dynes and A.C. Schlink, 'Livestock potential of Australian species of *Acacia*,' Conservation Science Western Australia 4(3) (2002):117-124.
- E.C. Lefroy, *Forage Trees and Shrubs in Australia – their current use and future potential*. RIRDC Publication No 02/039 (Barton ACT: RIRDC, 2002).

Chapter 11

Black Walnut

Juglans nigra

In 1939, an agricultural teacher named Andy Dixon climbed a nineteen-year-old tree growing on his farm in Ontario, Canada. He carried a handsaw with him and, starting high in the canopy, began pruning the branches off at the trunk as he worked his way back down to the ground. His saw was sharp and none of the branches were larger than about 6 centimetres in diameter so it wasn't a difficult task. Within a few minutes he'd transformed an open-grown branchy tree into a 'lollipop', with its small leafy crown sitting on top of an 8-metre clear trunk.

Fifty-two years later (in 1991), when Andy was eighty-four and the 71-year-old tree was 73.5 centimetres in diameter, he sold it for CAN$1500 (or the equivalent of $3065 in 2016 Australian dollars).[1] Accounting for bark and log taper, I estimated the volume of the pruned log would have been about 3.5 cubic metres which, if my calculations are correct, gives a current Australian standing value of more than $850 per cubic metre. Andy's aim was to demonstrate to other farmers that pruning Black Walnut could be quick and easy and, if you're prepared to wait, highly lucrative. To allow a Black Walnut tree growing on your farm to branch out freely, thereby greatly reducing the value of the timber, only breeds regret.

Being familiar with European or Persian Walnut (*Juglans regia*), the first Europeans who settled in Jamestown, Virginia, quickly took to the edible nuts of the local Black Walnut for sustenance and to its timber for commerce. Before the first commercial crops of tobacco were ready to harvest, it was Chesapeake Bay Black Walnut lumber that filled the hulls of the Virginia Company's supply ships on their return voyage to London. The timing was perfect. By the late sixteenth century Persian Walnut had established itself as the most desirable furniture timber amongst European nobility and was becoming difficult to source. This allowed its New World chocolate-coloured cousin to slot in as a fashion statement for the more flamboyant nouveau riche of the emerging commercial class. Even today, more than half the Black Walnut timber produced in North America is exported to Europe.

As its timber became popular in Europe so too did the Black Walnut tree itself, initially as a large garden specimen and later as a serious plantation option. Sadly, few of the early plantations ever reached maturity due to the recognised value of both types of Walnut (*regia* and *nigra*) as gun stocks. Walnut heartwood is strong yet relatively light, shock resistant and non-brittle. It is also durable and, most importantly for guns, stable across a range of moisture and

preceding: Measuring the diameter of our largest Black Walnut. It is now 35 cm in diameter at 30-yrs-old.

right: This 41-yr-old plantation in northeast Victoria is proof that the American Black Walnut can grow well in Australia.

temperature conditions. Peace never lasted long enough in Europe to avert a premature harvest and many private plantations were compulsorily acquired by government or invading forces to support their war effort.

In peacetime, these same qualities have ensured that the best figured Black Walnut lumber has a high value market for use in musical instruments and designer furniture. Naturally the highest prices are paid for large clean logs that are suitable for veneer, or the rare logs with outstanding grain patterns. Reports of individual Black Walnut trees being auctioned at the stump for US$30,000 (Ohio), poachers using helicopters to steal individual trees (Kentucky), and university students using DNA testing to match stumps against stolen logs (Indiana) has certainly helped fuel a fever of expectation amongst growers.

When assessing Black Walnut log value, size matters. The pruned Black Walnut tree I'm measuring in the photo at the start of this chapter is now thirty years old. Despite having a five-metre-long straight trunk and a diameter of

almost 35 centimetres, as a sawlog it is essentially worth nothing. But, if you give it another thirty years and let it double its diameter the volume of the pruned log would be more than 1.5 cubic metres making the tree worth as much as a return airline ticket to North America!

above: The mature Black Walnut fruit on the tree (left) and the dry nuts (right) ready for sale to farmers for planting.

opposite: To see how my pruning wounds were healing, I milled one of our 27-yr-old pruned Black Walnuts. I was shocked by the green colour of the heartwood (left). The next morning the colour had changed to the even dark chocolate colour I expected (right).

In 1987, I imported a kilogram of Black Walnut seed from New Zealand where I had spent a summer working, in part, with Ian Nicholas. Ian led the special purpose species program at the Forest Research Institute in Rotorua, which, back then, meant anything other than Radiata Pine. Being a researcher, Ian had to temper his enthusiasm for Black Walnut and focus on gathering objective data on growth rates, wood quality and production costs for secondary analysis by the economists. I was less guarded and lapped up his knowledge with little thought to how long it might take for a Black Walnut to reach a commercial size; I was young, I had time on my side.

When my nuts arrived I left them in the sealed plastic bag in the fridge until the end of August, to mimic a North American winter. Then, in the first week of spring, I sowed the nuts into a box of loose soil. As each seed germinated I carefully removed it and sowed it directly into the paddock, being sure to point the emerging white root down into the soil.

Direct seeding the nut allows the fragile taproot to develop freely. In the first season our seedlings were barely 30 centimetres tall, but when I dug one up I found that the taproot was more than 50 centimetres deep! For comparison, I also grew a few seedlings in our backyard nursery using deep containers but found that when I planted them out a year later they didn't grow at all in height over the next season.

Our Black Walnut trees grew very slowly. While I needed a ladder to high prune our eucalypts, our Black Walnut of the same age were barely above

head height. But I still visited every tree, every year. I would correct any double leaders by taking off the weaker shoot and remove any branch that was over about 2 centimetres in diameter. This form-pruning ensured that I would have a straight tree and no large branches that would be difficult to remove and leave a large wound.

I later read that Andy Dixon would recommend a similar pruning method to control the spreading canopy of Black Walnut in Ontario: 'No branch should be allowed to grow to a diameter exceeding two inches,' he wrote.[1]

Eventually our trees reached stem-pruning size and I began cutting off all the lower branches up to a point where the trunk was about 8 centimetres in diameter. Above that I would continue removing any large branches up to my final pruned height. The higher the better, but with Black Walnut a 2-metre-long log would still be worth growing. In addition to improving wood quality, pruning lifts the canopy, increasing light levels for pasture, and makes it easier to drive a tractor under the trees. I also think a high-pruned forest looks attractive, but then I'm a forester.

Regarding when to prune Black Walnut, Andy Dixon wrote: 'I recommend that you do it while the tree is dormant. Really can't give you any valid reason for choosing this time but the weather is nice, the ground is firm, and I feel that if a limb is removed the tree has more time to recover.'[1]

I also do all my pruning in winter. My reasoning is a little different. When a tree is dormant, even an evergreen species, the cambium is inactive. This means the bark is less likely to pop off the wood or strip off down the stem. If this happens the wound will be larger and take longer to heal. The weather in

Heartwood

left: Intercropping between rows of 17-yr-old Black Walnut at the University of Guelph's research farm in Ontario, Canada.

opposite: Our son, Tristan, beside his 7-yr-old Black Walnut tree in 1994.

Bambra is not so good in winter but the soft ground helps hold the ladder firm and the tiger snakes are in hibernation.

When my Black Walnut trees entered their seventeenth winter I visited the University of Guelph, Ontario, where another Andy (Dr Gordon) ran the agroforestry research program. He took me out to his research site in southern Ontario that included rows of Black Walnut interplanted with agricultural crops. His trees were seventeen years old too, averaged about 15 centimetres in diameter and were approaching 10 metres in height. They were the same age as my own trees, and a little bigger!

In my naivety, reinforced by my experience with pines and eucalypts, I'd come to expect that all tree species grew faster in Australia than they might in North America. I was genuinely surprised to see how big Andy's young trees were. As I felt beads of sweat running down my chest it suddenly occurred to me that summers in Ontario were perfect for tree growth: sixteen-hour days, good rainfall and high humidity.

While an evergreen eucalypt in temperate Australia might have the advantage of being ready to grow whenever conditions were right, a deciduous tree in Ontario has an assured growing season with near perfect conditions every day from bud-burst to leaf fall, no matter how short their season. And Black Walnut has a very short growing season.

While the dormant buds of the Black Walnut can survive the coldest Canadian winters, their spring shoots are very frost tender. Rather than invest in tough foliage that might survive the cold, Black Walnut has evolved an alternative strategy of waiting until the risk of frost has passed. The Black Walnut on our farm doesn't burst bud until mid-October. In Ontario, the humid conditions in spring mean there is little likelihood of a late frost. But in Bambra, if we have a dry spring and cold nights, we can experience a light frost in late October. Over a two-year period, the coldest frost I measured in our first few years on the farm was just -1°Celsius. This would hardly warrant a mention had it not disfigured some of my best Black Walnut trees.

The first buds to burst on a Black Walnut are those at the tip of the leading shoot, which allow the leader to assert dominance over all the lower shoots that will develop later. If the leader is killed off by frost, the next two buds down the stem are released from any suppression and immediately compete for supremacy. Without one being able to gain absolute control, the result will be a double leader. Once in full leaf it is hard to pick the double leaders and I've discovered that if I leave them uncorrected until the next winter, the trees develop a permanent kink in the main stem. I now recommend an extra form-pruning of young Black Walnut trees around Christmas time to correct any double leaders.

Andy Dixon died a couple of years before I visited Ontario. As I travelled through the state I looked for evidence of his legacy. Despite hundreds of farmers and forest owners having attended his field days and talks, all the Black Walnut trees I saw on farms were unpruned. Was it the message, its delivery, or the audience? Seeing the obvious similarities with my own story I couldn't help but consider my own legacy. Andy closes his book with an insightful comment that growing Black Walnut for timber was 'an old man's dream and a young man's opportunity'.[1] If the young will not listen to the old then maybe it is up to the old to do the work and then gift their well-pruned Black Walnut trees to the young that follow.

We held my fiftieth birthday party in our converted shearing shed. I started the evening with a relaxed pre-dinner tree tour. Our guests marvelled at the rate at which the Mountain Ash, Coast Redwood and Hybrid Poplars had grown. Even those that knew little about timber could see they might be a viable option. At the time, the best of our 25-year-old Black Walnuts had only reached about 20 centimetres in diameter. Later that night, our son Tristan told the crowd that it had just occurred to him during the tour that his Dad might never live to see the harvest of our mature Black Walnut trees.

I took it well. My trees were a gift to his generation. A well-pruned Black Walnut tree growing on your own land is not like a piece of antique furniture or a work of art that you can buy late in life when you've made some money doing something else. By spending a little bit of our time now, growing and tending trees that we will never live to see mature, we are giving our children, or the next owners of our farm, something they can't buy at any price. Only time can create this kind of value and only someone who receives such a gift understands its true significance. I don't just mean the money value of the tree or the land on which they grow, it is something more. We are all partly defined, and certainly remembered, by how we marry the stories we inherit with those that we write ourselves.

The reward that I seek—what motivates me—is how our children's children might think of the person who planted them: 'an old man's dream' indeed.

Hugh Meggitt didn't plant his Black Walnut plantation; he just bought the land on which one stood. Not that he knew it at the time. It was his dream to set up a trout farm that had attracted him to the property on the banks of the

Hugh Meggitt with one of his largest 44-yr-old Black Walnut trees on their farm in north east Victoria.

Goulburn River in north east Victoria. But the neglected 33-hectare plantation of fifteen-year-old trees soon caught his attention and became his distraction. The trees had been planted by a forestry investment company that had, characteristically it would seem, overstated the growth rates and exaggerated the returns. The investment was liquidated when the trees failed to achieve the unrealistic growth expectations. When the land hit the market the trees were seen as a liability.

As the new owner, Hugh began asking around in an endeavour to find out what the strange deciduous trees were. Hearing that they might have some value he then did the 1980's equivalent of an internet search (library books, newspaper cuttings and phone calls) and soon discovered that he was the owner of the largest Black Walnut plantation in the southern hemisphere and that, despite the failed prospectus, some areas of his forest were performing as well as the best plantations in North America. When Ian Nicholas heard about the plantation he came over, measured the trees and then set up a series of spacing trials in the plantation to monitor how Black Walnut respond to thinning.

The relative productivity of a site for growing timber is best judged by the height of the trees at a particular age. We use tree height, rather than diameter or volume growth, because in a sheltered plantation height growth is largely independent of spacing and management and reflects the intrinsic qualities of the soils (such as fertility, depth and structure) and the climate (including factors such as rainfall, humidity and temperature).

left: *Cattle grazing under 44-yr-old Black Walnut on Walnut Island, Victoria.*

opposite: *The American Site Index curves for Black Walnut. I have added the measured heights for Hugh Meggitt's plantation (Walnut Island) and our own trees. Site Index is the tree height at age 50-yrs-old.*

In our Australian pine plantations, foresters use the tree height at age twenty years as a standard measure of site quality, which they call Site Index. For plantation eucalypts grown for chipwood, Site Index is the tree height at age ten years. The Americans decided to use tree height at age fifty years as their Site Index measure for Black Walnut.[2]

A very good site for Black Walnut in the U.S.A. might have a Site Index of 80, suggesting that the dominant trees in a plantation would be expected to reach 80 feet, or just over 24 metres, by age fifty years. A marginal site for Black Walnut might have a Site Index of 40 (12 metres at age fifty), and anything less is generally considered non-viable for timber production. Growth curves based on many years of measurements across a wide range of sites are useful for predicting the future growth of young plantations. Measurements of Ian's trial plots at Walnut Island at age twenty-three years suggested that the best parts of the plantation were well on track to exceed more than 80 feet in height by age fifty years.

Hugh put the idea of a trout farm on the backburner and spent years under the Black Walnut spell. He travelled to America and met with growers who were more than impressed by his story and clearly envious of his apparent good fortune. With a commitment to silvicultural management, he returned to strip away the blackberry and began pruning and thinning. He also introduced cattle.

Being able to maintain agriculture production while your timber trees are growing can significantly improve the economics of forestry. In effect, the trees don't need to pay for the land on which they are growing. Unfortunately, most timber species grown in Australia, particularly eucalypts and pines, compete with crops and pastures for light, moisture and nutrients so pasture productivity declines as the trees grow larger.

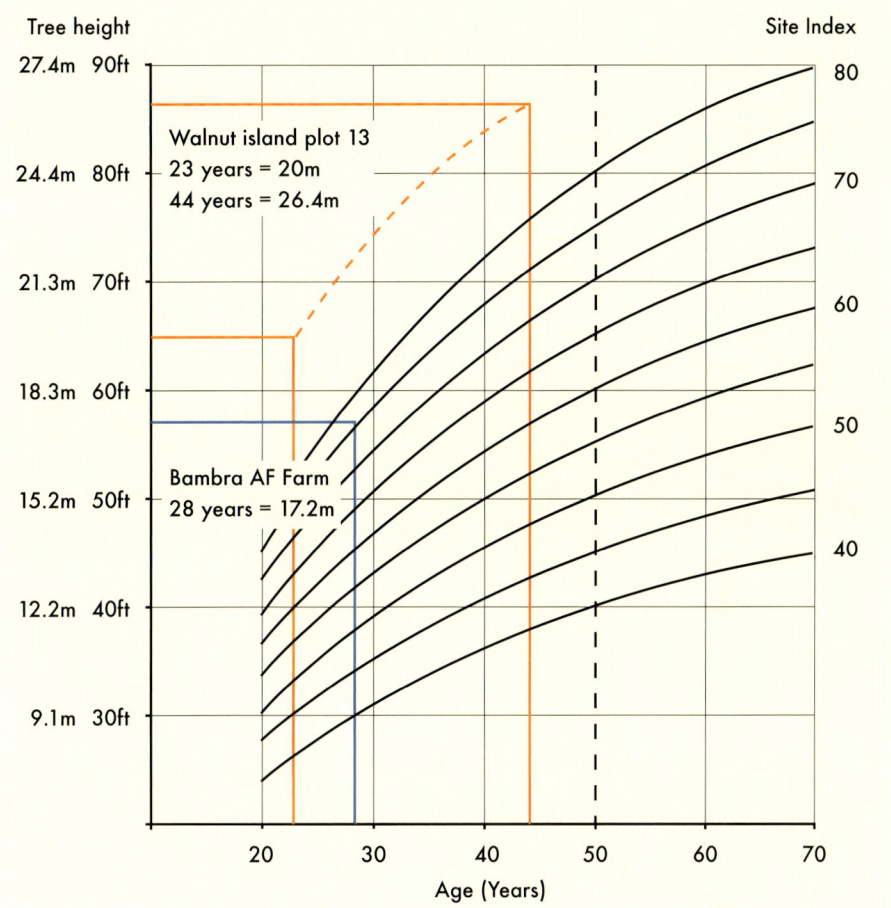

The deciduous Black Walnut is different. In summer the shade seems to help the grass stay greener for longer than out in the open paddocks. In winter the dormant leafless trees let in the light. Whilst they will only grow well on deep soils, Black Walnut do tend to have a deeper root system than a eucalypt or pine growing on the same site. They may also improve surface soil fertility.

When one of my students showed an interest in the potential for deciduous trees to enhance and sustain soil fertility, I set him up with a project to examine the impact of Black Walnut on soil nitrogen, phosphorous and organic matter. We chose the edge of Hugh's plantation beside open pasture and collected multiple soil samples from two depths (0–15 and 40–45 centimetres) at set distances out from the trees, along the edge and under the plantation itself. Although there was no apparent impact of the trees on soil phosphorous, the organic carbon content and nitrogen levels in the topsoil under the trees were significantly higher than under open pasture, suggesting that the annual dump of autumn leaves may be having a positive impact on soil fertility and carbon storage.

Just as important, although less obvious, is the contribution from the repeated growth and decay of fine feeder roots in the surface soil which may contribute as much organic matter and nutrients as leaf fall. Black Walnut are unable to fix atmospheric nitrogen so the increase in surface nitrogen had to come from another source. We found that the nitrogen levels in the subsoil (40–45 centimetres below the surface) were significantly lower under the trees than under open pasture. This suggests that the Black Walnuts were capturing leached nutrients from below the depth of the shallow pasture roots and bringing it back to the surface through leaf litter and the death of fine feeder roots. Although deciduous trees extract as much as fifty percent of the nitrogen and phosphorus out of their leaves before they let them fall in autumn, there is still a significant nutrient loading in their annual leaf drop. Calcium cannot be translocated out of the leaves or bark of all tree species so it all returns to the soil surface.[3] This may help improve soil structure and reduce acidity in forest and woodland soils.

In Ontario, Andy Gordon and his team were intercropping soybeans, corn and wheat in the alleys between rows of planted timber trees. Just prior to my visit, they had noticed large bare patches in the soybean crop around the base of the Black Walnut trees. They immediately suspected that it was a result of an allelopathic reaction. Allelopathy refers to a positive or negative interaction between two species resulting from the release of a chemical compound by one or both.

While many American farmers and horticulturalists had long suspected that there was an antagonistic effect of Black Walnut trees on tomatoes, potatoes and apples, it wasn't until the mid-1920s when researchers at the Virginia Agricultural Experiment Station published their paper in the scientific *Phytopathology* Journal that the concept of allelopathy gained scientific credibility.[4] In the grounds of the Virginia State University farm, a crop of alfalfa (lucerne) had been sown in a paddock containing two large Black Walnut trees. By mid-summer a large area, much greater than the extent of the tree canopies, was dominated by grass, leaving a clear line between it and the healthy alfalfa crop. The researchers carefully marked the irregular crop edge, or 'death line'. By digging around the tree they could confirm that the edge of the alfalfa crop perfectly matched the extent of the Black Walnut roots.

The researchers then ran several laboratory experiments. One involved cutting bark from the roots, soaking it in water then applying the solution to potted tomato plants. Within two days the treated plants began to wilt. In another trial they watered tomatoes with a solution made from soil taken from around Black Walnut trees, being careful to remove any roots, but none of the plants grown in the soil showed any signs of stress. They concluded that the toxic agent was either insoluble in the soil water or underwent some chemical change making it non-toxic shortly after leaving the root. Given what they

top: In 1987, we direct seeded Black Walnut between planted Poplars. I protected the trees from sheep using electric fencing loops and continued to graze sheep (photo taken in 1988).

bottom: The same paddock when the trees were 28-yrs-old.

knew about the chemical composition of walnut trees, they surmised that the substance juglone, which they knew was similar to other known plant toxins, might have been responsible.

It wasn't until the 1950s that the chemical composition of juglone was described. It has since been reported that juglone does have a selective toxic effect on other plant species including many broadleaf pasture weeds. Grasses grown close to Black Walnut seem immune, which may explain why the pasture composition under trees is often better than in open paddocks. Although some tree species are susceptible to juglone, including Black Alder (*Alnus glutinosa*), White Pine (*Pinus strobus*) and the Cherry cultivars (*Prunus*), many other tree

Using the through-and-through method I milled one of Hugh's 44-yr-old Black Walnut trees with great results.

species are unaffected, including American native White Oak (*Quercus alba*) and Northern Red Oak (*Quercus rubra*) and the Cottonwood.[5] Because Black Walnut take so long to grow, being able to farm crops, graze stock or plant other tree species amongst them provides an opportunity to generate short or medium term income.

While studying the interactions between trees and crops makes for exciting research, growing crops between rows of trees raises some practical challenges. The problem with trees is that they cannot be moved and the effect they have changes over time. Unlike conventional agriculture, where the crop is sown into a paddock that is relatively unchanged from year to year, in an intercropping system every season is different. As the trees grow larger, crop yields may initially increase due to the ameliorating impact of the trees, but there is likely to be a point at which yields reach a peak then decline due to competition.

Unless the farmer can freeze the system at this optimal point (by controlling the spacing or size of the trees and the extent of their root systems), net complementarity will invariably shift to net competition. For the same cost of sowing and tending the crop, yields per unit area will then begin to decline, resulting in a compounding negative impact on profits. At some point the farmer would be forced to decide whether to change from cropping to pasture production, prematurely harvest the trees, or retire the paddock from agriculture until the trees are mature.

There are also other problems inherent in mixing trees and crops such as the risk of spray drift, fertiliser intolerance and mechanical damage to the trees. Many farmers can remember picking up sticks in their parents' cropping fields and are now understandably reluctant to impose the same on their own children.

Andy Dixon began by growing corn, oats, wheat and pasture between his pruned Black Walnut trees in an attempt to maintain an income while his trees were growing. The trees had very little impact on agricultural yields during the first twenty years, as they had been planted at a spacing of 40 feet (12 m). But, the form of his widely-spaced trees was being affected by exposure and this increased his pruning costs. He was in his 90s when he modified his planting design, choosing to interplant faster growing species including Hybrid Poplar that could shelter the Black Walnuts. As if expecting tree planting to give him eternal life, he planned to remove the poplars when they reached about 60 centimetres in diameter in the anticipation of leaving a final spacing of 15 metres between maturing Black Walnuts.

Ten years earlier than Andy, I'd also decided to mix Hybrid Poplar and Black Walnut. I'd seen the impact of wind on the Black Walnut in New Zealand so I knew that shelter was important to protect the tender leading shoot and maximise height growth. But I was also exploring an idea of *transitional* forestry. Rather than assume that I would one day harvest all my trees and start again with an empty paddock—as is standard practice in conventional rotational forestry—I was interested in the idea of using fast-growing trees, such as poplars and eucalypts, to provide a physical, biological and economic scaffold on which I could build a more permanent forest. Instead of returning each block back to what it was like before, harvesting timber would take it to a new and more valuable state. Like Andy, I envisaged taking out the Hybrid Poplar for sawlogs and leaving the Black Walnut to grow on.

Fortunately, I started when I was young enough to see it happen. We are now harvesting the Hybrid Poplar so as to give the Black Walnuts more growing space. It's not easy. I need to be careful when felling the Hybrid Poplars, which are almost 30 metres tall, to avoid damaging the Black Walnut trees. I couldn't do it without using our tractor logging winch which allows me to direct the trees down into small gaps.

I recently revisited Hugh Meggitt's plantation. Many of the 44-year-old trees were over 50 centimetres in diameter with clear-pruned trunks up to 6 metres. They looked fantastic growing across what appeared to me to be a useful late season pasture. Hugh took me to Ian Nicholas' Plot 13. In 1994 (at age twenty-three years) the top height in Plot 13 had reached 20 metres. I identified what appeared to be one of the dominant trees, pushed the clip of my measurement

Sharing our 30 years of experience growing Black Walnut (the tree beside me and in the background) with another group of landholders (autumn 2017). Image courtesy of Ingrid Krockenberger.

tape into the bark and walked backwards to a point 30 metres from the tree where I had a clear view of both its top and base. Holding a clinometer to my eye, I could estimate the height of the tree. It was 26.4 metres tall. Although it had only grown 6 metres in 20 years it was already taller, at just 44 years, than that required for a Site Index of 80 (24.4 m by age fifty years).

Much has changed over the years since I planted our first Black Walnut seeds. Temperatures have increased, droughts have come and gone, and Ian Nicholas, with whom I shared a passion for specialty timber species and family forestry, has also left us. Yet, our Black Walnut trees have continued, slowly and quietly, laying down their wood. I last measured the height of my largest Black Walnut trees when they were 28 years old. The average was 17.2 metres (56 feet), which suggests my site is on track to achieve a site index of at least 75. It's an indication that the site is suitable for growing Black Walnut logs as large as the one Andy Dixon grew in Ontario. I just need to wait.

Fortunately, as I get older, I also become more patient. I can now see that the secret to growing Black Walnut is to plant them on a good deep well-watered loam on a sheltered site, prune the best trees to a single stem, follow up with timely stem pruning and thinning, and then, perhaps most importantly, find something else to take your mind off the trees for fifty years. When you look back you'll wonder why you didn't plant more of these aristocrats of the forest. If you don't get the opportunity then maybe your grandchildren will be the ones who look up at the large clean Black Walnut logs and marvel at your foresight in planting a tree you must have known you might never live to see reach maturity.

11 Black Walnut

White-throated Treecreeper (*Cormobates leucophaea*)

1   Andy Dixon, *A photographic treatise on how best to grow veneer quality lumber*, (Peterborough, Ontario: Northumberland Stewardship, Undated).

2   Wilard H. Carmean, Jerold T. Hahn, and Rodney D. Jacobs, *Site index curves for forest tree species in the Eastern United States*, North Central Forest Experiment Station, General Technical Report NC-128 (Minnesota: U.S. Department of Agriculture, 1992).

3   Peter M. Attiwill, H.B. Guthrie and R. Leuning, 'Nutrient Cycling in a *Eucalyptus obliqua* (L'Herit.) Forest. I Litter Production and Nutrient Return,' Australian Journal of Botany 26 (1978): 79-91.

4   A.B. Massey, 'Antagonism of the walnuts (*Juglans nigra* L. and *Julgans cinerea* L.) in certain plant associations,' *Phytopathology* 15 (1925): 773-784.

5   Johnson County Extension Master Gardeners *Gardening and landscaping near black walnut trees* (Kansas: Kansas State University, 2015).

Science and Practice

Pruning trees for sawlogs

The main purpose of pruning is to increase the proportion of knot-free clearwood in the lower log. The aim is to create a slender branch-free trunk, the scaffold, over which knot-free wood can be laid down with each year's growth. Here I present my standard approach to pruning for clearwood timber. Of course, in practice I do vary this a little to suit different species and product options but these notes provide a good starting point for growers.

My regular pruning of this Shining Gum confined the branch knots to an even core running up the centre of the log allowing clearwood to be cut from the surrounding clearwood zone.

When to start pruning

Visit every tree every winter to determine if it needs pruning. Check them again around Christmas time to remove any epicormic shoots or correct double leaders before the stems become too large.

Epicormic shoots often develop on the pruned stems of many hardwoods (top: Northern Red Oak) and softwoods (bottom: Hoop Pine). Cut them off close to the trunk as shown.

Which trees to prune

Don't prune trees that have a lean of more than about ten percent, bends or kinks that deviate outside the central axis, or show signs of disease or severe borer damage. Have a clear idea of the final stocking rate you plan to retain to avoid high-pruning trees that will ultimately be too close together. For eucalypts, I suggest not pruning two trees within a distance less than the height you are pruning to at the time. For example, if pruning a eucalypt to about four metres in a block plantation then do not prune another within four metres as the competition will reduce the diameter growth and the benefits of your pruning work. I thin any unpruned trees immediately after I have completed the pruning to ensure they do not dominate the pruned trees.

Double leaders

It is critical to remove double leaders early. A double leader can be identified by the lack of a branch collar. On a normal branch, the swelling at the base of the branch is an indication that the stemwood is overgrowing the branchwood. In a double leader, there are no interlocking wood fibres so there is a greater risk of the trunk splitting.

Pre-emptive form pruning

Each winter remove any branch on the stem, up to the anticipated pruned height, that is over about 2.5 centimetres in diameter. This measurement is taken a little out from the stem away from the swollen collar.

This Red Ironbark branch has a diameter greater than 2.5 cm so I removed it even though the main trunk at that point was less than 8 centimetres in diameter. If left to grow for another year, dominant branches like this can grow very large, increasing the workload later and affecting the shape of the main trunk.

A double leader in a young Tallowwood (*Eucalyptus microcorys*). Note how there is no swelling at the base of either stem. I have cut the weaker stem off perpendicular to the stem to minimise the area of exposed wood. In a year or two, the main stem will envelop the stub.

Stem pruning

Each winter remove every branch on the stem, up to a point where the trunk diameter is 8 centimetres. Stem pruning stops when you have reached the desired height. I make my own pruning gauge that has an 8-centimetre mouth on one side for stem pruning and a 2.5-centimetre mouth on the back for pre-emptive pruning.

Before and after I pruned a Coast Redwood up to a trunk diameter of 8 cm using a plywood gauge to determine where to stop. I then check for a double leader or any large branches (over 2.5 cm) above that point.

How high to prune

For special timbers like Blackwood, a pruned log of just 2 or 3 metres would be acceptable. For eucalypts, I tend to go to 6.5 metres to ensure I can produce one 6.1-metre-long log (the longest length I can mill on my bandsaw and fit in my kiln) or two 3.1 metre logs (close to the shortest practical length for most eucalypt timbers). The only species I prune higher is the Coast Redwood. I prune them to 8 metres because they are easy to prune and grow tall.

Where to cut

Remove the branch close to the trunk without cutting into the branch collar. The branch collar is the swelling at the base of the branch where the fibres in the trunk overlap with the branch fibres. If the collar is damaged, sugars flowing down the trunk cannot feed the cells that form the callus to overgrow the wound. Do not apply any coatings over the wound. A healthy tree will confine any decay to the branch stub and central core.

Before and after pruning a River Sheoak. Note how I have not damaged the branch collar.

The recovery one and two years after pruning a Black Walnut (not the same branch). If the collar is not damaged the callus growth will be shaped like a doughnut, evenly overgrowing the stub from all sides.

A section of Black Walnut (top) and Shining Gum (bottom) showing how the clearwood grows over the pruned stub. Note how any decay that enters the stub is confined to the branch and does not affect the new wood. The Shining Gum also shows how fiddleback can be initiated by pruning live branches and can continue to develop in the new wood.

Pruning tools

I use secateurs, long-handled loppers and a hand-saw. To work at height I use a vertical ladder and harness. The ladder is specially made to fit against the tree and is tied off to provide a firm footing. I fit the pole belt around the tree before I leave the ground. Rules regarding working at heights vary in different states.

Occasionally I use a pole saw instead of a ladder but only on species with small, horizontal branches, like Australian Silky Oak. Recently I purchased electric pole secateurs that can reach about 5.5 metres. These are ideal for double leaders and pre-emptive pruning. I do not use, nor recommend, a chainsaw. If you prune on time, every year, the branches should not get too large for hand tools.

High pruning a Shining Gum with a harness and ladder (left) and a Black Walnut with electric pole secateurs (right). Note, these are demonstration photos. When high pruning I do wear a helmet to protect myself from falling branches.

Chapter 12

Red Ironbark

Eucalyptus tricarpa and *Eucalyptus sideroxylon*

My building labourer, Wayne, stood astride a Red Ironbark telegraph pole and swung his adze downwards between his legs like a garden hoe. We were chipping off the white sapwood to make red heartwood beams. But Wayne misjudged the arc. Rather than the adze biting into the grain, it slid along the surface and deflected off to the right, into his leg. He had three stitches and a week off the build, leaving me to finish the job.

And that's how it came to be that Mum found me, late one afternoon, wearing cricket pads swinging an adze between my legs. We were six months into the project. The concrete slabs were down and the load-bearing walls were up. I thought we were making good progress. Mum saw it differently. She'd just been to visit Claire, who was nursing our first and pregnant with our second, in the uninsulated fibro rental up the road. 'Can't you just buy a bloody beam?' she scolded.

Well, no you can't, not really. Not a beam like this one: a 10-inch-square, naturally durable, immensely strong, hand-hewn Red Ironbark beam. This piece of timber would tell a story, our story, for generations to come. Mum, of all people, should have understood that. Besides, the beam had to carry its share of a forty-ton concrete roof and there are not many timbers that can be trusted to do that job.

The pine used in conventional house framing has a rating of F7. The 'F' stands for 'force' and the number is the amount of stress, in mega pascals, that the timber will withstand before it bends too much. Our clear, dried Shining Gum might reach F17, strong enough, in the right dimensions, for a window lintel in a brick veneer. Freshly cut, defect-free Red Ironbark is rated F27, and its strength, and hardness, only increases as it dries.

Wood scientists measure hardness using the Janka test, which determines the force required to embed half an 11-millimetre-diameter steel ball into the surface of the timber. Dry Radiata Pine has a Janka rating of 3.4 kilonewtons (think of banging a ball bearing into wood with a nail hammer) whereas Sydney Blue Gum is more than twice that at 9.0 kilonewtons (think of using a sledge hammer). The Janka rating for dry Red Ironbark is 13 kilonewtons (think of a hydraulic post rammer on the back of a tractor).

We lifted the 6-metre-long beam with the front-end loader and lowered it into place. One end rested on top of the 10-inch-thick stabilised mudbrick walls and the other on the top of two Red Ironbark posts. Between them was a free span of almost 4 metres that would open the kitchen to the lounge. It didn't

preceding: Measuring up a Red Ironbark beam beside our 29-yr-old Red Ironbark trees.

left: Wayne uses an adze to chip the sapwood off a Red Ironbark pole (1990).

right: My brother Tom helping with the lifting of the longest Red Ironbark beam (1990).

move at all when we poured the concrete roof and it probably never will.

Years later a friend gave me a book he found in his grandfather's library titled *Australian Timbers: its strength, durability and identification* (1900).[1] I immediately turned to the section on beams. Of the 42 native timbers assessed by the University of Melbourne's Engineering Department, Red Ironbark proved to be the strongest. I converted the imperial measures to metric: our 10-inch (250 mm x 250 mm) square Ironbark beam spanning 12 feet 6 inches (3.8 m) can safely carry a centre load of 6942 pounds (3149 kgs), double if the load is, like our concrete roof, evenly distributed. That's more than six tons on that one beam. A comparison of species in the book lists Mountain Ash and Messmate as being stronger than Red Gum and Jarrah (figure 1). The heaviest and hardest timbers are not necessarily the strongest.

I then turned to the chapter on durability and read that amongst the eucalypts:

> 'The red timbers are as a rule most durable, the lighter-coloured timbers of the same classes coming next, while those approaching a light straw colour appear to be the least durable. There are in all cases some exceptions.'

Fortunately, Red Ironbark is not an exception. I wanted our house, like the forest we were creating, to live on for generations. I needed Red Ironbark.

We began building the farmhouse in 1989. All the public Red Ironbark forests along the Otway coast had been locked up in nature reserves by then. The farm supply yard in town had Red Ironbark posts from central Victoria, but they had nothing longer than an 8-foot strainer. I began looking further afield. Then my friend Jason Alexandra called to tell me there was a stack of Red Ironbark poles in a timber yard near his farm in Gippsland. They were the leftovers after

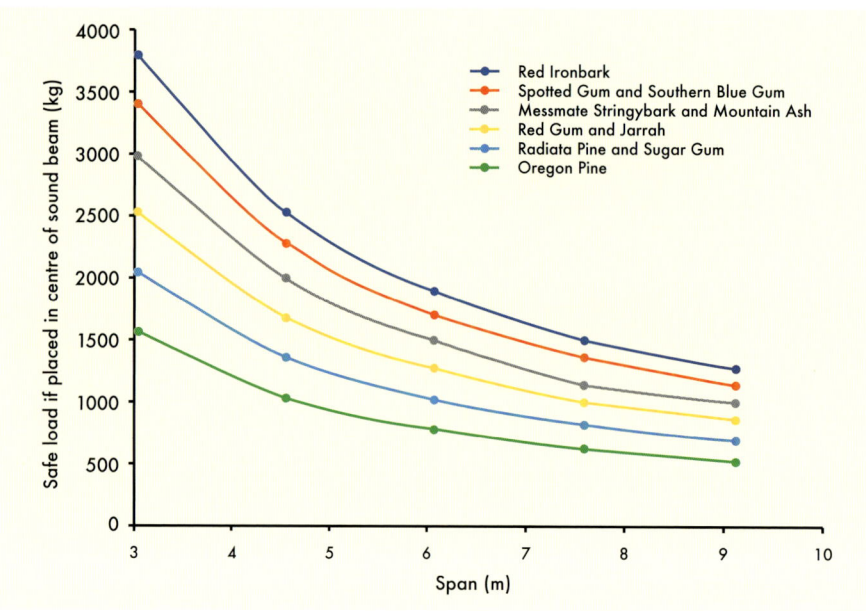

figure 1

figure 1: Loads which may safely be placed on the centre of sound 250 millimetre (10 inch) square beams of a range of timber species. For an evenly distributed load multiply by two.[1]

opposite: Clipping from The Age *(12th July 1990) shows Barry Donchi admiring the polished surface of a reclaimed Red Ironbark beam. Courtesy of* The Age/ *Catheryn Tremain.*

the State Electricity Commission had made their selection. I got twenty-six poles varying from 2 to 7 metres long for about $10 per metre.

Our choice of Red Ironbark for the posts and beams led us to seek out more seasoned red-coloured Australian hardwood for the doors and window frames. That's how I came to meet Barry Donchi. Barry had set up his recycled timber business in an old factory in Moama on the Murray River in the early 1980s, well before there was much interest in using recycled wood in buildings or furniture. He just loved the wood and the stories it told, and hated seeing it end up in landfill. Using a high-pressure sprayer, a sawmill and a heavy duty thicknesser, Barry was working his way through a stack of weather-beaten timber beams and posts that he'd salvaged from old bridges and warehouses.

    Barry sorted the eucalypts by their colours: reds, browns and blondes. Based on their origin, I judged his reds to be a mix of Red Ironbark, Red Gum and Sydney Blue Gum. We submitted our cutting order: lots of 5-by-3-inch sections, dressed all round, for the window frames, some wider boards for the sills, thinner sections for the doors, and a couple of hundred square metres of lining boards for the vaulted ceilings. Then I compromised on our red rule. To match our Australian Blackwood cabinets I went with the brown Spotted Gum for the kitchen floor. Knowing that Spotted Gum also had good bending properties, I got Barry to slice up some of his longest straight-grained 120-millimetre-wide beams into 10-millimetre-thick boards that I could then laminate back together to make the curved window heads. Recycled timber is

Mr Barry Donchi, the great-great-great-grandson of an Italian migrant, inspects a piece of Australian ironbark timber polished to mirror perfection by Mr Nicholas Dattner, a maker of furniture. The wood comes from Mr Donchi's timber-yard in Echuca. Much of the wood chosen for tables by Mr Dattner was felled for buildings by Mr Donchi's family who settled in the region in the 1850s. This piece was rescued from the Kiewa River railway bridge.

hard work. Before re-sawing and dressing, Barry had to use a metal detector to find every nail, which then had to be pulled out of the timber. The black stains where the metal had reacted with the tannins in the wood remained, verifying its recycled pedigree.

In early 1990, when we gave Barry our cutting list, his recycled timber cost about the same as freshly-harvested select-grade kiln-dried Mountain Ash. But, that was about to change. The Melbourne public was being skilfully trained to appreciate the character of Australian native timbers by a charismatic furniture maker named Nicholas Dattner. Nicholas celebrated everything that was considered wrong with our rough heavy eucalypts: defects like kino veins and knot holes became features, the density of the timber became a symbol of longevity, the diversity of colours and grain meant each piece was unique, and the utilitarian history of the recycled timber became a romantic story.

A clipping from *The Age* (12th July 1990), published a few weeks after I'd towed an overloaded tandem trailer back from Moama, might well have marked the moment that recycled Australian native timbers became a premium product. It shows Barry admiring Nicholas's work: a glassy marble-like finish on the top face of an otherwise weathered Red Ironbark beam that Barry had rescued from a railway bridge in the Kiewa valley of northeast Victoria. Within a few months, the value of recycled timber had increased dramatically.

Faced with increased competition for a limited supply, Nicholas had a choice: stick with recycled timber and pass the higher cost on to his customers or risk his environmental credibility by using native forest timber. Like straddling a Red Ironbark pole and swinging an adze, it takes skill and guts to cut through the extreme views on both sides of the native forest debate.

Nicholas convinced the timber industry and mainstream environmental groups to jointly promote high-quality native-forest timbers. The result was a glossy 100-page magazine called *Roots* (1994). In his editorial, Nicholas derided the way native forest logs were being sold off for low prices. He proposed a win-win solution that would involve reducing harvest volumes and a greater focus on value-adding: 'The environmental gain would be enormous for we would be harvesting less and selling it for more.' It was a conservation argument for logging native forests.

Then in 1999, Earth Garden Books produced the buyers' guide to *Forest-friendly building timbers*[2] which set out alternatives for every common purpose for which native forest timber was being used. Naturally, recycled timbers featured strongly but the book also advocated chemically-treated, industrially-grown Radiata Pine and imported, resin-impregnated, compressed bamboo flooring!

One of the editors, Alan Gray, made no secret of his intention to put the forest debate back on its traditional path: The Wilderness Society quote him as saying: 'This book will help clarify the forest debate, because from now on, you're either pro-native-forest logging, or you're against it.'[3] The gloves were back on. Now the press had their story, good versus evil, and ran with it.

Nicholas had suggested there might be a third way, but when the antagonists returned to their trenches he was left standing on his own in no-man's land. A generation on, we're still locked in the same debate over logging native forest. For many the answer is obvious; all native forest should be protected from logging. It would take a very special person to change this view and convince them that harvesting timber from native forests could provide the means of achieving the conservation outcomes they say they want. Maybe someone like Annabel Kater.

Annabel and I loaded up the Hilux with whiteboards, hard hats, cakes and ground coffee and headed up the Hunter Valley in northern New South Wales to run another Master TreeGrower course. Our work around the Hunter has always had a strong focus on the management of private native-regrowth forests because there is so much of it. Early in the twentieth century, most of the private land in the region was cleared for farming, but when the wars took the men away, the eucalypts, particularly the Spotted Gum and Grey Ironbark (*Eucalyptus paniculata*), took back the country. Now, after more than half a century of neglect, the regrowth forests are at a crossroads. We have a choice: we can naïvely sit on our hands and 'let Nature take its course'—thinking Nature knows where she is and where she is going—or we can steer these forests in ways that enhance their conservation and production values.

When we got our class out into the bush, Annabel encouraged the landholders to try to 'read' the forest, to interpret its history. There was no need for historical records; the structure and form of the trees tell the story. We

Annabel leads the discussion with a group of farmers in a regrowth forest in New South Wales.

started by identifying the various age classes. Diameter is not the best guide of age, but by looking at the height, branching habit and form, we could pick out the over-mature trees and a few distinct waves of natural regeneration. Scattered through the forest were some trees with a wide spreading canopy that suggested they might once have been growing freely in an open farm paddock. Matching the species, we deduced that much of the regrowth is their offspring, filling in the gaps that were once pastures.

Many of the younger trees were multi-stemmed from ground level, indicating that the regrowth itself had been harvested at least once or twice, maybe for fence posts, pit props or fuel, and then left to coppice. The youngest age class is made up of the shade-tolerant eucalypts such as the Grey Gum (*Eucalyptus punctata*), White Mahogany (*Eucalyptus acmenoides*) and Tallowwood that are now spreading through the regrowth from isolated remnants. What most of the participants initially saw as a natural, almost pristine, native forest was just an accident of human history.

All our native forests are the chance result of the natural processes of physiology, ecology and genetics being played out over time under the influence of biodiversity, geology, fire, climate and us. We live in the anthropogenic era; there is no wilderness in Australia, no forest that is untouched by humankind. For many, conservation is synonymous with removing any influence of people, whereas the decision to do just that is, in effect, a human act. The result will be no more natural than a forest created by logging, failed farming or fuel-reduction burning.

With new eyes for their trees and a licence to act, our landholders began to see opportunities to improve on Nature. They suggested thinning some of the poorly formed trees and cutting back the multiple stems on the coppice regrowth to reduce competition and stimulate growth on the retained stems. We discussed which trees to leave and the debate that followed highlighted the differences in the relative values they each place on timber, aesthetics and biodiversity. There is no right way but they all agreed there was a better way than doing nothing.

As parents, we don't stand back and 'let Nature take its course' with our children's futures—we intervene. Nor do we argue that all children should be treated equally—we celebrate their differences. We abhor the neglect of children and understand that without education, guidance and health interventions they risk floundering, wasting time and growing up lost or wayward. Yet, as a community, we seem to think it is more ethical to leave our damaged forests to their own devices. The result is there to see: millions of hectares of wayward forest right across the country on both public and private land.

Annabel's parents farm cattle in the Hunter Valley. She left to study agriculture then did a masters in forestry before returning home. She expected she'd help farmers plant more trees but after years of fighting drought, frost, weeds and cynicism it occurred to her that the problem was not the lack of trees, but the neglect of the ones that were already there. To prove a point, she and her partner James purchased a 300-hectare block of regrowth forest, followed by a tractor, sawmill and logging winch and then launched Australian Sustainable Timbers.

Annabel and James worked hard to prove their environmental credentials and became the first native forest logging and processing business in Australia to receive certification from the Forest Stewardship Council (FSC). This enabled them to compete directly with the plantation industry for commercial construction jobs where certification was critical. That's when the orders started. Annabel tells the story:

> *'We got a call from the multinational company that was building the Melbourne Convention and Exhibition Centre. They asked to speak to our sales manager. I told them to wait a moment, quickly put the baby down in the lounge room, ran back to the kitchen and, with my best sales voice, took the call.'*

They required thousands of square metres of premium grade FSC certified Spotted Gum veneer for the ceiling of the grand auditorium. 'Yep, we can do that,' she answered, without pausing to think.

And they did. They sent clean sawn boards to a veneer factory and followed the process right through to the buyer. At the National Landcare Conference in 2016, I pointed to Annabel and James' timber on the ceiling of the grand auditorium and suggested to the audience that in its beauty was a message: helping farmers find markets for the products of our native trees and shrubs could be the key to enhancing the biodiversity value of private native forests.

James and Annabel thinning their native forest in the Hunter Valley to improve timber growth and biodiversity.

James and Annabel aim to ensure that every harvest leaves the forest in a better condition. By carefully selecting trees for culling, they can create small gaps, encourage natural regeneration, improve the timber value of the forest, and tweak the mix of plants to ensure all native species, both understorey and trees, are well represented. Their approach reminds me of the American ecologist and forester Aldo Leopold who described the natural environment as a complex machine with many cogs. Just because he might not know what all the cogs do, a wise mechanic would not discard those he didn't understand (the over simplification of natural systems), and neither would he use his ignorance as an excuse not to try and fix the machine (the precautionary principle). Leopold advocated an approach to ecological management that he called 'intelligent tinkering' where we engage with the landscape, making small interventions and observing the results, always seeking to learn.[4]

James and Annabel's tinkering has brought a stagnant forest to life. Before they intervened, the trees were growing less than five millimetres in diameter each year and the intense overstorey competition was suppressing understorey biodiversity. Thinning doubled the growth rate on the retained trees, stimulated flowering of the understorey plants and triggered a wave of natural regeneration. They tickled the forests with a chainsaw and unlocked its potential for growth and diversity.

At the sawmill James tries to create value from whatever logs need to come out of the forest. As a sawmiller he would prefer to get his hands on the biggest and best trees but as a forest owner and father he agrees with Annabel when she says:

> 'You wouldn't let someone come in to your cattle yards when you were away, allow them to take all your best cattle, pay you what they thought they could get away with and break the legs of the ones they didn't want as they left. So why do we let this happen in our forests?'

Over a bottle of red wine, Annabel, James and I went through the figures. They have 300 hectares of mixed species native forest of which 240 hectares is harvestable regrowth. The rest is unavailable to logging because it is too steep, too rocky, unproductive, within the designated riparian zone, or classified under the forest management code as old-growth or rainforest. Based on their growth measurements within the areas they have already thinned, Annabel estimated they can produce 60 to 65-centimetre diameter logs within a rotation of 60 years. This final harvest of mature trees would involve creating gaps in the forest about 1 to 2 tree heights across, within which every tree would be cut down.

Selectively harvesting is a tool for encouraging diameter growth on the retained trees. To regenerate eucalypts you need seed, bare soil, moisture and sunlight: you need to create a gap in the forest. The seed comes from the surrounding mature trees and from the canopies of those that are harvested. The regrowth will reflect the mix of species that Annabel chose to retain through the thinning phase. Millions of seeds will be released but those that fall too close to the edge of the gap will never develop into healthy trees because of shade and competition. Where the sun can reach the ground, the determinant factor will be competition from weeds. Harvesting and patch-burning creates a mineral earth seedbed that favours the tiny eucalypt seed.

We opened a second bottle and got into the detail. After years of selective thinning, James was confident that every hectare of harvested forest would provide at least ninety tall sawlog trees averaging over 60 centimetres in diameter at breast height and with more than 15 metres of clear stem up to the first branch. Accounting for the bark and stem taper we estimated that the mid-length diameter underbark of the 15-metre logs would be about 45 centimetres. I got out the calculator: 45-centimetre mid-log diameter gives a cross-sectional area of 0.16 square metres $((45/200)^2 \times 3.142)$. Multiplying this by the length of the log gave us a conservative estimate of log volume as being 2.4 cubic metres per tree.

Based on current government royalties and mill-door prices, James suggested we work on a standing value of $100 per cubic metre for sawlogs. I said I'd want more than that for Class 1 and 2 durable timbers. Annabel said she was hoping for more, and certainly expected it, but added that when you're doing the numbers you can't assume the best. Multiplying the yield and prices, I calculated a return of $21,500 per hectare. This translates to a perpetual annual return of $86,000 from harvesting four hectares, or less than two percent of their forest, every year, indefinitely.

'What if you do the milling yourselves?' I asked. James replied, 'Based on our current equipment and market prices we'd be looking at a forty percent recovery of green sawn timber valued at $1,600 per cubic metre.' I tapped the keypad, 'That's about one cubic metre of sawn timber per tree: $1,600 per tree, $144,000 per hectare and $576,000 per year.' Annabel smiled, 'That should be enough to cover us, a couple of mill workers, machinery costs and the inevitable breakdowns.'

'So, when will the money start to flow?' I asked. The silvicultural work to upgrade the forest started ten years ago so if all goes well they expect to have some of their forest ready for gap harvesting in about ten or fifteen years. Such is the state of their forests, and most others. Once their ecological and commercial value has been restored, forests have enormous potential to produce high quality timber on a sustainable basis.

Which raises the question: Who in our community would be prepared to invest the time and the money required to lift the capital value of our native forests to the point where they can provide a perpetual dividend, both financial and environmental? Annabel and James are doing it for their own and their children's future, but they are taking a big risk, a sovereign risk. Most private native forest owners don't believe the community will allow them to harvest their native forests in the future. Their rational reaction is to high-grade their forests—take the best and leave the rest—or just neglect them. In effect, the push to lock up native forests for conservation is undermining their conservation value.

Despite their initial apprehensions, our rural council eventually approved Peter Lockyer's architectural drawings for our house. The plans certainly gave the impression we knew what we were doing. Essentially the structure involved load-bearing walls set on a split-level concrete slab, capped with a series of north-facing concrete vaults.

Like our Red Ironbark beams, concrete vaults are inherently strong and durable. Boat hulls have been made of concrete for decades so we know they can be watertight. Our concern was bushfire and the roof would be our defence against ember attack. Yet, my attraction to Peter's drawings was not entirely practical or rational. The plans immediately appealed to me because I could see that this building would reflect us, portray us and, over time, fashion us. Its fireproof construction and passive solar design spoke of my past. Its aesthetic, derived from function rather than convention, spoke to how I saw my role in helping create new futures for our rural landscape. Our house would represent no period or trend. Like our forest, it would be unique, personal and part of our story.

When Darius Bartlett, an experienced earth builder, saw the plans

he immediately approached us. The drawings had passed his test, now our capability was being assessed. Darius was understandably wary of my skills but agreed to work on the project on an ad hoc basis; he would show us what was required at each step then leave us to finish it. Just pouring the split-level slabs was enough to prove to me that we were out of our depth. I had never built anything more complex than a billycart or a cubbyhouse. We could never have tackled the roof on our own.

For the roof structure, we made thirty-five arched beams by overlapping three layers of curved timber segments. If I were doing it today, I'd use Monterey Cypress (*Cupressus macrocarpa*). It is durable above ground, light and strong. The short wide clear sections we required could have been milled out of windbreak trees growing on the farms across the district. But we never learnt anything about the timber qualities of Monterey Cypress at university and I didn't own a sawmill, so we used Oregon (*Pseudotsuga menziesii*) from the regrowth forests in North America.

We locked the arched beams together with short hardwood purlins and laid recycled pine wafer-board over the frame, then foil, plastic, steel reinforcement and wire netting. A local company that made concrete water tanks then sprayed the roof. No one working on site had ever done anything like it before. It could have gone so wrong: forty tons of wet concrete suspended on a curved roof frame supported by adobe walls and Red Ironbark posts and beams. It held.

With the roof on, Darius and I returned to the timberwork. We laminated-up the curved window heads out of Barry's Spotted Gum and fixed them on top of the window frames made from his native reds. Underneath the

opposite: Our concrete-vaulted, load-bearing adobe brick and Red Ironbark post and beam house.

top: Darius Bartlett and Tom discuss the next step in the building of our vaulted roof frame (1990).

bottom: Darius oversees the spraying of the concrete roof.

beams, we nailed up his Sydney Blue Gum, River Red Gum and Red Ironbark lining to create a vaulted ceiling. Starting from one wall, the panelling rose like a wave over my head as I added each board, engulfing me in a tube that would become our living room; this house was consuming me.

Our young Red Ironbark (Eucalyptus tricarpa) grown from seed I collected near my surf beach.

Our Red Ironbark poles were most likely *Eucalyptus sideroxylon* from New South Wales, the same species name used for the Red Ironbark that I'd grown up with on the coast. But as we were chipping off sapwood and lifting the beams into place, two Australian botanists, Hill and Johnson, were preparing their argument for splitting the species *Eucalyptus sideroxylon* in two. My coastal Red Ironbark's new name was *Eucalyptus tricarpa*.[5] To distinguish the species you count the number of flower buds: always three on the *tricarpa* versus seven to nine on *sideroxylon*. The same two botanists went on to further discredit the taxonomy I learnt at university by publishing a paper in 1995 that moved more than thirty species out of *Eucalyptus* group to create an entirely new genus. When I laid the Spotted Gum for our kitchen floor it was *Eucalyptus maculata*, it's now *Corymbia maculata*.[6]

The species name may have changed but the Red Ironbark forest behind my surf beach is still there, still changing. Each summer, on the days when there is no surf, I walk the same tracks and read its history. The dominant trees have grown, many are now over 50 centimetres in diameter, but they are no good for timber. Before I was born, the forest was selectively logged; most likely high-graded. The loggers took the best and left the twisted, damaged or diseased to grow on, suppressing and distorting the regrowth.

The harvested trees coppiced and, although multi-stemmed and struggling to find the light, they are now producing seed. Assuming the trees they harvested had the best genetics, I collected capsules from the regrowth. I only needed a handful from ten or so trees. I put the capsules in a paper bag to dry. Within a few days, they released their seed, which I gave to Mike Robinson-Koss. Eight months later he gave me back 100 Red Ironbark seedlings for my new forest.

I planted them in a mixed plantation with Hickory Wattle on some of our infertile duplex sandy loam. The site needs lots of fertiliser to grow pasture, but it will grow trees without me needing to add any nutrients. It turned out to be the driest ever spring on record (2015). Still, they've done well in my plastic wallaby guards and I'm now form pruning them to a single stem, dreaming of a big tree and wishing I'd done it all twenty-five years earlier.

Designing and growing a forest is like designing and building your own home. You can copy others but it is more rewarding to create a unique forest that reflects your interests and personality. Just doing it is a valuable experience, learning along the way is enlightening, living with it provides utility, looking after it is nourishing, and looking back on your work is gratifying. How much more satisfying would it be to build a house from trees that you planted and nurtured yourself? Or, as is more likely in our case, leave a patch of high pruned, straight Red Ironbark trees to grow on after we've gone that might inspire a grandchild to do just that? The hand-hewn, 10-inch square Red Ironbark beam in our farmhouse may well be their inspiration.

Wedge-tailed Eagle (*Aquila audax*)

1   James Mann, *Australian Timber: its strength, durability and identification* (Melbourne: Walker, May & co., 1900).

2   Alan T. Gray and Anne Hall (eds), *Forest-friendly building timbers* (Trentham, Victoria: Earth Garden Books, 1999).

3   'New buying guide for forest friendly building timbers released,' The Wilderness Society, accessed May 18, 2017, https://www.wilderness.org.au/new-buying-guide-forest-friendly-building-timbers-released.

4   L.E. Leopold (ed.) *Round River: From the Journals of Aldo Leopold* (New York: Oxford University Press, 1972).

5   K.D. Hill & L.A.S. Johnson, 'Systematic studies in the eucalypts - 3. New taxa in *Eucalyptus* (Myrtaceae),' *Telopea* 4(2) (1991): 247.

6   K.D. Hill and L.A.S. Johnson, 'Systematic studies in the eucalypts 7. A revision of the bloodwoods, genus *Corymbia* (Myrtaceae),' *Telopea* 6 (1995): 185–504.

Durability of timber

In Australia, wood is rated for its resistance to fungal decay and insects, including termites, on a scale from Class 1 (very durable) to Class 4 (non-durable). The heartwood of a Class 1 species is expected to remain serviceable in the ground for at least 25 years and above ground for more than 40 years. Class 2 should provide 15 to 25 years in the ground and 15 to 40 years above ground, Class 3 and 4 timbers are not suitable for use outdoors. The ratings are based on mature heartwood.

The sapwood of all species is rated as having a durability of Class 4. For internal use the more important consideration is whether the sapwood is susceptible to *Lyctus* beetles and, if so, whether there is any starch present in the sapwood. *Lyctus* will only attack dry timber. To test for the presence of starch, apply an aqueous iodine solution to the sapwood. If starch is present, the liquid will develop a blue-black colour. The better option is to treat the sapwood of all susceptible species. I soak the freshly cut timber in a 5 percent solution of Sodium Borate (Disodium Octaborate Tetrahydrate). The salts move into the wet sapwood by osmosis and remain trapped in the timber when dried. It seems to be a safe and effective method for timber used indoors.

The question facing many of us who are growing Class 1 or 2 durable species is whether the heartwood of young fast-grown trees has the same durability as mature trees. In 1984, John Wilkes took samples from 40-year-old multi-stemmed Red Ironbark coppice regrowth to test the effect of growth rate on wood colour and durability.[1] As all the stems originated from the same stump, they were genetically identical. The only difference between them was their rate of diameter growth, which is based on environmental factors. He found that the larger stems had a higher concentration of extractives—the compounds deposited in the heartwood that give the timber its colour and durability. A more recent study of plantation grown Red Ironbark (*E. sideroxylon*) in South Australia compared heartwood density and durability of 30- to 40-year-old trees with 90- to 110-year-old trees of similar size.[2] Although the heartwood density of the younger trees was 10 percent less (1022 versus 1144 kgs per cubic metre at 12 % moisture) decay rates and termite resistance were similar.

[1] J. Wilkes, 'The influence of rate of growth on the density and heartwood extractives content of eucalypt species,' *Wood Science and Technology* 18 (1984):113-120.

[2] K. McCarthy, L.J. Cookson and D. Scown, *Natural durability of six eucalypt species from low rainfall farm forestry*. RIRDC Publication No 08/161 (Barton ACT: RIRDC, 2009).

Red Ironbark sawn from one of our 20-yr-old trees showing the red coloured heartwood and white sapwood. The sapwood has been attacked by *Lyctus*.

Species	AAD kg/m³	D	T	L
Red Ironbark *Eucalyptus tricarpa*	1130	1	R	S
English Oak *Quercus robur*	700	2	NR	S
Australian Red Cedar *Toona ciliata*	420	2	NR	S
Spotted Gum *Corymbia maculata*	950	2	R	S
Blackwood *Acacia melanoxylon*	640	3	R	S
Sydney Blue Gum *Eucalyptus saligna*	850	3	NR	S
Southern Blue Gum *Eucalyptus globulus*	900	3	NR	S
Manna Gum *Eucalyptus viminalis*	750	4	NR	S
Shining Gum *Eucalyptus nitens*	700	4	NR	S
Mountain Ash *Eucalyptus regnans*	680	4	NR	NS
Silky Oak *Grevillea robusta*	620	4	na	S

Species	AAD kg/m³	D	T	L
Tallowwood *Eucalyptus microcorys*	990	1	R	S
Coast Redwood *Sequoia sempervirens*	450	2	R	NS
Black Walnut *Juglans nigra*	600	2	na	S
River Sheoak *Casuarina cunninghamiana*	770	2	na	NS
Messmate *Eucalyptus obliqua*	780	3	NR	S
Flooded Gum *Eucalyptus grandis*	620	3	NR	NS
Queensland Kauri *Agathis robusta*	480	4	NR	NS
Hoop Pine *Araucaria cunninghamii*	530	4	NR	NS
Radiata Pine *Pinus radiata*	500	4	NR	NS
Hybrid Poplar *Populus*	440	4	NR	S
Pear *Pyrus communis*	700	4	na	NS

Table: The density and durability of some of the tree species we grow.
From: Keith Bootle, *Wood in Australia, 2nd Edition* (Sydney: McGraw Hill, 2005).
Air Dried Density kg/m3 (AAD) at12% moisture content (average)
Durability (D): Heartwood durability class (1 – 4)
Termites (T): Resistant (R) or Not Resistant (NR), Not available (na)
Lyctus (L): Sapwood Susceptible (S) or Not Susceptible (NS)

Chapter 13

English Oak

Quercus robur

On the island of Visingsö in Lake Våttern, Sweden, there is a 400-hectare forest of mature English Oak that provides credible witness to a remarkable story. In 1980, the admiral-in-chief of the Swedish Navy received a letter from his nation's Forestry Department informing him that the plantation commissioned in 1829 was now ready for harvest![1] In the wake of the Napoleonic Wars (in 1815), Sweden lost access to the quality English Oak forests of northern Germany that had supported their naval shipyards for more than a century. Forced to look in their own backyard, the navy undertook an inventory of all the English Oak trees in their southern provinces of Sweden. The survey, completed in 1825, found that there were only 40,000 trees left in the whole country that could be considered fit for ship building. It took 2000 large oak trees to build each battleship.

The need was clear: thousands of oak trees had to be planted to ensure the future defence of the country. Parliament agreed and Visingsö was chosen as a secure location, deep within the interior of the homeland where it would be safe from invading armies and their own oak-hating Swedish peasant farmers. The first trees were established on the island in 1831, with planting continuing through to 1857.[2]

With the discovery that metal boats could float, the navy soon lost interest in their forest. Like most Swedes, the admiral-in-chief who received the letter in 1980 only knew of the Visingsö forest as a popular tourist attraction. The parkland of mature trees draws thousands of visitors every year, supporting a thriving food, recreation and accommodation industry. On realising how it had come to be, he wrote back congratulating the generations of foresters who had stubbornly pursued the goal of creating such a fine naval forest. The needs of the community may have changed but he was sure that the forest would delight visitors for centuries to come.

The best oak for battleships grew on the best land. Naturally the trees grew taller and fatter but there is also an important structural difference between the wood of a fast-grown and a slow-grown English Oak. A fast-grown tree produces wood that is denser and more watertight. All the deciduous oaks have

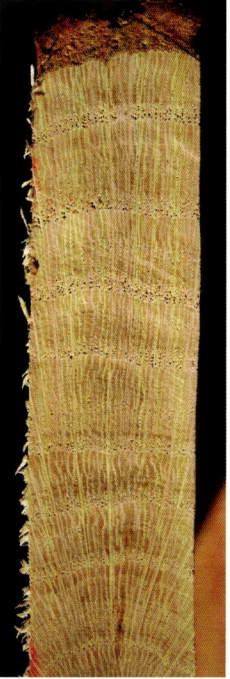

preceding: Amongst our 21-yr-old English Oak with a small oak log growing Shiitake mushrooms.

left: The end section of our young English Oak showing the rings of large pores that form at the start of each growing season. If the annual growth is greater, the average wood density increases because there are less rings of low-density pores.

right: Planted and managed for naval timber, the large English Oaks on the island of Visingsö in Sweden are now a tourist attraction. Image courtesy of Gert Albertssonn.

a ring-porous wood structure, meaning that they lay down a band of large open pores or vessels in a complete ring at the beginning of each growing season. The new pores can carry a stream of water with its dissolved sugars up to the developing leaf buds. Then, over the course of the season, normal wood cells are laid down to provide strength. Although some new pores will be added before the next winter these tend to be much smaller and have relatively thick cell walls compared to the pores produced in early spring.

In a fast-growing English Oak the growth rings are further apart so there is a greater proportion of tightly packed wood cells between the rings of pores than occur in a slow growing tree. I have seen reports of open-grown English Oak trees in New Zealand achieving a wood density of more than 750 kilograms per cubic metre (at 12 % moisture content) compared to the reported 720 kilograms per cubic metre for the fastest growing trees in Britain and 670 kilograms per cubic metre in Europe.[3] Most evergreen hardwood trees, including eucalypts and wattles, lay down similar sized pores throughout the growing season (diffuse-porous). In this case, increasing the annual growth rate seems to have no impact on overall wood density.

The naval engineers of pre-industrial Europe were aware of the defence advantages of fast-grown oak so they purposely targeted widely spaced trees growing on fertile, well-watered sites. French wine makers also knew about the relationship between the growth rate and wood density in their Sessile Oak (*Quercus petraea*), a close relative of the English Oak. Unlike the naval engineers, they purposely selected slow-growing oak trees from dense forests for wine barrels. By maintaining a high level of competition between the trees, the foresters could produce logs that had growth rings less than two millimetres apart. This resulted in timber with a density of less than 600 kilograms per cubic metre (at 12 % moisture content) that was easy to carve and bend to make barrel staves.

Oaks are the eucalypts of the northern hemisphere. There are more than 500 species within the genus *Quercus*, covering an equally diverse range of environments as the 800 or so species of eucalypts. Botanically, the oaks can be divided into three groups: white oaks, red oaks and live oaks. The live oaks are evergreen, or near-evergreen, holding their leaves all year round. The best-known commercial species of the live oak group is the Cork Oak (*Quercus suber*), which has a peculiar outer bark that can be harvested without damaging the inner bark or the cambium.

Deciduous oaks are separated into the red and white groups on the basis of their leaf shape and wood characteristics. The oak that the Swedish Navy were after was the English, European or Pedunculate Oak (*Quercus robur*), which is in the white oak group along with Sessile Oak, the species the French used for their wine barrels. In North America, the Burr Oak (*Quercus macrocarpa*) and the American White Oak (*Quercus alba*) are also from the white oak group. Most of the red oaks originate from North America and, not surprisingly, include the American Northern Red Oak (*Quercus rubra*) and Scarlet Oak (*Quercus coccinea*), along with the common Australian street tree, Pin Oak (*Quercus palustris*). The leaves of the red oaks are more deeply indented and often have small points on the end of each lobe, which help with identification. For woodworkers, ship builders and wine drinkers there is one critical difference between the wood structure of the red and white oaks.

Tylosis is an active process that occurs in the woody stem of some hardwood trees, quite independent of heartwood formation, that fills the pores in the sapwood with balloon-like growths that block the tiny pits between the cells. In short, it makes the pores impervious to water. In most of the red oaks there is virtually no active tylosis and the pores remain completely open even in the heartwood zone. To demonstrate the impact of tylosis, an American colleague gave me a thin cross-section of Northern Red Oak and told me to hold the end grain up to the light. I could see straight through the pores, which stood out like stars in an unfamiliar night sky. He then gave me a longer piece of straight-grained heartwood and showed me how I could blow air through the end grain. This lack of tylosis is a common characteristic of the red oaks from North America and makes the timber easier to dry but no good for boats or barrels.

We planted our first English Oak in the winter of 1991 when, for my thirtieth birthday, my friend and nurseryman Jason Alexandra gave me some advanced open-rooted seedlings he'd grown from acorns in his nursery. He also gave

Light shining through the annual rings of open pores in Pin Oak. Because the pore are open, red oaks cannot hold water.

me some American White Oak, Swamp Oak (*Quercus bicolor*) and Pin Oak. We planted them all into the heavy wet clays in front of the house, partly as ornamentals but also for fire protection. They would also provide shade in summer and let the sun through in winter. I have been pruning them all for clearwood, except one. With visions of grandchildren climbing through the branches and riding a rope swing, we are letting one English Oak develop a broad low canopy.

In 1995, I bought one-year-old open-rooted seedlings of the narrow Lombardy Poplar-type form of English Oak. It is commonly known as Cypress Oak and botanically as *Quercus robur* var. *fastigiata*. The varietal name comes from the botanical term *fastigiated*, which refers to the branches growing out almost parallel to the main stem. The original parent tree was discovered growing in the forests of Germany in the eighteenth century and propagated by grafting for gardens around Europe. Ours are grown from acorns and, although there is some variability in their form, most tend to run true to their mother's fastigiated habit. My hope was that the more upright form might provide a longer, straighter trunk before it spread its branches. The plan worked to some extent but the numerous acute-angled branches do make pruning more difficult.

I have been impressed with how tolerant the English Oak are to the annual cycles of waterlogging and drought on our heavy cracking clay soils. I measured our 1995 planting in 2017. At age twenty-two years, the forty high-pruned trees averaged 21 centimetres in diameter. When they were twelve years old the average was 13 centimetres—they have grown less in diameter in the last ten years than they grew in the first twelve years. To get the plantation back on track I need to thin out half the trees. If I cut them in late winter when the starch content is at its highest, the logs will be ideal for growing Shiitake mushrooms. I will then allow the stumps to coppice to provide an understorey that I can manage for Shiitake logs. This will mimic the coppice-with-standards model used in England to produce a mix of sawlogs (over a long rotation) and fuelwood (on a short rotation).

left: Our 6-yr-old English Oak (variety fastigiata). I planted the trees as 1-yr-old open-rooted seedlings using our tall tree guards to protect them from the sheep.

right: Milling a 100-yr-old English Oak that fell over in a neighbour's garden.

opposite: Alive but not growing. The English Oak trees in this 126-yr-old plantation in central Victoria have virtually stopped growing in diameter because of the intense competition for light.

I recently got the chance to put a mature English Oak across my sawmill while our own trees were still in their infancy. Sandy Stewart, a neighbour of sorts, called to let me know his 100-year-old English Oak had fallen over in the cattle yard after a wild winter storm. While the tree was still fresh, we focused on recovering short logs from the spreading canopy for Shiitake mushroom production. Then we milled the trunk in slabs and boards and stacked them to dry in the shed.

    Sandy's ancestors had planted the English Oak shortly after the First World War. When his own father returned from the Second World War, the tree was large enough to cast a shadow for both man and beast, so he built the stockyards around it. No farmer plants an oak with the expectation of ever harvesting the timber. It takes too long, longer even than they might hope to live. One generation of the Stewarts planted the English Oak because they dared to dream of a large shady tree. For the next, it was just a permanent and valued feature of their farm landscape. And for Sandy and his siblings, its death created new opportunities. After three years drying, the timber is down to ten percent moisture and ready to be made into furniture.

    Sandy's tree was growing out on its own, free of competition. I needed to know how close together I could grow our trees without compromising their diameter growth. I recalled there was a small English Oak plantation near the forestry school in central Victoria and went to see what it might teach me. I set up a plot amongst the trees that were planted in 1890. After 126 years, the

average diameter was just 29.3 centimetres! It wasn't a site problem; the trees are growing in a well-watered valley and there are other English Oaks growing nearby that are well over 70 centimetres in diameter. It was competition. The stocking rate was 376 trees per hectare and the basal area was 27.2 squaremetres per hectare. The plantation was stagnant. It might have looked pretty but, unless some trees die or are thinned, there will be very little diameter growth on the surviving trees.

Using indicative log prices for English Oak in the United Kingdom (figure 1) a 3-metre-long log from the average tree in the 126-year-old plantation would be worth less than £8 (approx. AU$14) stacked at the roadside. I doubt a farmer could harvest, dock and drag a log to their front gate for much less than that. Had the plantation been thinned, it could have produced many 60-centimetre-diameter logs over the years which (using the same figures) could have been worth more than £125 (approx. AU$216) each.

In Europe, there has been a long-standing debate between those foresters who support conventional close-spaced plantations of oak and those who advocate wider spacing or even free-growth regimes.[4] The close-spaced oak plantations use competition to control branch development. Frequent, light thinning to promote diameter growth may not start until the trees are fifty years old. The annual diameter increment in these close-spaced plantations can be less than 5 millimetres per year and it is common for it to take more than 150 years to produce sawlogs of 60 centimetres in diameter.

Advocates of early thinning of English Oak argue that wider growth rings do not affect wood quality. By giving the trees space to grow, they can produce logs of the same diameter in less than 100 years. But, the branches and epicormic shoots must be pruned or the timber will be of very low quality. In both cases the final spacing between mature trees might be as much as

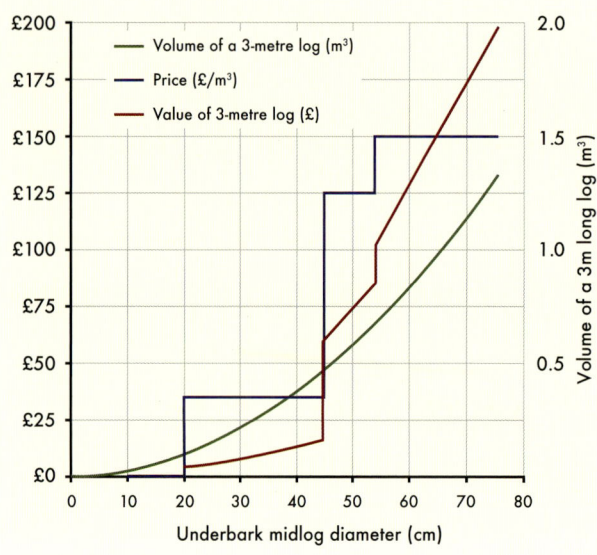

Doubling log diameter quadruples log volume resulting in a huge increase in value. I could use almost any sawlog market to illustrate the impact of diameter on log value but have chosen to use indicative British roadside prices (which include harvesting costs) for English Oak. Assumptions: log length is three metres. Prices: firewood £35/m³ (assumed to be a minimum of 20 cm diameter), small sawlog (45-55 cm) £125/m³ and large sawlog (>55 cm) £150/m³.

opposite: A sheep eyes off one of our Burr Oak (Quercus macrocarpa) growing in our flexible tree guard.

14 metres (only 51 trees per hectare)—it is just a question of which route is taken (self-pruning or manual pruning) and how long it might take to reach the same tree diameter. I prefer the latter. Having pruned my trees for wood quality, I now need to give them space to spread their canopy. If I do, I have no doubt I'll be harvesting 60-centimetre-diameter English Oak logs before my hundredth birthday!

For now, each autumn I compete with the sheep to get a share of the acorns to extend our English Oak forests. Hungry sheep on dry autumn pastures vacuum up every acorn on the ground and then wait for the next acorn to drop. The fodder, along with the shelter and fire protection they provide, make English Oak a great tree to have on the farm.

Prior to the eighteenth century, Swedish peasants were happy to allow some English Oak to grow on their poor-quality grazing land. They valued the acorns, shelter, fuel wood and nutrient cycling. But that changed when the government, faced with a shortage of naval timbers, introduced laws giving the crown legal rights over all English Oak trees growing on private land. Being unable to clear the trees, some peasants cut the branches in an effort to reduce competition with their crops.

Having no legal stake in the wood, the farmers had no reason to care for their oak trees. In 1741, botanist Carl Linnaeus expressed his frustration at the state of the trees:

> *The oaks hereabouts are many but are ill managed and in poor condition. The thick boughs were hacked off a handbreadth from*

the trunk, but far too late. For this reason, many oaks are quite decayed and dried up.[2]

The years of antagonism between the navy and farmers over the property rights to the trees growing on their land gave rise to a deep-seated hatred of English Oak amongst farmers. So, when the foresters went looking for a place to establish a new plantation, they chose an island in the middle of a lake.

When the English Oak plantation on the island of Visingsö was just twenty years old, a German forester published a paper that challenged the prevailing paradigm that underpinned plantation forestry at the time. Martin Faustmann used financial discounting to demonstrate how long rotations, like those inherent in the production of high quality English Oak timber, eroded forest value and profitability. At the time, rotations of more than 100 years were considered quite acceptable. It was the King's money and the foresters got paid their salary. Besides, the oak was grown to defend the country. But with peace and democracy came accountability and competing demands on government funds. The foresters had to demonstrate that the public expenditure in tree growing was a good investment.

Faustmann simply proposed that the time spent waiting for a plantation to mature should be acknowledged as a cost of producing timber, along with the cost of the land, labour, fencing and seedlings. He calculated the opportunity cost of the investment—the interest foregone on the funds that were tied up for the period of the rotation—so he could determine the cost of waiting for the trees to mature.

Some of the more progressive wine producers in France had already begun exploring the same question. Although it was well accepted that cellaring a bottle of wine would improve its quality, they wanted to be sure that the increase in price not only covered the cost of building and servicing the cellar but also the risks involved and the opportunity cost of their investment. If they sold each vintage immediately, rather than leave it in the cellar, the price would be lower but at least they would have the money in their hand to invest in other ways. Their initial calculations on the cost of waiting were rudimentary, but having asked the question, they had already changed the way their financiers looked at long-term investments.

There are few investments longer than growing English Oak so it's not surprising that it was foresters who refined the mathematical calculations required for discounting future costs and revenues. Their work provided a means of directly comparing alternative investment scenarios including species choice, site selection, planting design, pruning and thinning options, and rotation length. What they found dramatically changed the species foresters planted, where they planted them and how the trees were managed.

If we assume a climate of positive interest rates (to which we have become accustomed), the real value of a future sale of timber diminishes with increasing rotation length. Discounting future values is the opposite of compounding a current sum into the future, and the impact is just as significant. Talking specifically about the problem of compounding in forestry, Nobel Laureate economist Paul A. Samuelson, once said:

> 'At six percent interest, money doubles in twelve years, quadruples in twenty-four, grows sixteen-fold in forty-eight years, and 256-fold in ninety-six years. Hence, the present discounted value today of $1 of timber harvested ninety-six years from now is, at six percent, only 0.4 of one cent!'[5]

Samuelson also questioned the use of such low discount rates saying:

> 'The notion that for such gilt-edge rates (just 6 percent) I would tie up my own capital in a fifty-year (much less a 100-year) timber investment, with all the uncertainties and risks that the lumber industry is subject to, at first strikes one as slightly daft.'

Using our own 1995 plantation of English Oak as an example, I know that each bare-rooted seedling we planted cost me $0.80. For every tree I expect to harvest, we planted four or five at a regular spacing to allow for selection based on vigour and form. We protected the seedlings using a tall plastic sleeve at a cost of about $1.20 per tree. With the additional costs of herbicide (used for the first two years), the total costs of establishment, including my labour but ignoring the cost of the land, was in the order of $25 per harvestable tree. The cost of pruning was spread over the next fifteen years and might have amounted to about 45 minutes work per harvestable tree; let's say another $25. This brings the total cost of each mature tree to $50. All this money was spent in the first fifteen years and now that the trees are high pruned, all I need to do is wait. If I maintain a diameter growth at over 1 centimetre per year they might be ready to harvest in 2055 when they are sixty years old, and I am ninety-four.

Even with a conservative discount rate of four percent (which excludes inflation as it is expected to impact both the costs and returns to the same extent), just to get my money back the standing value of each mature oak tree would need to be $520.[6] Any more than that would be a profit. It sounds possible. But my analysis ignores the cost of the land on which the trees are growing, both the purchase and holding costs. I'm happy with that, we own the land anyway and the trees are providing shelter, fire protection, Shiitake logs from thinnings, shade for our trial crop of Goldenseal (*Hydrastis canadensis*) and acorns for the sheep. Together, all the non-timber values more than covers any loss in pasture production.

But what if I use a more realistic discount rate of eight percent? This figure is still moderate for corporate investments in risky enterprises like tree growing. I would need to achieve a final price of $5,062 per tree in today's money, just to break even. At twelve percent, which might better reflect an individual's time preference for money, and is probably what Samuelson would have thought was more realistic, the future break-even price is $44,879 per tree! To grow English Oak for timber you clearly need to be both patient and optimistic.

Not surprisingly, once discounting became the accepted method for assessing the viability of growing timber, funding for English Oak plantations in Europe dried up. Norway Spruce (*Picea abies*) grew faster, so despite producing a lower quality timber it could be shown to be a more profitable investment. Faustmann also developed formulae for calculating the optimum harvest age for a timber plantation, which led to trees being considered profitable to harvest years before they had reached their highest value. To wait any longer for quality would be irrational.

Faustmann's laws of economics spread throughout the new world and have dominated the thinking in contemporary plantation forestry ever since. While we know what a quality plantation might look like—the species, the size of the trees and their age—having developed a mechanism for understanding its worth, economists ensured that no rational investor, including government, would consider growing one.

Discounted cash flow analysis provides a clever mathematical way of collapsing many years of costs, and the long wait for a return, into a single number called the Net Present Value. But, if a grower plants trees for timber

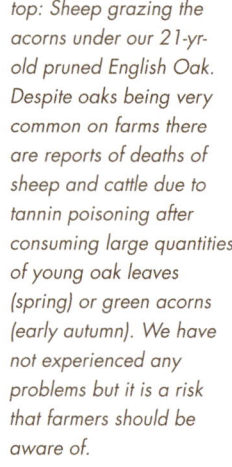

top: Sheep grazing the acorns under our 21-yr-old pruned English Oak. Despite oaks being very common on farms there are reports of deaths of sheep and cattle due to tannin poisoning after consuming large quantities of young oak leaves (spring) or green acorns (early autumn). We have not experienced any problems but it is a risk that farmers should be aware of.

bottom: Under our oaks we have trialled growing the medicinal herb Golden Seal. Unfortunatley it failed due to moisture competition from the trees.

there is no way of collapsing time itself. They still need to wait and, while they do, they will grow older. Discounting does not solve the long investment problem inherent in forestry; it only serves to highlight it as a problem. If farmers are going to plant high-quality, long-rotation forests for timber they will need an alternative economic paradigm.

I was filming my friend Andrew Stewart out in his paddock surrounded by his recently planted multipurpose belts of trees when he said something to camera that shocked me:

> 'Long-term rotations don't really present a problem to me because, well really … I think there's an opportunity there because, while the trees are there improving the farm productivity and the environmental integrity of the property, they're growing into timber … we're currently making our living from prime lambs and beef and the trees are assisting in that process so we have assured income, but the next generation, they'll gain the benefit of harvesting those trees, then perpetuating the system by replanting.'

Wow! I'd never heard my friend say that before, and I'd certainly never heard a forester say anything like that.

I tried the same technique with another farmer who had been planting trees for shade, shelter, timber and seed production for more than fifteen years. After filming Noel Passalaqua amongst his various plantings on his farm in southern New South Wales, we went to his favourite spot overlooking the front valley of his property. Noel turned to the camera and said:

> 'Here is something that I never get sick of. You know, I have lived on this farm for twenty-two years and it just gets better and better. It gives us a great feeling every time we come up here. It's a beautiful landscape and it's improving every year. How do you value that? How do you quantify that? I guess, in simple terms, this is the place we live, this is our life. People try and design a good life in many different ways, and often it revolves around income. But, you know, improving the landscape value gives you a better feeling about where you live. It's not something that you can value with money, it's just a feeling. It's where you live, and if it improves your quality of life, it's a great thing.'

As their trees had grown, so too had Andrew and Noel's confidence to talk about what it feels like to grow a forest. Of course, it takes time. But *time* is just something that passes while we live out our lives. *Time* is not just a cost, it is also an *opportunity*: an opportunity to grow forests that not only give purpose and meaning to our own lives but that also provide the prospect of a cash return, and leave a legacy. For me, the key to understanding the economics of tree growing lies in the *other* distinguishing feature of a forest: it cannot be moved. Forests are part of the land on which they grow. If a farmer can establish multipurpose forests that sustain or improve agricultural productivity, enhance landscape values and offer the promise of future income this will be reflected in their feelings for the land and its value. For those hoping to pass their farm

Noel Passalaqua tells other farmers what it feels like to change a landscape with trees.

on to the next generation, what greater gift is there than thirty or forty years of time wrapped up in living trees firmly rooted in their land?

People value the English Oak forests of Visingsö, the tall Coast Redwood groves in California and the massive Kauri (*Agathis australis*) trees of New Zealand *because* they are old, *because* of the time that has passed in bringing them to their grandeur. By putting a cost on time, mainstream forestry has proved that it is more profitable to grow a series of short rotations of fast growing species that produce mediocre timber rather than take the time to produce a quality forest. Dennis Hocking, a second-generation farm forester in New Zealand, explained how the latter might actually be economically rational for private landholders when he told a professional foresters' conference that their approach was wrong and that 'forest growing was a capital, rather than a cash flow, business'.[7] Why would a landholder spend a lifetime building an asset that could deliver cash and non-cash values for generations then clear it and go back to what they had before?

This conflict, between what we know is *quality* and what is perceived as *profitable,* only serves to undermine the attractiveness of plantation forestry to the very farmers and communities we need to engage. Faustmann understood the difference. While preparing his famous 1849 paper he published another less widely read article under a pseudonym in which he points out that the forest valuation methods he was advocating could not fully represent 'the special economic interests or preferences of individual forest owners'.[8] He then demonstrates how his optimum harvest model could be used to show that it would be more profitable for a farmer to clearcut his 24-hectare forest prematurely and start again rather than have let it mature and manage it for a perpetual return of high quality timber. Most significantly, he notes that his model simply demonstrates what someone might do if the *only* thing that matters to them is the financial return from the timber.

When thinking of planting a tree for our grandchildren, even if they're not yet born, many of us consider planting an English Oak. In the small seedling we can see a mature tree: we might see a child on a swing, a couple picnicking in the shade, or even, an extended family of our descendants sitting around a beautiful oak table; a piece of timber that puts us right there amongst them, linking our lives with theirs. Though few doubt it is possible to grow a quality oak forest, or the value of a mature oak tree, few ever bother to plant an acorn. Those that do will be long remembered.

King Parrot (*Alisterus scapularis*)

1   G-A. Morin, K. Kuusela, D.B. Henderson-Howat, N.S. Efstathiadis, S. Oroszi, H. Sipkens, E. v. Hofsten and D. W. MacCleery 'Long-term historical changes in the forest resource,' *Geneva Timber and Forest Study Papers*, No. 10, United Nations, 1996).

2   Eliasson and S.G. Nilsson, 'You Should Hate Young Oaks and Young Noblemen: The Environmental History of Oaks in Eighteenth-and Nineteenth- Century Sweden,' *Environmental History* 7(4) (2002): 659-677.

3   N.C. Clifton, *New Zealand Timbers – The complete guide to exotic and indigenous woods.* (Wellington: GP Publications, 1994).

4   Giulia Attocchi, *Silviculture of Oak for High-Quality Wood Production. Effects of thinning on crown size, volume growth and stem quality in even-aged stands of pedunculate oak (Quercus robur L.) in Northern Europe* (Doctoral Thesis, Swedish University of Agricultural Sciences, 2015).

5   Paul A. Samuelson, 'Economics of forestry in an evolving society,' *Economic Inquiry* 14(4) (1976): 466-492.

6   To calculate a present value (PV) of a future value (FV) at a particular discount rate (r) for a known number of years (n): PV = FV/(1+r)^n. The current value of $1000 obtained in 60 years' time based on a discount rate of 4 % = $1000/(1+ 0.04)^{60} = $1000/10.52 = $95.

7   Denis Hocking, 'Bigger role for smaller growers,' *New Zealand Journal of Forestry*, May (2003): 11-12.

8   E-J. Viitala, 'An early contribution of Martin Faustmann to natural resource economics,' *Journal of Forest Economics* 12 (2006): 131-144.

Growing Shiitake mushrooms on logs

My introduction to growing Shiitake mushrooms came through a Bhutanese student of mine who later became a refugee. After graduating, Parsuram Sharma-Luital had a job training Burmese refugees how to grow Swiss Brown and Oyster mushrooms. He was keen to add Shiitake and contacted me to source logs. Our reunion led to a research project trialling Shiitake mushroom production on a range of Australian farm-grown timbers.

We compared two eucalypts (Shining Gum and Sugar Gum (*Eucalyptus cladocalyx*)), Blackwood, Hybrid Poplar, Black Alder and English Oak. We cut fresh clean logs from healthy trees in late winter. The Shiitake (*Lentinus edodes*) mycelium feeds off the sugars and starch stored in the sapwood so the ideal time to harvest is when the concentration of carbohydrates in the wood is at its peak. This is usually in winter when the tree is dormant. As spring approaches the food stores in the sapwood are converted to soluble sugars that move up the stem to drive bud burst and leaf growth. Fast-grown trees with a wide sapwood band are best. For ease of handling, the logs were cut about 1 metre long and between 100 and 150 millimetres in diameter.

We drilled about 30 eight-millimetre diameter holes into the sapwood of each log and inserted a small wooden dowel that carried the Shiitake mycelium. We imported the impregnated dowels from North America. Melted bees wax was then applied to the ends of the logs and over the drill holes to seal in the moisture and keep out any competing fungi. The logs were stored in loose stacks in a shade house with a misting system to maintain a high humidity and prevent them from drying out.

Over the first summer we could see the white mycelium spreading through the logs. Then, in autumn, we soaked the logs in cold water for 24 hours to induce fruiting and compared the yields. Differences between the species were evident immediately, with 70 % of the English Oak logs producing mushrooms on their first fruiting, compared to less than 30 % for all the other species. We then rested the logs for a few months to allow the fungus to continue consuming the carbohydrates in the logs before soaking them again. There is no need to re-inoculate the log between each fruiting cycle.

The eucalypts improved with time, suggesting the mycelium was taking longer to fully impregnate the sapwood. By the third fruiting in spring almost all the eucalypt logs were producing mushrooms. Despite a poor fourth harvest in late summer due to the logs drying out, the average for the 2-year trial was about 1.3 kgs of fresh mushrooms per log for the English Oak and 600 grams for the Shining Gum and Sugar Gum. By the sixth fruiting cycle, a full two years after the logs were initially inoculated, the Blackwood, which had barely produced 100 grams of Shiitake per log over the first four fruiting cycles, suddenly flourished.

Since our first trials, farmers around Australia have had success with other native species including Southern Blue Gum, Flooded Gum and Swamp Sheoak (*Casuarina glauca*). Yields vary enormously. I have often harvested more than a kilogram from a single fruiting of a eucalypt log while other logs in the same batch barely produce any. This can make commercial production difficult and home production interesting and fun.

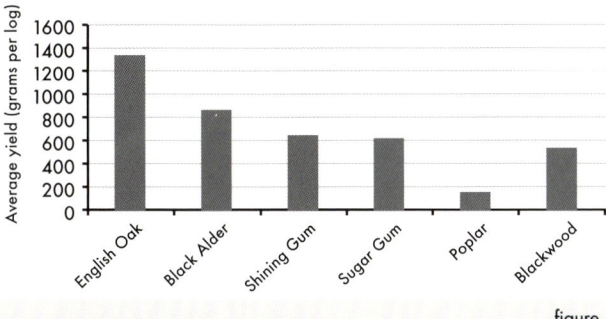

figure 1

Parsuram Sharma-Luital and Rowan Reid, *Log-Grown Shiitake Mushrooms: An Australian Grower's Manual* (Birregurra, Vic.: The Otway Agroforestry Network, 2009).

1: Ready to harvest Shiitake mushrooms on an English Oak log.

2: Parsuram Sharma-Luital inspecting the growth of Shiitake on English Oak.

3: The Shiitake mother spawn on wooden dowels.

4: The CERES Shiitake trial shade house showing how the logs were stored between fruitings.

5: Shiitake mushrooms growing on one of our Shining Gum logs.

figure 1: The average total yield per log for different tree species over six fruitings (CERES Shiitake trial, Melbourne).

Chapter 14

Spotted Gum

Corymbia maculata

We often see our lives as a series of finite games: completing school, growing a crop, building a house. They have an end, a point when we stop studying, working or building. To 'win' is to pass, to profit or be in on time and under budget. Finite games are good; they help us map our progress and measure our achievements; but they are not the whole story. They are just one part of the larger game we are all playing—our life's journey. Together they form an infinite series of games that are too complex and dynamic to be constrained by rules, and the running score never tells the full story.

American forest scientist and woodland owner Dr Jim Finley knew little about growing trees on Australian farms when I brought him out to join us for a national series of field days and workshops. Bags jammed into the back of the four-wheel drive, we drove out of Melbourne Airport on what was, for Jim, the wrong side of the road. For him everything was wrong: the trees, farms and wildlife. One night, just a few days into our tour, we were on a pitch-black road in the Western Australian wheatbelt when Jim asked me to stop the car so he could get out; he'd never seen the southern night sky. I started doubting my decision: What advice could Jim offer an Australian farmer?

We held our final event in the Otway Ranges. The room was filled with local tree growers and a few special guests from further away, including David Jenkins. Jim usually began his presentation by apologising for his ignorance; if they had come to learn about what species to plant and how to manage their trees, they would be disappointed. Then he'd talk about the forests he had worked in and some of the landholders that had inspired him. Despite the obvious differences in species, climate and markets, Jim gently drew out the similarities between the family forest owners of Pennsylvania and the Australian farmers he had met. Wherever we live, he said, we share a certain meaning in our relationship with our landscape. Then, almost as if wondering to himself, he added that maybe it was because trees took so long to grow that farmers seemed to have the time to develop a special relationship with their forests.

Jim finished his presentation by challenging the very reasons why we plant trees at all: 'Growing a forest on your own land is not really about the trees, or the timber, wildlife, soil protection, water quality or carbon sequestration that they provide,' he said. 'These are just the things that give it value. What gives the act of planting, managing and caring for a forest meaning is the personal history it allows us to write on the landscape.'

The room applauded. Jim invited questions. I heard a familiar voice and turned to see David. He was clearly moved. Thanking Jim, David said *preceding: The farmer and the forester. Andrew Stewart and I beside our largest high-pruned Spotted Gum (29-yrs-old).*

left: Professor Jim Finley, Pennsylvania State University, with American private forest owners. I was listening as he explained how thinning would encourage canopy development and increase diameter growth on their hardwoods.

right: Jim showing me a good size American Black Cherry in Pennsylvania.

that in his many years as a tree grower he had never heard anyone express what he himself had come to *know*: that the trees he was growing for timber were more than just another crop. Jim, the professor, the forest scientist, the teacher from afar, had told him that it was okay to be emotionally engaged with his trees, even if he was planning to harvest them. Indeed, his participation in the harvesting and milling of timber from the forest that he himself had created had interwoven part of himself even more tightly into the story of his land.

You could have heard an American Black Cherry (*Prunus serotina*) leaf fall to the ground.

A few days later Jim gave me a copy of Aldo Leopold's *A Sand County Almanac* in which he had written the inscription: 'This book contains many parcels of knowledge—most of which you know'. Yes maybe, but did I know that I knew these things before I read Leopold's words or heard Jim talk of them? Like Leopold's explanation of a conservationist: 'I have read many definitions of what is a conservationist, and written not a few myself, but I suspect that the best one is written not with the pen, but with the axe. It is a matter of what a man thinks while chopping, or deciding what to chop. A conservationist is one who is humbly aware that with each stroke he is writing his signature on the face of his land.'[1] I thought of David harvesting his trees, his chainsaw was his axe. Then I read the next line: 'Signatures of course differ and this is as it should be.' *That's it!* I thought, *there is no right way to grow trees, no right species or right purpose, just an opportunity to be the author of a never-ending story, if only for a short time.*

Andrew Stewart understands what it means to take a turn at writing a story on a landscape. His family purchased a block off the first settlers a hundred years ago and Andrew's grandchild is the sixth generation to live on the farm. After studying, working and travelling, he returned about the same time we bought our block in the next valley. Today, their 230 hectares look completely different, transformed from three-and-a-half percent tree cover to more than seventeen percent, with the establishment of over 40,000 trees and shrubs. The family now turn off about 1,500 prime lambs each year and they are beginning to generate some income from their trees. At first it was just the sale of Radiata Pine Christmas trees, but since then there has been a commercial harvest of Southern Blue Gum pulpwood that yielded almost $30,000 and small spot sales of River Mint (*Mentha australis*) and Banksia flowers. Because they grow trees, some handy income has also come from conducting farm tours to share their experience.

Andrew tells his guests that despite fencing out more than seventeen percent of the farm for trees, there has been no loss of agricultural production. He acknowledges that this is partly due to their improved pasture and grazing management and their use of deep-rooted perennial summer crops for feed, but the trees play their role. Along with the sale of seed, flowers and bush food, Andrew calculates that the trees are adding more than 100 green tons of harvestable timber to the farm's asset value each year. Then there are the 106 species of native birds that have been spotted on the property, including large flocks of Ibis that search out the Redheaded Pasture Cockchafer grubs that might otherwise destroy the pastures. The trees may also be helping increase and sustain the populations of predatory spiders that control the Red-legged Earth Mite that can devastate their pasture clovers. The waterlogging, soil erosion and dryland salinity, which had been slowly eating away at the family's resource base, are now under control and their carbon budget is in the black. But the main benefit of the trees is the shelter they provide for the stock.

Animal physiologists use the concept of a neutral temperature range within which animal growth, fertility and behaviour are unaffected by either hot or cold stress. At temperatures below the neutral range, sheep and cattle endeavour to maintain their core body temperature by eating more, increasing their metabolic rate (by shivering) and seeking shelter from the cold. In hot weather they pant, reduce their feed intake, increase water consumption and seek shade or windy areas to cool their core body temperature. In each case, physiological stress and behaviour change can reduce growth, fertility, milk production and the birth weight of their offspring. In some cases, severe stress can lead to death.

Andrew joins his rams to the ewes in February (the hottest month), which means they'll lamb in August (the coldest month). This strategy increases the risk of heat stress affecting ram and ewe fertility—due to a lower viable sperm count and longer oestrous cycle—and of cold stress reducing lamb development and survival. In the lead-up to joining, Andrew holds the rams in a well-treed paddock to maintain their sperm count and the ewes in large shady

By carefully integrating trees into the landscape for shelter and conservation, the Stewart family have achieved 17 percent tree cover without any loss of agricultural production.

paddocks. Twelve weeks after joining, the ewes are scanned with an ultrasound and separated into three mobs: those with single embryos, those with twins or triplets and the barren ewes. Ewes carrying multiple lambs get priority through the winter and then access to the best sheltered pastures for lambing.

Across southern Australia as many as ten percent of all lambs die of cold stress within their first few days of life. The greatest risk is in the period immediately after birth when the lamb is wet and weak. Once they are up and suckling, their chances improve but cold wet windy weather during the first two days of life can be devastating. Twelve days after the first lambs drop on the Stewarts' winter pastures, lambing reaches a peak. If wet cold weather was to hit right then, more than 200 day-old lambs might be at risk of dying from the cold. As a small boy, Andrew recalls going out on a cold wet night with his father to save the lambs. With a thermos of warm milk and brandy, Lindsay walked amongst the ewes searching out the weakest newborns to give them a drink. Those that couldn't stand were taken back to the homestead, given a warm bath and left to dry beside the stove.

A good lambing paddock has lush pastures and good shelter, which can be provided by tree belts on all sides. But trees also provide cover for foxes so Andrew runs a few South American Alpacas with each mob of lambing ewes. A trial undertaken on working farms in central New South Wales found that running Alpacas with ewes increased the weaning percentage from seventy to eighty-three percent.[2] The difference was attributed to a reduction in fox and dog predation. Without a statistically valid trial, Andrew can't prove that the Alpacas, or the trees, are improving their weaning rates but he believes they do make a difference. In 2016, their lambing rate was over ninety percent for

singles and 160 percent for twins. One mob of twinning ewes yielded 183 percent, a result that Andrew attributes to the fact the mob was small and were put into a well-sheltered paddock that had about 1700 kilograms per hectare of pasture dry matter and a couple of Alpacas.

Wool is a very good insulator against the cold. In full wool, a mature sheep can feel quite comfortable at temperatures below zero, even if it is raining. But after shearing they can suffer from cold stress, particularly if it is wet. The most critical period is the first 24 hours, while they replenish their cover of waterproofing lanolin, but they remain susceptible for a week or so until there is some reasonable wool growth. The Stewarts now shear all their ewes and rams in one frantic week in late November. Had they done so back in 1987, they might have experienced a massive loss of stock. On 1 December 1987, we were ready to shear our 400 young wethers. When it started raining we were forced to abandon our plans. Only 10 sheep were shorn that day but that night we lost four of them in our treeless paddocks. Across the region more than 50,000 sheep died.

The air temperature that night was quite mild, about 10°Celsius, but the wind and the rain were ferocious. Had we had belts of trees around a paddock boundary they wouldn't have kept the sheep dry but they would have reduced the windchill. Although we know we feel colder when standing out in the wind, scientists have been unable to measure the windchill effect. Think of it this way: if you put two thermometers outside, one in a sheltered location and one out in the wind, they read the same temperature, but that's not how it feels. Meteorologists and physiologists have developed models that seek to describe how cold animals *feel* when exposed to different wind speeds. They make many assumptions. For example, the Australian Bureau of Meteorology uses the Steadman model[3] of 'apparent temperature', which is based on an adult walking

opposite: Even in bad weather, winter lambing is now a joyous occasion on our well sheltered farm.

top: Rod Bird (centre right) and farmer Don Jowett (centre left) explain the shelter benefits of widely spaced high-pruned Spotted Gum to a group of western Victorian farmers. Don grew Lucerne under the trees to create a safe and productive lambing paddock.

outdoors at about five kilometres per hour, in the shade, on a day of seventy percent humidity, wearing dry clothes 'appropriate for the conditions'. Based on this model, if the temperature was 10°Celsius and we were out in a paddock where the wind speed was 50 kilometres per hour it would feel like -1°Celsius. If we then moved behind a shelterbelt where the wind speed was 25 kilometres per hour the effective temperature would increase to 4°Celsius. The effect would be much greater for wet sheep.

Animal physiologist Dr Rod Bird spent years measuring the impact of shelterbelts on wind speeds and pasture production in Western Victoria. His results show that well-structured shelterbelts can reduce wind speeds to well below fifty percent of open conditions for up to ten times the height of the trees out into the paddock (see science and practice section at the end of this chapter). Wind, like water, seeks the path of least resistance so if there are gaps between or under the trees, the air will tunnel through at speeds much higher than open conditions. Rod's message to farmers: 'effective shelter is best obtained by establishing tall, dense windbreaks and excluding browsing livestock.'[4]

For recently-shorn sheep, the lower the wind speed the better. Just off his laneway that links the shearing shed to the paddocks, Andrew has a patch of trees and shrubs that the family established around a salty swamp. The mix of native species, long rank grass, the presence of water and its location within the landscape has resulted in the site having the greatest diversity of bird species found on the farm. It also plays a strategic role in Andrew's shelter plan: if the weather turns cold during shearing he runs the off-shears sheep into the block for a night or two. The feed is rough but there is good shelter. It happened in Spring 2012 and not a single sheep was lost.

I first met Andrew in 1987, when he'd just returned home from his solo trip working on cattle stations in the north, exploring the highlands of Papua New Guinea and backpacking through Southeast Asia. Travelling through unfamiliar landscapes changed the way he looked at what was familiar. Despite having fond memories of a productive family farm, what he saw on his return was waterlogging, encroaching dryland salinity, expanding gully and stream bank erosion, and a lack of shade and shelter for stock. He became uncomfortable about his future; should he stay or should he go?

Andrew was drenching sheep in the stockyards when I approached him. My interest was the Italian Stone Pine (*Pinus pinea*) growing nearby. I was surprised when the farmer seemed to know who I was, or at least to know of my first book. Working as a teacher, Andrew had been using *Agroforestry in Australia and New Zealand* (1985) as a text for his year 10 agricultural class. We talked about trees when we first met and have probably done so every time since, as friends and colleagues. Ours is a perfect, albeit accidental, partnership: Andrew, with his degree in agricultural science and a credible family history growing up on the farm—in a landscape that needed trees—and me, the forest scientist who grew up on the coast but was looking for a landscape that needed a tree grower.

It could have been very different. Not long before we met, Andrew and his new wife Jill recognised that, run as it had been, the farm had little potential to support another generation of the Stewart family. They decided that their best option was to sell up and move north onto a larger grazing property. Fortunately, for me at least, the sale failed. With one dream thwarted, a new one rose to take its place. Andrew and Jill would stay and fight the adage—*get big or get out*—and make small-scale family farming work for their generation, and the next. They recognised that things would have to change; farming would mean more than just growing pastures for sheep, cows and hay.

Andrew started by leading the family through a whole-farm planning process. Using a large aerial photograph and plastic overlays, they began by drawing in the key landscape features, such as the contours and drainage lines. They then divided the farm into its various land classes based on its inherent capabilities and weaknesses. Lines were drawn to mark the boundary between the heavy clay loams that would get waterlogged in a wet spring and the light sandy loams higher up the slopes that dried off early in the season. Dams, remnant trees and salt affected areas were also marked on the base map, along with assets that couldn't be moved—the two houses and the 100-year-old shearing shed.

A farmer's thinking can be easily led by their existing fence lines. Andrew's planning process drew attention to the fact that their fences crossed land type boundaries and enclosed contrasting soil types in the one paddock, trapping conflicting problems together. He knew that if they fenced the farm to reflect the land, he could better match the pasture species and grazing management to its capability, thereby reducing overgrazing, maximising animal productivity, minimising weed growth and restoring soil health. They would

Andrew (right) shows a guest how they used an aerial photograph and plastic overlays to develop their whole farm plan.

also put in laneways for stock movement. The role of trees and their place in the landscape became obvious.

They began by fencing out the creek and planting a mix of native trees and shrubs to control erosion, trap nutrients, and provide wildlife habitat and a corridor for its distribution. Andrew included tall trees to maximise the shelter out into the adjacent paddocks and began managing them for timber. A native understorey would fill the gaps beneath their canopies. He had seen our multipurpose creek planting but he wasn't copying my design. He adapted it to suit his site and the requirements of the funding agency. As he explains it:

> 'The Landcare grant paid for the fencing material and indigenous trees and shrubs. We did the work, but rather than just focus on conservation we chose to move the fence out further into the paddock and plant a few rows of timber trees on the edge.'

By differentiating between the trees and shrubs for conservation and the family's private investment in timber production, Andrew placated the departmental officers who were concerned that it might look like public funds were being misdirected to support timber harvesting. But, in doing so, he had also reinforced the fallacy that timber production is incompatible with conservation.

Direct incentives, such as grants to cover the cost of seedlings and fences, are widely used to encourage farmers to plant trees. In fact, most landholders

The Stewarts' multipurpose creek planting has Spotted Gum for timber planted close to the fence and native shrubs for biodiversity and soil conservation along the drainage line.

expect them. Similar cash or in-kind inducements have also been used to encourage households to install water tanks, rooftop solar panels and low energy light bulbs. The argument is that the people who need to adopt the favoured practices—in order to help achieve the desired public benefits—are either unable or unwilling to pay the full cost themselves. What makes these preferred practices or innovations unattractive is usually obvious: high up-front costs; loss of existing production potential; long investment periods; high social, environmental or market risk; or a perception of low private benefit.

My concern is that direct incentives almost always result in a range of perverse outcomes that mean they often do more damage than good. Mine is not a popular view, even amongst my professional and landholder peers. So, when I was invited to present at the 1st World Congress of Agroforestry in Florida back in 2004, I took the challenge of presenting the case with a paper titled: *Direct Subsidies for Agroforestry Technologies - Is it a case of The Emperor's New Clothes?*

Striding up to the stage I was sure I had a winning hand; ten no-trump tricks. I presented my hypothesis: direct incentives do not drive spontaneous agroforestry adoption, in fact, they can prevent it. I began with the simplest tricks. I argued that direct incentives:

1. stifle, rather than drive, innovation and adaptation by only supporting technologies or methods approved by the funding agency;
2. actively discourage farmers from implementing alternative practices that provide the same public benefits;
3. support only a few of the potential recipients while alienating the majority who miss out because of the program's timeframes, conditions, preferred location or eligibility criteria;

4. reward, rather than discourage, mismanagement, neglect or inappropriate farming systems by supporting landholders who continue practices that are known to contribute to the problem;
5. encourage farmers to overcommit by requiring a particular level of adoption, such as a minimum area of revegetation;
6. undermine early adopters by not acknowledging or rewarding those farmers who have implemented similar technologies without having received public funds; and,
7. discourage third party investors who might have been willing to jointly fund multipurpose plantings that deliver both public and private benefit.

Without giving my opponents the opportunity to respond, I cleared my seven tricks off the table and reconsidered my hand. Which argument should I play next?

I am often told that supporting farmers with cost-share grants creates working examples that will act as demonstration sites for others. But how can that be?

8. the fact that a farmer requires a grant or free inputs to implement the promoted practices provides a clear signal to other landholders that the innovation is not worth funding privately.

There, another trick in the bag!

I then moved on to the negative social engineering impact of subsidies. Some of the extension agents who have been relying on handing out grants to attract farmers into their programs have told me that landholders often ask them: 'What do you have funds to support this year?' So:

9. over time a welfare mindset tends to develop amongst farmers to the point that many assume that investing in conservation practices is a public rather than a private responsibility. Many farmers would not consider planting trees at all without first receiving some form of financial support, even if they thought it would be worthwhile.

Nine tricks down, one to go. My audience was silent. I was touching a raw nerve amongst the researchers and extension agents from both the rich and poor countries. Government and conservation groups back home have come to rely on providing grants to get their preferred land management practices adopted by farmers. The agencies celebrate the trees they funded but rarely follow up a few years later to see if they had achieved the outcomes they anticipated or considered the impact their program might have had on other farmers. I could see I wasn't making any friends.

To ease the tension, I showed some beautiful pictures of the Stewarts' farm and described how the family had worked together to design unique agroforestry systems that reflected their needs and aspirations. I focused on one of their more recent designs which was established without public funding. Along a land class boundary they had established one fence for stock management and a second, 15 metres back onto the less productive land. Between the fences, they planted a five-row multipurpose shelterbelt. The outside and middle rows were planted with Spotted Gum in pairs at wide spacings and the other rows planted more closely with understorey shrubs for low shelter and biodiversity.

Paired planting involves establishing two trees close together, in this case about 75 centimetres apart, and having a large gap between the pairs. They used a 6-metre spacing between the pairs in the outside rows and increased this to 8 metres in the centre row to balance the competition. When the trees were about 5 or 6 metres tall they removed the poorer performing tree in the pair, and began pruning the retained tree for timber. The design was born out of a need to protect sheep yet was also focused on creating new opportunities. In both respects, it was about reducing risk and uncertainty.

Whether it is climate, markets, disease or roaming stock, risk is inherent in farming. It's not something I fully appreciated when I started planting trees. Sure, we planted a wide range of species—I was hedging my bets—but like others, I was enticed by the fast early growth rates and optimistic predictions of some of the southern eucalypts (the hares), and overlooked the tortoises that were right there in front of me. Andrew's father Lindsay planted his first Spotted Gum in the 1960s. I saw the same trees, standing taller than any other eucalypt, as I drove past their farm almost every day on my way to the shop, kindergarten and school in those early years. But I didn't, or couldn't, read their story. When the Millennium Drought hit, bringing with it moisture stress, insect attack and wildfire, our Southern Blue Gum and Shining Gum plantations struggled while Lindsay's Spotted Gum grew on.

It wasn't until Russell Washusen ran a series of milling trials of farm-grown eucalypts, including Spotted Gum, that I started thinking my focus on fast early growth rates may have been misguided.[5] Even when backsawn, Russell was able to produce a recovery of about 25 percent select grade timber from small-diameter trees (average 40 cm underbark). When he milled some larger pruned Spotted Gum from Richard Moore's research trials in Western Australia the results confirmed his view: Spotted Gum can be backsawn for furniture and flooring without experiencing problems of collapse or checking. Russell used the timber for flooring in his own farmhouse. It looks fantastic.

I ran a video of Andrew's image on the screen. He told the audience: 'I see using commercial trees and habitat trees as part of the risk management strategy for our property.' I explained; if trees are going to be added to the farming landscape they should reduce, rather than increase, the environmental, economic and social risks. For Andrew, Spotted Gum grown in shelterbelts along land class boundaries with an understorey of native shrubs, was not so much a new venture but a way of sustaining and enhancing the old—the family farm.

But what of the timber? I let Andrew's image explain: 'We have trees integrated into the landscape for their multiple values,' he said, 'but if, at

top: Andrew's multipurpose shelterbelt soon after planting (left) and about 8 years later (right). The Spotted Gum were planted in pairs in three rows with understorey between them to fill in the gap caused by pruning.

bottom left: Having done the milling research, Russell Washusen chose to plant Spotted Gum in his own multipurpose creek planting on his farm in north east Victoria.

bottom right: Researcher Richard Moore amongst his trial of pruned Spotted Gums in Western Australia.

the end of the day for whatever reason the trees aren't harvested they're still performing jobs for the farm. Any income from timber is a bonus. I prune and thin just to keep that opportunity alive.'

I then presented my final trick to the conference delegates:

10. when offered cost-share grants, farmers will see little point in engaging in community networks that build their own knowledge and confidence in tree growing and support the development of sophisticated and resilient agroforestry designs that are appropriate to each family and their landscapes.

I then explained how, when Andrew and I set up the Otway Agroforestry Network, our focus was on helping landholders develop forestry options that were attractive to them. We did not provide any grants or free trees.

left: More than 200 local landholders are members of the Otway Agroforestry Network and many of them have completed the Australian Master TreeGrower course. We now have a team of about 30 peer group mentors who help other landholders design and develop their tree projects.

opposite: Belts linking together to form a web of trees across the Stewart family farm that provides shelter, land degradation control and corridors for wildlife. The pruned Spotted Gum belt (centre) links the roadside trees with an old shelterbelt at the top of the hill.

If the farmers themselves felt that trees really did have a place on their family farm, and were prepared to make the investment of land, time and money, they would lead far-reaching and enduring landscape change.

That's not to say we don't welcome public money. There are essentially three alternatives to direct incentives that governments and NGOs can use to support tree growing on farms:

1. developing the physical and legal infrastructure required to support the industry, such as port facilities for exports or enabling legislation;
2. establishing fair and open markets for environmental, social and commercial services that reward farmers for the public goods their trees provide, irrespective or how the outcomes are provided; and
3. building the capacity of farmers, and those that service the sector, so that they are all able to make better decisions.

As a community group, our focus is on supporting farmer education and knowledge sharing and developing a strong knowledge network across our community. We are particularly excited about our peer mentoring program that trains, and then pays, experienced tree growers to work beside other landholders as they explore, design and implement the revegetation and forest management projects that they are willing to invest in.

I had been schooled in conventional 'finite' plantation forestry where trees are treated as a crop; planted, managed, harvested and the cycle repeated. For me, finite forestry missed an opportunity to build landscape capital and create something new, a better launch pad for future generations. A farmer who plants trees because they want shelter for stock and soil erosion control doesn't anticipate clearing the trees, and returning the land to what it looked like before, even if they prune them for timber. They know they are playing a longer and less certain game.

My hand exhausted, I invited questions. I only got comments: One extension agent told the room that their farmers were different, they needed grants: 'Your model would never work in our region.' Another said that their grants were only part of a comprehensive package that also included research and training. The money was just a teaser to attract landholders 'into the fold'.

I made my final point: Across the world, in Africa, Australia, Asia, Europe and America, I had seen how projects that provide substantial direct incentives to farmers to plant trees undermine initiatives that focus on providing support and education to farmers to do what they want to do. You can't have both.

I finished with a story. A neighbour had called me up and asked if I'd come over and look at a large Blackwood that had fallen over in her paddock. She thought it might be worth something. She was a local with family going back generations to when the country was first settled by Europeans. I told her I thought the tree was too rotten and not worth milling. 'That's fine,' she said, then added, 'You know, I was worried about you when you came to Bambra. I thought you were going to try to change people.' 'Thank you,' I replied, for we both knew that the landscape had changed. Hundreds of farmers, including many from the families of long-time locals, had planted thousands of trees. It was change from within.

Eastern Great Egret (*Ardea modesta*)

1   Aldo Leopold, *A Sand County Almanac* (New York Oxford University Press, 1947).

2   S. Mahoney and A.A. Charry, 'The use of alpacas as newborn lamb protectors to minimise fox predation,' *Extension Farming Systems Journal* 1(1) (2005): 65-70.

3   Robert G. Steadman, 'Norms of apparent temperature in Australia.' *Australian Meteorological Magazine* 43 (1994): 1-16.

4   P.R. Bird, T.T. Jackson, G.A. Kearney and A. Roache, 'Effects of windbreak structure on shelter characteristics,' *Australian Journal of Experimental Agriculture* 47 (2007): 727-737.

5   Russell Washusen, *Evaluation of product value and sawing and drying efficiencies of low rainfall hardwood thinnings*. A report for the RIRDC/Land & Water Australia/FWPRDC/MDBC Joint Venture Agroforestry Program. January 2006.

Shelterbelt design

Dr Rod Bird used anemometers (spinning meters that measure wind-run) to study the pattern of wind flow behind real farm shelterbelts. His results confirm wind tunnel studies and provide a basis for understanding how shelterbelt design and management can change the pattern of wind flow. Here, I use Rod's photographs and measurements to illustrate the science of shelterbelt design.

Wind speeds begin to fall before the wind reaches the belt, suggesting the trees act as a physical barrier to the movement of air. This forces the moving air to go over, through or around the structure in a similar manner to water flowing over a barrier in a stream. The greatest reduction in wind speed is not immediately behind the barrier but further out on the leeward side. The wind speed then gradually returns to open field strength at a point more than 30 tree heights away from the belt.

The extent of wind speed reduction at any point behind a shelterbelt is known to be a function of shelterbelt height and porosity. The Cypress shelterbelt is 10 m tall and has a relatively dense and even foliage cover down to ground level (figure 1). If the shelterbelt shown was 20 m tall, rather than 10 m, the greatest reduction in wind speed would still have been less than 40 % but this would have occurred at a point 120 m (6 tree heights) from the belt rather than at 60 m. Because of this relationship, height is used as the measure on the horizontal axis of shelterbelt graphs.

Shelterbelt porosity refers to the proportion of the air flow that travels through the belt rather than over or around the obstacle. Shelterbelts with a lower porosity result in a greater reduction in wind speed, however they do not change the distance at which the winds returns to open field speed. In the above example, the wind speed falls to less than 40 % of open wind speed at around 6 tree heights (or 60 m). Had the foliage been more open, the reduction in wind speed would have been less.

Open areas under the canopy of a shelterbelt can lead to increased wind speeds as the air tunnels through the gaps. This is a common problem in unfenced shelterbelts or those dominated by species like the eucalypts that tend to self-prune. Rod found that tunnelling under the canopy of a single row of Tuart (*Eucalyptus gomphocephala*) trees increased wind speed by as much as 15 % (figure 2). This could be a death trap for stock pushed up against the fence by driving wind and rain. Nonetheless, the same belt still provided reasonable shelter out in the paddock between 4 and 12 tree heights.

Aerodynamic porosity is often estimated from the proportion of direct light that can be seen through the belt (optical porosity). This may be appropriate for two-dimensional, even textured barriers, such as shade cloth, but is unreliable in irregular or wider tree belts. Despite being unfenced and having little foliage close to ground level, a 20-m-wide belt of direct seeded Sugar Gum had a wind speed profile that suggests that there was very little wind tunnelling under the canopy (figure 3). Judging by the level of wind speed reduction (40 % of open wind speed at 6 tree heights) the wide Sugar Gum belt had a similar aerodynamic porosity as the single row Cypress belt.

The longer the shelterbelt the less impact any wind flowing around the end of the belt will have on the sheltered area. However, with any end there is a risk of increased wind speed. To avoid this, try to create a network of vegetation across the landscape which links shelterbelts to remnant forest areas, riparian plantations and woodlots. The risk of wind tunnelling through gateways can also be avoided by locating them in naturally sheltered areas such as beside a perpendicular shelterbelt or abutting a forested area.

When wind flows across a series of parallel shelterbelts, each subsequent belt becomes less effective in reducing wind speed. This is because the belts are inducing greater turbulence in the approaching wind, which reduces both the percentage of wind speed reduction and the distance at which the wind will return to open wind speed. As the belts become closer they do begin to mimic what occurs in an open woodland or wide spaced plantation. Wind speeds measured under a range of pruned *Pinus radiata* tree stockings in New Zealand showed wind-run reductions of around 40 % by age 10 at only 100 trees per hectare. Increasing the stocking to 200 trees per hectare had no additional effect, suggesting that the roughness caused by the trees was encouraging the bulk of the wind to flow over the tree tops. Rod measured wind speeds in a paddock of widely spaced mature River Red Gums (only 17 trees per hectare) and found a relatively even wind speed reduction across the paddock of around 40 %.

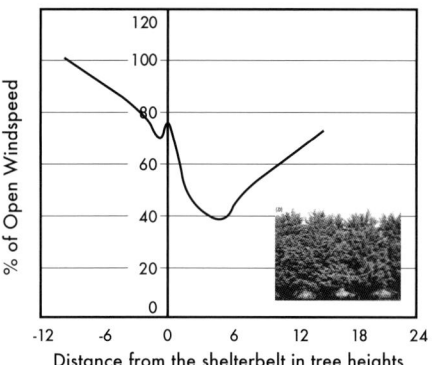

figure 1

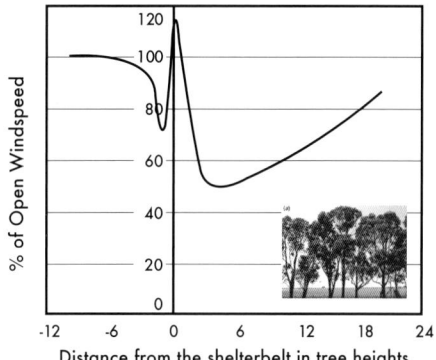

figure 2

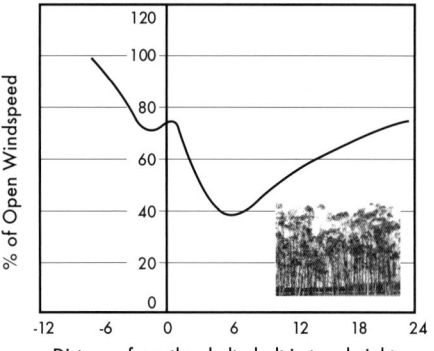

figure 3

figure 1: Wind profile for a single-row Monterey Cypress windbreak (Height = 9 m) in Western Victoria.

figure 2: Wind profile for a single-row Tuart windbreak (Height = 15 m) in Western Victoria.

figure 3: Wind profile for a direct seeded belt of Sugar Gum (Height = 18 m width about 20 m) in Western Victoria.

(Photo and data: Rod Bird[4])

Chapter 15

Australian Red Cedar
Toona ciliata var. australis

When we started planting trees I didn't really have a plan—either on paper or in my mind—of what our farm might eventually look like. I'd try something, learn from the experience and then adapt. It's how I was trained; it's the scientific process. If you think you know the answer you may never discover anything new, but if you focus on the process—the journey—where you end up can be a pleasant surprise.

The changes in our landscape were subtle at first. If they were there to see, they were masked by the work I had to do to protect our young trees and direct their early growth. It wasn't until our trees were about ten years old that I started to see glimpses of something extraordinary happening. I know it now as the point where a young plantation changes from being something that must be continually nurtured, into an autonomous and dynamic forest. Instead of being a composer setting down an imagined symphony, I had become a conductor without a score.

As I write, it is late winter 2016. It's my birthday; I'm fifty-five years old. To mark the occasion, I'm going to plant some trees; Australian Red Cedars. As I plan my day—gumboots, spade, seedlings and tree guards—it suddenly occurs to me that my choice of species reflects just how far I have come, what I have learnt and how much I have changed, along with the climate, since I was twenty-five.

In those early years—between working around the district as a farm labourer and planting trees on our own property—I got my first professional job as a technical adviser for an anthropologist, as she documented community concerns about family farms being bought up for government pine plantations. The farmers in the areas being targeted were outraged; they blocked the valley roads to prevent the 'dozers and planting crews getting to the sites. Dr Lea Jellinek and I were sent in behind the blockades to document their concerns.

They had a long list: increased fire threat, cover for wild dogs, the spread of noxious weeds, soil acidification by pine needles and the decline in the number of farming families, which threatened the viability of their schools and postal services. There were also arguments about the impact of the plantations on land prices and whether governments should be growing timber at all. Lea

preceding: Planting another Australian Red Cedar. Our 10-yr-old Red Cedars are behind me.

above: The beauty that some see in a monoculture plantation (industrial aesthetic) or a messy farm (ecological aesthetic) rely equally on the perspective and knowledge of the observer.

and I worked through the issues. My job was to make sense of the science and practice of forestry, her's was to understand the social issues. The government's scientists dismissed each of the community's concerns in turn. But the facts, as they were presented, didn't sway the farmers. There was clearly more to it than just weeds, vermin, fire and soil, and, of course, the farmers knew that population decline was already happening in their communities. This was different. Lea and I were witnessing a deeper discomfort, a real pain that was hard for the farmers to describe; the government plantations and the change they represented were just *ugly*.

For the foresters, their monoculture plantations were a thing of beauty, arguably more productive and sustainable than many of the agricultural practices they would replace. My training had given me an appreciation of the importance of homogeneity in the genetic selection, site preparation and spacing required to achieve maximum productivity and ensure uniform log quality. I also understood, given the focus on commodity products, the need for scale. But '*beauty is bought by judgement of the eye*' [1].

Years later, I watched ecologist Dr David Lindenmayer make a presentation to farmers in Tasmania. David argued that what we needed to support our native wildlife was *messy* farms.[2] But, most farmers see fallen logs, dead trees, scruffy shrubbery and rank tussock grasses as a sign of neglect or poor farming practices; a reflection on them and their capacity as a good land manager. David's ecological aesthetic, like the industrial aesthetic of the foresters, was informed by his knowledge and interests. Unless farmers shared David's perspective—*knew* what he *knew*, and *cared* for what he *cared* for—they couldn't *see* what he *saw*.

The ugliness farmers are fleeing is not inherent in forestry. Forestry (whether for conservation or profit) is just the growing of trees and can not by its own nature be ugly or there would be no beauty in gardens, which also involve growing trees.[3]

Melbourne Botanic Gardens. Gardening, like forestry, involves the science and practice of growing trees.

Soon after European settlement, the British navy officers found something attractive in the Australian bush. It was the wood of a large mahogany-like tree they found growing on the river banks, which looked like the Indian Red Cedar, known to the British shipwrights as Toon. Along with samples of other colonial timbers, Governor Phillip sent a small parcel of Australian Red Cedar back to England for evaluation.

But the private merchants didn't need to wait for a response. Having seen similar timbers being traded across the Empire—African Mahogany (*Khaya senegalensis*), the Cigar-box Cedar (*Cedrela odorata*), and the West Indian Mahogany (*Swietenia mahagoni*)—they immediately recognised the potential of Australian Red Cedar. A freight ship called *The Fancy* was loaded up with logs and left the colony in 1795.[4] Sensing the competition, the admiralty ordered that the empty convict ships be loaded with pit-sawn planks of Red Cedar and shipped back to the naval dockyards of South Africa and England[5]. The Red Cedar rush had started.

At first, the trees were easy pickings. Red Cedar grew right down to the river's edge and could be felled or rolled into the water where the logs were tied into a raft and towed out to sea then back into Port Jackson (Sydney Harbour). In 1802, concerned about the rate of harvesting, the governor passed an order reserving every Red Cedar tree of commercial value in the Hawkesbury valley for the crown.[6] They then confiscated any illegally harvested Cedar logs or planks as they were moved down the river. The ban just pushed the cedar-getters further north into the Hunter Valley. Rather than chase them down, the authorities saw an opportunity to get the private sector to do the hard work whilst raising revenue for the colony. A resource tax was introduced—our first government timber royalty—and collected as the logs were floated out the river mouth.[7]

Small Red Cedar trees, even those that are straight and clean, have very little heartwood and were of no value to the cedar-getters so it is not fair to blame the timber cutters for the virtual disappearance of the species. With the native Red Cedar being concentrated on the alluvial flats and basalt soils it was farmers, again, who followed the first wave and cleared any trees that might one day make a sawlog. But, what choice did they have? The governor had introduced a clause to all grants of land '*expressly reserving, under pain of forfeiture, for the use thereof such timber as might be growing or to grow hereafter upon land so granted, which should be deemed fit for naval purposes*'.[8] He even instructed that any promising Red Cedar tree on private land be 'marked' as the property of the crown.

The British were making the same mistake as their colleagues in Sweden, ensuring that any rational settler would make sure there were no Red Cedar trees worth saving on their land, and no regeneration. Within just fifty years of European settlement, the first opportunity to build an ecologically and economically beneficial relationship between farmers and the Australian forest had been lost, along with most of the Red Cedar.

Once classified as a distinct species, *Toona australis*, Australian Red Cedar is now recognized as a local variant of the Asian Red Cedar (*Toona ciliata*). The Meliaceae family, which comprises more than 50 genera including *Toona*, *Cedrela*, *Swietenia* and *Khaya*, originated in the African Rift Valley and spread north to Europe and across to North America when they were a tropical oasis with rainforests and coral reefs. Fossil records suggest that the closely related *Toona* and *Cedrela* may have separated in North America with the *Cedrela* moving south to their current location in Central America and the *Toona* crossing back into China through Alaska.[9]

Whatever the evolutionary pathway, *Toona ciliata* was clearly the most adventurous child of the family. Breaking away from its closest relative (*Toona sinensis*) in China, it travelled south, spreading west to Afghanistan and east to Papua New Guinea, and eventually across the land bridges that occasionally opened to Australia. Once on Cape York, we know it moved slowly down the east coast as our continent drifted north, almost making it to Victoria. Given time, and a warming climate, Red Cedar may well have reached Bambra without my help.

top: This Red Cedar I am measuring is on the Atherton Tablelands in Far North Queensland. The plantation is now a tourist attraction and is celebrated as a native rainforest.

bottom left: Digby Race measuring the diameter of an Australian Red Cedar in the Albury Botanic Gardens in 2016 (104 cm). Image courtesy of Digby Race.

bottom right: The original leader on this young Red Cedar growing in the Hunter Valley was damaged by tip moth. One of the lower branches and a secondary leader are now competing for dominance, resulting in a tree of very poor form for sawlog production.

In its natural Australian habit, large Red Cedar trees are usually only found on deep well-drained basalt soils or alluvial flats that have a high summer rainfall. But, Red Cedar may be much more tolerant than its rainforest habit implies. There is a Red Cedar growing in the Albury Botanical Gardens which is now 104 centimetres in diameter. Although the gardens are located on deep Murray River alluvial flats, Albury is well inside the Great Dividing Range and experiences hot, dry summers and frequent winter frosts. The largest planted Red Cedar on the National Register of Big Trees is in the Adelaide Botanical Gardens; Australia's driest capital city. First recorded as being present in 1859, the tree has a clear trunk up to about 6 metres and was more than 120 centimetres in diameter in 2010.

While the nineteenth century gardeners were planting Red Cedar well outside its natural range, clearly with some success, foresters in New South Wales and Queensland were trying to establish it in timber plantations on some of the best tropical rainforest soils. They failed spectacularly. Their problem was the Asian Cedar Tip Moth (*Hypsipyla robusta*). The moth lays its eggs on the tree's leading shoot and the larvae burrow into the stem, causing dieback of the leader. The attack rarely kills the tree but it does cause the release of secondary buds just below the original leading shoot resulting in a multi-leader tree. Repeated attacks cause multiple deformities, destroying the form of the tree for timber production. The difficulty for growers, even those well-away from any affected trees, is that the moth appears to have learnt to sense the chemicals produced by a healthy Red Cedar tree as it puts on a spurt of height growth.

Once inside the stem the insect is impossible to control using contact insecticides.[10] Even systemic chemicals have shown limited value, particularly in larger trees. Current research is exploring the potential of using artificial pheromones to trap the male moths, or at least make it hard for them to find their females—a method that is commonly used to control Codling Moth in apple orchards—but so far scientists have been unable to unravel the complex chemistry of the attractants released by the Red Cedars.

The presence of large, straight Red Cedars growing alone in mixed species rainforests led to the suggestion that planting the trees under a canopy or in mixed species plantations may reduce the incidence of attack. Fortunately, young Red Cedar are shade tolerant and height growth can be as fast under a canopy as it might be in full sunlight; often better if frost or dry winds are a problem. However, diameter growth under shade is restricted, leading to tall slender trees. To achieve sawlog size, the Red Cedar would either need to be able to grow up through the canopy into full sunlight, as it often does in a rainforest, or the competing overstorey would need to be removed.

I planted our first Red Cedars when I was forty-five years old. I had no idea how they would perform. Fortunately, we don't have Cedar Tip Moth at Bambra. In 2016, I finished pruning one of our ten-year-old Red Cedars up to 8 metres. It was perfectly straight, and so easy to prune. The large compound leaves often develop straight off the main stem and simply fall off at the end of

the season, leaving only two or three real branches that need to be cut off each year. I've also found that Red Cedar coppices well so if a young tree is damaged by wind, I just cut it off at ground level and grow a new trunk.

Red Cedar is a phototropic species; meaning that the leader will tend to grow towards the light. In a rainforest, this allows the tree to bend towards any small gap in the canopy. That's fine for survival, but the resulting bend in the stem reduces its value for timber. I made the mistake of planting a Red Cedar on the sunny side of a large Black Walnut and it has grown to about eight metres with a sweeping bend away to the north. I now only plant Red Cedar in full sunlight or the even shade of a eucalypt canopy. In both cases, I'm achieving good straight growth.

Growing Red Cedar in full sunlight has its own risks including, surprisingly enough, sunburn. Jenny Dewing and her partner Mick planted and pruned Red Cedar on their farm near Bridgetown in Western Australia. I visited in early spring one year as their trees were just coming into leaf. They had painted the stems white. Walnut growers do the same to their Persian Walnut trees to reflect the heat off the trunk. Sunburn occurs late in the dry season when the tree is unable to draw sufficient moisture to maintain a cooling flow of water up the stem. In the heat of the afternoon, the dry cambium layer can be 'cooked'. The damage isn't evident at first but as the cambium dies, the bark peels off leaving a long thin scar down the western side of the tree.

We did have sunburn damage occur on some of our young English Oak and Blackwood trees after a very dry summer. The wounds are healing over now and, as the bark thickens, I'm hoping they will be well protected before the next drought. Because the damage occurred when the stems were only about 10 centimetres in diameter I don't think it will affect their sawlog value. I made a note, when planting Red Cedar in the open, target sites where they will have afternoon shade.

left & middle: I planted this Red Cedar in 2006 and it was well above the tree guard by 2009 (left). By 2017 (middle) it was 15 cm in diameter and I had pruned it up to 8 m.

right: Jenny and Mick Dewing's Red Cedars coming into leaf in early spring on their Bridgetown farm. The white paint will reflect the heat of the afternoon sun and reduce the risk of sunburn on the unshaded lower trunk.

opposite: Plantation grown Australian Red Cedar being sold at auction on the Atherton Tablelands in 1997.

I don't know if the Cedar Tip Moth will ever reach the Otways. Given the changing climate and increasing interest in growing the species in Victoria, it probably will. Meanwhile, I'm planting as many Red Cedars as I can, testing how the species performs on a range of soil types, from our best alluvial creek flats to our heavy wet clays and free draining sands, and in mixtures with different species. It seems to do well on our heavy clay soils. I am confident I can maintain a diameter increment of about 1.5 centimetres per year if I provide space for the canopy to spread.

But what of the wood quality of a farm-grown Red Cedar from southern Victoria? No one knows; it hasn't been done before. But, like English Oak, we do know that Australian Red Cedar is ring porous, which means the wider the growth rings, the higher its wood density. Keith Bootle implied as much when he wrote of Red Cedar: '*Fast-grown timber seems to have at least as good, probably better, mechanical properties than the average material from large logs.*'[11] Whilst this sounds promising, timber harvested from fast-grown plantations in Hawaii was rated poorly on sawing due to problems of growth stresses and branch defects.[12] A photograph in the report shows a dense plantation of tall unpruned trees. Red Cedar is a hardwood. Like a eucalypt, it will develop tension wood in tall, skinny trees. Our trees will be straight, clean and fat. For an American, Australian Red Cedar is just another exotic timber. For an Australian, it is an iconic species. Even if our trees grow slower than I hope, I have no doubt that some well-managed Red Cedar will add value to our farm.

Farmers often say they plan to leave their farm in a better condition than when they inherited or bought their land. This suggests many landholders do recognise they have land management problems, but it may also offer an excuse to defer any action. Family farming has caused massive soil degradation, many local plant and animal extinctions, reduced water quality in our waterways and increased the severity of downstream flood events. It is the same around the world. Other than climate change itself, the greatest conservation issues affecting rural landscapes are a result of what has happened, and what is happening, on family farms.

Canadian academic Stephen Sheppard explored what it was that allowed farmers to get away with it; why we tend to find family owned farms attractive even if the land management practices are causing degradation. He called it '*visible stewardship*' and argued that we find landscapes more attractive if it looks as though '*real* individuals care for the land or place, that there are people who are linked to it, rooted in it, *from generation to generation*'[13].

Does this explain why many in our community seem relaxed when a farmer ploughs a steep paddock for a crop but are uneasy when a plantation company rips up a flat paddock for trees? Or why the logging of public forests fuels such outrage while we turn a blind eye to the farmer who lets their cattle ringbark a patch of remnant forest? Land managed by farmers or indigenous communities is not necessarily better (ecologically or economically) but it does look and feel different because we tend to identify with the human attachment to the land. Just the presence of a house, farm animals, sheds, gardens or even a letterbox provides the vital signs of a visible and permanent stewardship that can *excuse* cattle grazing in an eroded gully and make a monoculture of highly-bred canola look more attractive than a corporate-owned plantation of native eucalypts.

I'm not suggesting we apply greater regulation on farmers. In fact, I see their own stated objectives of *passing the farm on in a better state* and the public licence they are afforded as an opportunity. Just a week before my fifty-fifth birthday, our local council abandoned an amendment that sought to 'protect' the biodiversity values of forests on private land. The proposed overlay included the very forest we had created along our bare eroded creek, and another 100 hectares of planted trees on other farms in our area. If it had passed, the amendment would have meant that we would need to apply for a permit to harvest the trees we had planted.

One of our local old-timers wasn't surprised. Stan has been farming and logging the forests around Bambra for more than sixty years. He survived the Ash Wednesday fire (1983) by sheltering under a blanket with his dog on a burnt patch of pasture. He loves this country; he knows it well. Even after the fire he didn't take the opportunity to clear his native forest for grass like others did. He knew the value of the timber and chose to let the trees recover and grow on as his retirement package. Now he's not so sure he'll ever be allowed to harvest them.

As a community, we tend to give family farmers a social licence that is not afforded to industry or government. Rather than abuse this gift, we should see it as an opportunity.

'Remember when you started planting trees,' he said to me, 'I told you this would happen; they'd come and tell you that you can't harvest them because they were doing something good for the environment.' I told him I was confident we'd win this one; the wider community would back us as long as we distanced ourselves from the corporate and government timber industry. We are family farmers exploring new ways of marrying conservation and production. Our farmland, including our remnant forests, is already degraded. Surely the public will understand that growing trees for timber could help drive landscape restoration.

The Otway Agroforestry Network invited the councillors to come and see it for themselves. As well as our planted forests along creeks and up steep slopes, we showed them eroded gullies on the farms where the landholders had done nothing. What affect might the proposed amendment have on their behaviour? The perverse outcome of trying to *save* biodiversity would most likely result in farmers neglecting their native forests and eroding creeklines. And, if they planted trees at all, they'd probably only grow exotic species. The damage to the English Oak trees on the farms in Sweden, the premature clearing of the Red Cedars in Australia, and the land degradation on farms in the Otways are not the fault of the farmers. They are simply the outcome of their rational response to the social, cultural and economic environment in which they make their land management decisions. You cannot legislate against neglect.

As a group of tree growers, we believe we have found a way of inspiring farmers to plant trees and manage their forests. What they choose to do doesn't always look like a conventional conservation planting or a commercial plantation but, as we have seen in our region, when many landholders plant many trees and shrubs for many reasons the landscape scale impacts can be

significant. The key to reducing soil erosion, improving the quality of the water running off farmland, rejuvenating remnant forests and enhancing biodiversity is to help farmers achieve their own goals and ensure they and their children believe they will retain the property rights to harvest the trees on their land, even if they have no intention of doing so.

Progress is not about going further down the same path; it is about changing paths. The well-worn tracks of commercial forestry and conservation-focused revegetation or reservation that have served us well in the past have reached their limits. In a world where our footprint is greater than what our planet can produce, we no longer have the luxury of just picking sides—conservation or production—and dividing our landscape up into single-purpose fragments. Governments, industry and interest groups need to let go of their preferred options and engage the wider community of rural landholders in the exploration and implementation of approaches to establishing and managing forests which are attractive to them.

When Jenny and Mick purchased their farm in 1986 they immediately saw a need for trees. They planted local natives for conservation and, separately, eucalypts and poplars for timber production. I met Jenny when she did our

above: If a farmer believes they will not retain the property rights to the trees growing on their land, whether natural or planted, their rational reaction might be to let the cows in. It might look pretty but this native forest of Messmate Stringybark is being ringbarked by the cows.

opposite: Jenny and Mick's farm near Bridgetown, Western Australia. For me, this photo epitomises the great potential for trees to reflect the interests and aspirations of farmers.

Bridgetown Master TreeGrower course in 1997. Seeing what has happened since then, I suspect the course and the community of tree growers it spawned gave her the knowledge and confidence to do more. It also gave her the licence to do it her own way.

In 2010, I took a photograph looking across their revegetated dam. It tells a wonderful story. Where once there was degradation and decay there are now trees and shrubs protecting the soil, improving water quality, enhancing biodiversity, sheltering stock, growing timber, and creating special places for relaxation and contemplation. Everyone knows that trees can provide these things, but still most landholders don't plant many trees or even manage the ones they already have. What's stopping them? It can't be just the lack of time and money, or even knowledge and skills. There must be something else they need. Something Jenny has. Something I captured in that photograph.

Jenny's forest is much more than the sum of its many values. It has a quality that is obvious to the eye but so difficult to describe. I think it is the evidence of the tightly interwoven relationship between a forest and the people who created it and cared for it over a period of time. Unlike the agricultural seasons or geological time, the rate of change in a forest is comparable to our own. Given time, the choices a tree grower makes—the species they plant and their management decisions—result in a forest that becomes a unique expression of an individual's, or a family's, relationship with their land. The beauty we see in Jenny's forest is the marriage between the science of trees and the art of being a tree grower.

The catalyst that will drive spontaneous investment in tree planting and

The view across our dam to our trees.

management is the belief that, as landholders, we can create unique landscapes that reflect our own needs and aspirations. This is the new and powerful tale that is so persuasive that it sweeps away the myth that there is a right way to grow a forest and that it must be either for conservation or profit. Growing a forest is not about following a dictum or trying to recreate a museum exhibit of an imagined past. It is about growing trees to fashion a new landscape that gathers all the bits of our past and our present into a coherent whole.

If our Red Cedar grow well and the timber looks good, it may turn out to be my favourite species. But then, I'm also trialling some other shade tolerant native timbers. One possibility is our local Otway Satinwood (*Nematolepis squamea*), which has a beautiful white durable timber; but I'll save that one for my next book. To be honest, I really don't know where my trees, my science or my heart will take me.

For those of you who are just beginning your tree growing journey, and for those who have already started, I hope that my story, the science and our little farm has helped shed some light so that you can take the next step forward and find your own path through the bush. Timber may not be part of your solution, but for many farmers it will be. Nonetheless, together, our many varied forests, planted and managed for many different reasons, will slowly spread across the farmlands of the world creating a tapestry that protects and enhances our land, livestock, lifestyles, wildlife and livelihoods. All the while, all our trees will be laying down heartwood that can become a wooden table, a warm fire, a bed or even a home. Whether we harvest or not, just by planting and managing our own trees we will be helping others uncover opportunities for growing trees on *their* land. Our legacy may not just be in the trees *we* leave behind, but also in those that others grow in other landscapes for other reasons.

Red-browed Firetail (*Aegintha temporalis*)

1   *Shakespeare,* Love's Labours Lost, *1588*

2   David Lindenmayer, M. Crane, D. Michael and E. Beaton, *Woodlands: A Disappearing Landscape* (Melbourne: CSIRO Publishing, 2005).

3   Robert M. Pirsig, *Zen and the art of motorcycle maintenance: an inquiry into values* (New York: Morrow, 1984).

4   Richard T. Baker, *Cabinet Timbers of Australia*. Technological Museum Sydney, Technical Series, No. 18 (Sydney: Government Printer, 1913).

5   Morris Lake, *Australian Rainforest Woods – Characteristics, uses and identification* (Melbourne: CSIRO Publishing, 2015).

6   Ida Lee, *The Coming of the British to Australia 1788 to 1829* (New York: Longmans, Green and Co, 1906).

7   John McPhee (ed.), *Red Cedar in Australia (*Sydney: Historic Houses Trust of New South Wales, *2004).*

8   David Collins, *An Account of the English Colony in New South Wales, Volume 2* (London: T. Cadell Jun. and W. Davies).

9   E.J.M. Koenen, J.J. Clarkson, T.D. Pennington, L.W. Chatrou, 'Recently evolved diversity and convergent radiations of rainforest mahoganies (Meliaceae) shed new light on the origins of rainforest hyperdiversity,' *New Phytologist* 207 (2015): 327–339.

10 F.L. Bygrave and P.L. Bygrave, *Growing Australian Red Cedar and Other Meliaceae Species in Plantation* (Canberra: Rural Industries Research and Development Corporation, 2005).

11 Keith R. Bootle, *Wood in Australia – Types properties and uses*, *2nd Edition* (Sydney: McGraw-Hill, 2005).

12 R.G. Skolmen, *Some Woods of Hawaii Properties and Uses of 16 Commercial Species.* Pacific Southwest Forest and Range Experimental Station, Berkeley. USDA Forest Servo General Technical Report PSW-8 (California: USDA, 1974).

13 Stephen R.J. Sheppard, 'Beyond Visual Resource Management: Emerging theories of an ecological aesthetic and visible stewardship,' In: S.R.J. Sheppard and H. Harshaw (eds.), *Forests and Landscapes: Linking Ecology, Sustainability, and Aesthetics.* IUFRO Research Series (Wallingford UK: CABI, 2000).

How to plant a tree

The choice of planting stock

For each species you may be faced with a range of options: pots, tubes, cells or open rooted trees. The cheapest are likely to be 1-year-old open-rooted seedlings (for conifers and deciduous trees) or trays of seedlings grown in small cells for most native species. Both must be handled carefully and planted quickly but they do have the advantage of being light and easy to carry. Special planting tools are available for the cells, which means you don't even need to bend over.

Tubes and pots are more robust and versatile and can be held on site with occasional watering in anticipation of planting. Advance trees, those larger than a metre tall or so, are rarely worth the additional cost and labour. Small healthy seedlings will generally outgrow advanced trees quickly.

What I do: All the eucalypts and wattles we buy are grown in small cells. They are cheap and easy to plant using a poker stick or simple tree planting tool. We usually purchase pines and deciduous trees as open-rooted 1-year-old stock and plant them carefully using a spade. I often buy specialty trees in small individual cells and then replant them into 6 or 8-inch pots to grow on for a second year before planting out.

We buy our plants in a range of pot types including cells (middle), tubes (left) and pots (right). Image courtesy of Otway Greening.

Getting them in the ground

I like to start by identifying the factors that are likely to impact tree survival and early growth. Invariably it gets back to four elements: weed control, soil conditions, climate and protection.

1. Weed control

When planting trees, a weed is anything that competes with the seedling for moisture. Removing competition using chemicals, mulch, weed mats or cultivation is almost always essential to ensure survival and will certainly improve growth. Almost every novice tree grower makes the mistake of not having sufficient weed control.

Simply mowing the grass is not weed control. In fact, this will only encourage the grass to stay green longer and dry the soil out more.

Fertilising and watering also encourages the weeds and should not be done unless the weed control is perfect. We are talking here about the *total elimination of all plants that draw moisture from the soil around the seedling*. If you don't want to use herbicides you must find an alternative—be it mulch, weed mats or cultivation.

The area of weed control required and how long it must be kept weed-free depends on the rate of growth of the trees and the predominant weed types. In most cases trees provided with a full growing season of weed control (within 75 to 100 cm of the tree) will be strong enough to fend for themselves. Weed control in the second and subsequent years is only justified where tree growth is very slow or there is extremely vigorous competition from deep rooted grasses or woody weeds.

What I do: I do use herbicides. I've tried mulching and weed mats but it's just too slow and laborious so I only use them for food producing plants. I mix a knock-down with a pre-emergent in a knapsack and spray spots (about 1.5 to 2 m in diameter) a month or so prior to planting so that the grass is dead at the time of planting. This provides a weed free area for up to 12 months. For the deciduous trees and slow-growing specialty species, I often spray carefully around the tree prior to the second growing season, being careful not to allow the chemical to contact the tree. Our tree guard makes this easy as it protects the young seedling.

2. Soil conditions

On some sites, survival and growth will be very poor unless something is done about soil structure or drainage. Commercial plantation companies often rip to more than 60-cm depth with dozers and build mounds more than 50cm high. You may well need to invest in this type of soil preparation but it can be expensive so it is worth testing whether this is necessary. The best way to find out is to ask around; neighbours, commercial contractors or Landcare groups. If they do deep rip or mound then ask why and whether or not they have tried planting without it.

What I do: Given our use of a range of species and irregular planting patterns, I cannot justify the cost of bringing in a contractor to rip and mound prior to planting. I also don't like the lumps and bumps mounding leaves in the paddock and the thistles that come up after cultivation. I have found that I can achieve reasonable survival and growth by planting into undisturbed soil following spot herbicide application.

I have seen many sites like this where the farmer has followed best-practice plantation establishment (ripping and mounding) only to find that the trees don't grow straight and they are left with bumps through the paddock.

3. Weather conditions and when to plant

In the southern states of Australia, trees are usually planted in winter when the soils are moist and there is little risk of a hot dry wind. Open rooted deciduous trees and conifers are best planted in mid winter when the days are short because their roots tend to start growing earlier than their shoots. Most of our native species are opportunistic growers and are better planted just prior to when the growing

Science and Practice

conditions are best. Leaving them wallowing in wet cold soils over the winter seems to set them back a little. Frost sensitive species, like Spotted Gum, are best planted later in the season. This can work if the weed control is done early.

What I do: I like to plant my native trees, like eucalypts and wattles, in spring into a warming soil that has a good store of moisture. This ensures I have good control of the spring weeds prior to planting. If the soils are wet, planting in winter or early spring means that there is usually no need to water the trees at all.

4. Protection

Rabbits, hares, deer, kangaroos and wallabies are common browsers of young trees. Domestic stock can be a serious problem if poorly controlled and this includes the landowner's own stock as well as those of neighbours. Options for browsing control might include shooting and poisoning (where acceptable), repellents, tree guards or fencing.

Defoliation of young leaves and shoots by caterpillars, beetles or fungal infection can affect the growth and form of young trees. Although most species can tolerate some damage, landholders should look out for repeated defoliation, in which case some form of treatment may be warranted. If the problem persists it may be worth considering an alternative species.

What I do: My worst browsing pests are wallabies. If I can effectively guard the trees from them, I needn't worry about rabbits or sheep. In the Australian Blackwood Chapter I describe my wallaby guard. Defoliating insects have caused problems in our young eucalypts but I tend to accept a degree of damage in preference to using insecticides. In most cases our trees seem to recover in the next season although I may need to do more form pruning.

A circle of weed control and our tall flexible guards protect the seedling from stock (top). Note I added a small stick to hold the guard away from the seedling until it is safely growing up the tube. I often spray again to provide a second year of weed control (bottom).

Fertilisers and watering

On most ex-pasture sites there is little to be gained by adding fertilisers at the time of planting. If anything, you could add a handful of N-P-K or an organic equivalent but the risk is that you will only encourage weeds that then compete with the seedling for moisture. The exceptions to this would be on leached sandy soils or sites with a proven deficiency in trace elements like boron. In this case seek advice from experienced tree growers in the region. If I do fertilise, I prefer to do it when the trees are 2 or 3 years old and are competing well against the weeds.

Watering at the time of planting is worth doing if planting on a warm day. Ongoing watering is expensive and can lead to the tree becoming dependent on supplementary watering.

What I do: Nothing. I have seen cases where very rapid early growth driven by soil preparation, fertilisation and watering has increased the risk of the seedlings toppling or leaning over in strong winds, leading to poor stem form. Weed control is the most important factor in achieving good tree establishment.

One of our early English Oak plantings (1994) where I trialled various guards, including electric rings (foreground) and the corflute 'tree shelters' from United Kingdom.

Plant it and see

As farmers gain experience in tree growing they tend to refine their establishment methods. Low-cost options, such as direct seeding, can be effective but the methods need to be appropriate for each district. Techniques involving a high-labour requirement (such as mulching instead of herbicides) are an option, but it is up to the individual to decide what they are prepared to do.

Landowners should attend field days and visit other farms and industrial plantations in their area to see what works for others on similar sites. At each site try and identify what the grower's objectives are. Think about what might be their limiting resources and note how they have chosen to deal with the issues of weed competition, soil factors, weather and protection. Then, if possible, start small and learn from your own experience.

What I do: I like to spread my risk. I plant a few hundred trees of a range of species every year across a number of sites. I prefer to do all the work myself and not do so much that it becomes a chore. After 30 years of tree growing, we are now seeing lots of natural regeneration of eucalypts, wattles and even some exotics. If the regeneration occurs in a good location, I will often just put a guard around the seedlings and treat it as one of my planted trees.

Acknowledgements

So many people to thank.

I mention many tree growers in this book: Andrew, David, Annabel, Mike, Noel, my brother Tom and others. But, I cannot name the hundreds more who have shared their time, farms, knowledge and experience with me. We are all learning from each other and that's what will ultimately drive landscape change. Thank you.

My science comes from both practitioners and researchers. Some researchers I have known for years, like Richard Moore, Russell Washusen and Rod Bird, and many I don't know at all. They have done the experiments and written the papers that fed my need to understand. I hope that I have understood. If there are mistakes of nomenclature, biology or fact, I apologise, they are entirely mine. If my explanations and interpretations are proved wrong, I will be the first to celebrate. In science, being corrected is a worthy lesson. Thank you.

I have been working on this book for so long now that I'm at risk of forgetting all the people who have worked on it. Joanna Moore (The Improving Pen) helped massage my ramblings-of-a-tree-grower into something worthy of presenting to a publisher. Friends Mike Robinson-Koss and Jason Alexandra read draft chapters; they kept me grounded. Then, it was David Tenenbaum of Melbourne Books who was the first to see the potential. His editor Raphael Solarsh guided me through the production process and designer Ellen Cheng brought all the components together into the book you hold. Thank you.

Of course, what you see in front of you is more than just words. Cormac Hanrahan (Cormac Photography) took photos for the cover and chapter openings. His brief was to convey the art and emotion of being a tree grower, and the many hats we all wear. These are our trees, but I wanted the reader to imagine being amongst their own. As growers, we are part of the story. Thank you.

Michelle Stewart's wildlife drawings that close each chapter are very special to me. I am so impressed by her talent. I wanted to remind the reader that this book is as much about improving the environment as it is about growing wood. I cannot walk around our farm without sharing my time with the birds. It is one of the hidden pleasures of being a tree grower and, for me, a perfect link back to my Mum who was a passionate bird watcher. Thank you.

Through it all, going back to the day we planted our very first tree, there has been my wife, Claire. Together we have grown a forest, built a home and raised a family. Now we have nurtured a book. Thank you.

To my children and their children and beyond. You are the ones who will inherit the story we are writing on the landscape. May your trees grow tall and wide.

Index

Note: Italicised page numbers denote photos.

A

Acacia falciformis (Hickory Wattle), *50*–1
Acacia koa (Koa), 50
Acacia mearnsii (Black Wattle), 43–4, 65
Acacia melanoxylon See Blackwood (*Acacia melanoxylon*)
Acacia stenophylla (River Cooba), 49–50
acacias, suitability as sawn timber, 49–51
Acer saccharum (Sugar Maple), 44
aerodynamic porosity, 276–7
African Blackwood (*Dalbergia melanoxylon*), 38
African Cherry (*Prunus africana*), 96
African Mahogany (*Khaya senegalensis*), 282, 283
Agathis australis (Kauri), 256
Agathis robusta (Queensland Kauri), 75
Ai-Kakeu (*Casuarina junghuhniana*), 149–50
Albizia (*Paraserianthes falcataria*), 140
Albury Botanic Gardens, *284*
Alexandra, Jason, 246–7
all-backsawn pattern, 178, *180*
allelopathic reaction, 214
allergens See Silky Oak (*Grevillea robusta*)
Allocasuarina fraseriana (Western Australian Sheoak), 156
Allocasuarina littoralis (Black Sheoak), 148, 151
Allocasuarina luehmannii (Buloke), 148
Allocasuarina torulosa (Forest Oak), 148
Allocasuarina verticillata (Drooping Sheoak), 10, 152, 156
Alnus glutinosa See Black Adler (*Alnus glutinosa*)
Alpine Ash (*Eucalyptus delegatensis*), 59, 60
aluminium sulphate, 77
American Cottonwood (*Populus deltoides*), 184, 215
  genetic breeding program, 188–90
Amyema pendula (Drooping Mistletoe), 121–2
Angophora, 24
Araucaria cunninghamii (Hoop Pine), 75
Araucaria heterophylla (Norfolk Island Pine), *109*
Ash Wednesday 1983 (Vic), 112–14
Asian Cedar Tip Moth (*Hypsipyla robusta*), 285
Asian Red Cedar (*Toona ciliata*), 283
Atriplex (Saltbush), 14
Australian Bureau of Meteorology, 64, 266–7
Australian Master TreeGrower program, 172–3, 230–1, 291
Australian Red Cedar (*Toona ciliata* var. *australis*), 108, 280–93
  during colonial days, 282–3
  diameter of trees, *284*
  pruning, 285–6
  shrinkage rate, 35
  sunburn, 286
  tension wood, 287

Australian Stream Management Conference 2001 (Brisbane), 128, 132
Australian Sustainable Timbers, 232
Australian Tax Officer (Dandenong), *142*, 143
auxin hormones, 99, 108, *109*

B

backcut, 53
backsawn boards, 29
  cathedral grain, 176
  English Oak, 99
  furniture making, *129*
  ghost knots, 141
  recommended wood for, 34
  River Sheoak, 156
  shrinkage, 34
Balsawood (*Ochroma pyramidale*), 75
Bambra Agroforestry Farm
  1987 and 2001, *20*
  scoping land for, 115–18
  soil tests, 118
bark, 43–4
  components, 52
  fire-tolerance, 169
Bartlett, Darius, 235–6, *237*
Basal Area, 85–6, 194–5, 249
Beefwood (*Grevillea striata*), 15
Bird, Dr Rod, 156–7, 159, 267, 276–7
bird habitats, 79
bird's-eye grain, 47, 140
Black Adler (*Alnus glutinosa*), 215
  for shiitake growing, 258
Black Cockatoos, 148
Black Friday 1939 fires (Vic), 114
Black Poplar (*Populus nigra*), 184
  genetic breeding program, 188–90
Black Saturday fires 2009 (Vic), 58, 114
Black Sheoak (*Allocasuarina littoralis*), 148, 151
Black Walnut (*Juglans nigra*), 121, 204–24
  allelopathic reaction, 214–15
  backsawn boards, 178, *179*
  effect of frost, 209
  effect on soil, 213–14
  fodder value, 201
  fruit, *206*
  heartwood in boards, *207*
  intercropping, *208*, 214, 216–17
  market value of timber, 204, 205
  pruning, 206–8, 209
  shrinkage rate, 35
  use in gun-making, 204–5
  using height to measure site productivity, 211–13
Black Wattle (*Acacia mearnsii*), 43–4, 65
Black Willow (*Salix nigra*), 194–5
Black Wooded Acacia, 38 See also Blackwood (*Acacia melanoxylon*)
Blackbutt (*Eucalyptus pilularis*), *71*
Blackwood (*Acacia melanoxylon*), 38–52, 108
  backsawn boards, 178
  bark, 52
  as export in colonial days, 38

guard design trials, 40–2
heartwood, 44–6, *45*
pruning, 48–9, 221, 222
self-thinning lines, 88, *89*
for shiitake growing, 258
shrinkage rate, 35
tree-felling methods, 42–3, 47, 48–9
blue-green algal bloom, 129
Bootle, Keith, 287
borers See longicorn bull's eye borers; *Lyctus*
Brachychiton populneus (Kurrajong), 200
Bradbury, Dr Gordon, 46
brittle-heart, 153, *163*
Brown, Robert, 38
Bryant and May Ltd, 185, 187
Buloke (*Allocasuarina luehmannii*), 148
Bureau of Meteorology, 64
Burr Oak (*Quercus macrocarpa*), 246
bush fires, 112–15, 167–8
  crown fires, 167
  historic chart analysis, *113*
  places identified for extreme, 170
  regeneration after, 59–60, 115, 166
  salvaging logs from, 168–70
bush foods, 15, 115

C

Californian Coast Redwood forest, 56
Callitris species (Cypress Pine), 15, 75, 101
cambium, 44, 52
Campbell, Andrew, 157, 159–60
Campbell, John Archibald, 16, *17* See also Dungalear Station (NSW)
Canada
  Black Walnut growing conditions, 208–9
  Black Walnut market, 204
carbon dioxide stored
  in Coast Redwood, 83–4
  in soil, 119
carbon sequestration, 119–20
Carr, John, 156, *156*
Carsan, Sammy, 94–5
case hardening, *67*
Castanea sativa (Chestnut), 121
Casuarina cunninghamiana See River Sheoak (*Casuarina cunninghamiana*)
Casuarina glauca (Swamp Sheoak), 259
Casuarina junghuhniana (Ai-Kakeu), 149–50
Casuarina oligodon (Yar), 149–51
Cedrela odorata (Cigar-box Cedar), 282, 283
chainsaws, conventional and ripping chains, 96–7
Chamaecytisus proliferus (Tagasaste), 200
checks (small cracks), *67*
Cheney, Dr Phil, 167
Cherry cultivars (*Prunus*), 215
Chestnut (*Castanea sativa*), 121
Christmas Beetles, 100
Cigar-box Cedar (*Cedrela odorata*), 282, 283
circular swing-blade mill, 175, 176
climate change, impact on farmlands, 15–16, 104

Coast Redwood (*Sequoia sempervirens*), 56, 74–90, 108
    Diameter of trees, 84–5, *86*
    pruning, 80–*1*, *221*, 222
    self-thinning lines, *89*
    shrinkage rates, 35
    stages of growth, *85*
    stocking rates, 60–1, *82*
    use in controlling soil erosion, 75–9
collapse, timbers susceptible to, 66
common names for trees, 25
compression wood, 162–3
    shrinkage rate, 162
cork cells, 43
Cork Oak *(Quercus suber)*, 246
Cornell, Wade, *79*
Corymbia, 24
Corymbia calophylla (Marri), 166
Corymbia maculata See Spotted Gum (*Corymbia maculata*)
Costello, Tim, 21
cost-share grants See funding grants
Crack Willow (*Salix fragilis*), 190
    hybridising potential, 195–6
    impact on aquatic wildlife, 192
    leaves for livestock fodder, 190–1
    weed status, *191*–2
Cremer, Kurt, 196, 199
Cricket Bat Willow (*Salix alba* var. *caerulea*), 192–9
    catkins, *195*
    hybridising potential, 195–6
Crockett, Bob, 192
crownsawn boards See backsawn boards
Cupressus macrocarpa (Monterey Cypress), 74, 236
curly grain, 137
Cypress Oak (*Quercus robur* var. *fastigiata*), 247, *248*
Cypress Pine (*Callitris* species), 15, 75, 101
cytokinin, 108

D

Dalbergia melanoxylon (African Blackwood), 38
Dann, Paul, 190–2
Dattner, Nicholas, 229–30
Davies-Colley, Peter, *175*, 176, 179
Davies-Colley, Richard, 171, 175
Davies-Colley, Wilma, 171, 175
deciduous oaks, 246
detannification agent, 201
Dewing, Jenny, 286, 290–1
Dewing, Mick, 286, 290–1
Diospyros crassiflora (Ebony), 188
direct incentives See funding grants
direct seedling, *215*, 297
    Black Walnut, *206*
Dixon, Andy, 204, 207, 210, 217
Dock (*Rumex* species), 120
Donchi, Barry, 228, *229*
double leaders, 221
Douglas Fir (*Pseudotsuga menziesii*), 74 See also Oregon Pine (*Pseudotsuga menziesii*)
Drooping Mistletoe (*Amyema pendula*), 121–2
Drooping Sheoak (*Allocasuarina verticillata*), 10, 151–2, 156–7 See also Shingle Oak
droughts, 63, 135
drying techniques
    Mountain Ash, 66–8
    Silky Oak, 98
Dungalear Station (NSW), 16, 17–18, *17*

E

earlywood cells, 44, 52, 66
Ebony (*Diospyros crassiflora*), 188
Eden woodchip export facility (NSW), 12
Emu Berry (*Podocarpus drouynianus*), 78
English Oak (*Quercus robur*), 244–60 See also Cypress Oak (*Quercus robur* var. *fastigiata*)
    backsawn boards, *179*
    commercial value of, 249, 250
    discounting future value, 251–3
    fast-grown and slow-grown differences, 244–5
    pruning, 249–50
    ray cells, 99
    relaxing tension wood in, 153
    ring shakes, 26
    self-thinning lines, 88, *89*
    for shiitake growing, 258
    shrinkage rate, 35
    stocking rate, 249
epicormic shoots, 80–1, 100, *220*
Eucalyptus See also *Angophora*; *Corymbia*
    fire tolerant species, 170
    fodder value, 201
Eucalyptus acmenoides (White Mahogany), 231
Eucalyptus camaldulensis (River Red Gum), 80
Eucalyptus cladocalyx See Sugar Gum (*Eucalyptus cladocalyx*)
Eucalyptus delegatensis (Alpine Ash), stocking rates, 59
Eucalyptus globulus See Southern Blue Gum (*Eucalyptus globulus*)
Eucalyptus gomphocephala (Tuart), 276
Eucalyptus grandis (Flooded Gum), 25, *71*
Eucalyptus maculata, 238 See also Spotted Gum (*Corymbia maculata*)
Eucalyptus marginata (Jarrah), 166, 177
Eucalyptus microcorys (Tallowwood), *221*, 231
Eucalyptus nitens See Shining Gum (*Eucalyptus nitens*)
Eucalyptus obliqua (Messmate Stringybark) See Messmate Stringybark (*Eucalyptus obliqua*)
Eucalyptus paniculata (Grey Ironbark), 230
Eucalyptus pilularis (Blackbutt), *71*
Eucalyptus punctata (Grey Gum), 231
Eucalyptus radiata (Narrow Leafed Peppermint), 118
Eucalyptus regnans See Mountain Ash (*Eucalyptus regnans*)
Eucalyptus saligna See Sydney Blue Gum (*Eucalyptus saligna*)
Eucalyptus sideroxylon, 238, 240 See also Red Ironbark (*Eucalyptus tricarpa*)
Eucalyptus tricarpa See Red Ironbark (*Eucalyptus tricarpa*)
Eucalyptus viminalis See Manna Gum (*Eucalyptus viminalis*)
European Walnut See Persian Walnut (*Juglans regia*)
evergreen oaks, 246

F

Faustmann, Martin, 251–2, 253, 256
Fethers Veneers, 140
Fibre Saturation Point (FSP), 65
fiddleback grain
    Blackwood quartersawn, *47*
    as feature in furniture making, 137–*8*
    impact of pruning on, 138–9
    Shining Gum, *136*–7, *223*

Finley, Dr Jim, 262, 263
Fisher, Lachlan, 192, 193
flat cut board See backsawn boards
Flinders, Matthew, 38
Flooded Gum (*Eucalyptus grandis*), 25, *71*
force rating, 228
Forest Fire Danger Index (FFDI), 114
Forest Oak (*Allocasuarina torulosa*), 148, 156
Forest Research Institute (NZ), 206
Forest Stewardship Council (FSC), 232
forestry
    dualisms in, 11–12
    long-rotation, 254–5
    moving beyond dualisms, 21
Forestry Tasmania, 57
forestry wars, 12, 172–3
Formply, 187
form-pruning, 207–8, 209
Frankia bacteria, 150
Fritz Wonder Plot (US), *86*
funding grants, 269–75
    alternatives to, 274
fungal rust, 185, *186*
fungi damage to trees, 135
furniture making
    Blackwood, 48
    fiddleback as feature, 137–*8*
    Hybrid Poplars, *187*
    Mountain Ash, *54*
    Shining Gum, 128
    using kino as feature, 26, 30–1

G

Gadubanud people, 114
genetic breeding program, 188–90
geotropic trees, 99, 108–9
ghost knots, 141
Gingko (*Gingko biloba*), 78
Gingko biloba (Gingko), 78
Gloucester Tree fire tower (WA), 28–*9*
Gordon, Dr Andy, 208, 214
grass as buffer for capturing run-offs, 130–1
gravitropic trees, 108
Gray, Alan, 230
Greenaway, Simon, 172–3
greenhouse gases, 119
Greenwood, Tom, 56, *57*
Grevillea striata (Beefwood), 15
Grey Gum (*Eucalyptus punctata*), 231
Grey Ironbark (*Eucalyptus paniculata*), 230
growth rings, 52
guards
    design trial and error, 40–*2*, *297*
    planting tips, 296
gypsum, 77

H

Hairsine, Dr Peter, 128–31, *129*, 132
hardwoods, 75, 152, 287
    epicormic shoots, *220*
    horizontal bandsaw patterns, 178
    quartersawn boards, 178–9
    tension wood, 152, *163*
    tylosis, 246
harvesting trees, rights to, 288–9
heartwood, 52 See also truewood
    Black Walnut, *207*
    Blackwood, 44–6
    colour changes, 154–*5*
    durability, 240
    Walnut, 204–5
heatwaves, effect on Mountain Ash, 63–4

height of trees, 56–8
    Coast Redwood, 82–3
    contributing factors, 70–1
    as measure of site productivity, 211–13
hemiparasites, 121
Hickory Wattle (*Acacia falciformis*), 50–1, 239
Hill, Hamish, 128
hingewood, 53
Hocking, Dennis, 256
Hoop Pine (*Araucaria cunninghamii*), 75
Hordeum marinum (Sea Barley Grass), 120
horizontal bandsaw mill, 175, *181*
    hardwood sawing patterns, 178
house building
    fireproof designs, 235–7
    timbers for, 226–9, 235–9
humidity, effect on drying timber, 30
Hybrid Poplars (*Populus x euramericana*), 121, 185, *189*–90
    in furniture making, *187*
    as livestock fodder, 190, *199*
    pruning, 190
    relaxing tension wood in, 153
    rooted cuttings, *193*
    as shelter for Black Walnut, 217
    for shiitake growing, 258
hygroscopic timbers, 65
Hyperion Coast Redwood forest (US), 56

I

India, Kerala community forestry research project, 173–5
insect pests, 63, 98, 134, 154, 168, *241*
Italian Stone Pine (*Pinus pinea*), 268

J

James, Dr Ken, 27
James, Will, 140–3
Janka test, 226
Jarrah (*Eucalyptus marginata*), 166, 177
    F-rating, *228*
Jellinek, Dr Lea, 280–1
Jenkins, David, 140, 166–8, *172*, 175, 176–7, 262–3
Jigsaw Farms, *159*, 160–1
Juglans nigra See Black Walnut (*Juglans nigra*)
Juglans regia See Persian Walnut (*Juglans regia*)
juglone, 215–16
Juncus species (native rush), 120

K

Kakadu Plum (*Terminalia ferdinandiana*), 15
Kantor, Eve, 158, 160–1
Karri (*Eucalyptus diversicolor*), 28, 176
Kater, Annabel, 230–5 *See also* Australian Sustainable Timbers
Kauri (*Agathis australis*), 256
Kenya *See also* World Agroforestry Centre (Nairobi)
    Silky Oak as shade tree in food gardens, 92–4
    subsistence farmers, 18
Khaya senegalensis (African Mahogany), 282, 283
kilns, solar-powered, 65, *67*
kino, 24, 25–6
    as feature in furniture, 26, 30–1
Kiumbe, Anthan, *96*
Koa (*Acacia koa*), 50
Kurrajong (*Brachychiton populneus*), 200

L

Lacewood, 31
Land & Water Australia, 148
land degradation, 16, *117*, 288–9
    water-related, 76–7
Landcare, 104–5
landslides, contributing factors, 102–3
latewood cells, 44, 52
Leopold, Aldo, 233, 263
L'Héritier de Brutelle, Charles-Louis, 24
Light Detection and Ranging (LiDAR) technology, 57
lignotubers, 78, *79*
Lindenmayer, Dr David, 281
Linnaeus, Carl, 250–1
livestock
    acorns as fodder, 250, 254
    shelter belts, 264–6
    tree foliage as fodder, 190–1, *199*, 200–1
    windchill factor, 266
livestock disease outbreak, 14
Lober, Keith, 186, 187
Lockyer, Peter, 235
Logosol Timberjig, *98*
Lombardy Poplar (*Populus nigra* var. *italica*), 184
    disease outbreak, 185–6
London Plane (*Plantanus orientalis* var. *acerifolia*), 31 *See also* Lacewood
longicorn bull's eye borers, 134, 168
Lophozonia cunninghamii (Myrtle Beech), 61, 63
Lunt, Ian, 148
Lyctus
    trees susceptible to, 98, *241*
    trees tolerant against, 63, 154

M

MacLaren, Archie, 192
Maiden, Joseph, 25, 51
Manna Gum (*Eucalyptus viminalis*), 112–23
    hollow formations, 122–3
    parasite threats to, 121–2
    shrinkage rate, 35
    summer branch drop, 122
    in waterlogged areas, 121
maple syrup, 44
Marr, Robert, 30
Marri (*Eucalyptus calophylla*), 166
mass dampening effect, 27–8
McKay, Vic, 148
McKendrick, Alistair, *139*
Meggitt, Hugh, 210–11, 212, 217–18
Melampsora larici-populina, 185
Melampsora medusa (Poplar Fungal Rust), 185, 186
Menezes, Justino Monteiro, 149–50, 151
Mentha australis (River Mint), 264
Meru Oak (*Vitex keniensis*), 95
Messmate Stringybark (*Eucalyptus obliqua*), 24–33
    dominance in Australian landscape, 24
    effect of pruning on, 26–*7*
    F-rating, *228*
    kino in, 24, 25–6
    lifespan, 33
    shrinkage rate, 35
    summer branch drop, 31–2
    tangential shrinkage, 30, 34-35, *65*, 155, *156*, 162, 178,
Mifsud, Brett, 57–8
Millennium Drought, 63, 272
Mistletoebirds, 121, 122

Mitchell, Thomas, 16
moisture content, 144
    firewood, 145
    Messmate Stringybark, 30
moisture meters, 65, *67*, 144
Mollongghip Coast Redwood plantation (Vic), 74, *75*, *82*, 83
    diameter of trees, *86*
Monterey Cypress (*Cupressus macrocarpa*), 74, 236
Moore, Richard, *172*, 177, *272*, *273*
Mountain Ash (*Eucalyptus regnans*), 56–72
    climbing tips, 56–7
    effect of heatwave on, 63–4
    F-rating, *228*
    resistance to *Lyctus*, 63
    seedling germination post-fires, 59–60
    self-thinning lines, 88, *89*
    shrinkage rate, 35
    stocking rate, 60–1
    tallest specimen, 56, 57–8
    tension wood, 153
multipurpose planting projects, 157–8 *See also* Potter Farmland Plan Project (Vic)
mutual shelter effect, 70–1
Mwanza, Eli, 18
The Myer Foundation, 172
Myer, Kenneth, 171
Myer, Phillip, 171–2
Myrtle Beech (*Lophozonia cunninghamii*), 61, 63

N

Narrow Leafed Peppermint (*Eucalyptus radiata*), 118
National Landcare Conference 2016, 232
native birds, 79, 121, 122, 148, 159, 264
native fodder, 14, 15
native regrowth forests
    commercial value, 234–5
    ecological management, 232–5
    logging debates, 229–32
native rush (*Juncus* species), 120
Nematolepis squamea (Otway Satinwood), 292
New Zealand
    Blackwood plantations, 39
    English Oak density, 245
    Sydney Blue Gum plantations, 171
Newnham, Adam, 137–8
Nicholas, Ian, 206, 211
    Walnut Island trial, 212
    Walnut Island trial Site Index, 217–18
nitrogen capture, 157–1, 213–14
Norfolk Island Pine (*Araucaria heterophylla*), *109*
Northern Red Oak (*Quercus rubra*), 215, 246
Norway Spruce (*Picea abies*), 253

O

Ochroma pyramidale (Balsawood), 75
O'Connor, Paddy, *39*–40
O'Meara, Dr Tim, 172, 173, *174*
open-rooted seedlings, 294
optimum harvest models, 253, 256
Oregon Pine (*Pseudotsuga menziesii*), 74, *228*, 236
Otway Agroforestry Network, 273–4, 288
Otway Ranges
    dominant species in, 61, 63, 118
    fire towers, 28
    rainfall, 118
Otway Satinwood (*Nematolepis squamea*), 292

P

Papua New Guinea, 150–51
Paraserianthes falcataria (Albizia), 140
Passalaqua, Noel, 255
Persian Walnut (*Juglans regia*), 204–5
Peter, Elizabeth, 15
Peter, Jane, 16
Peter, John, 14–15, 16 *See also* Tubbo Station (NSW)
Phillip, Governor, 148, 281
phototropic trees, 108–*9*, 152
    growth of leaders, 286
Picea abies (Norway Spruce), 253
Pin Oak *(Quercus palustris)*, 246, *247*
Pinus insignis See Radiata Pine (*Pinus radiata*)
Pinus pinea (Italian Stone Pine), 268
Pinus radiata See Radiata Pine (*Pinus radiata*)
Pinus strobus (White Pine), 215
pith, 52
plant toxins, 215–16
Plantanus orientalis var. *acerifolia (*London Plane), 31, 41
plantation investment schemes, 12, 159
plantations, 20
    Black Walnut, 211
    Blackwood (South Africa), 46
    Coast Redwood, 74
    community concerns about, 280–*1*
    Cricket Bat Willow, *193*
    criticisms, 100–1
    English Oak, *249*
    optimum harvest models, 253, 256
    Silky Oak, 101–2
    softwood, *75*
    spacing trials, 70–*1*, 160–1, 195
    susceptibility to disease, 185–6
    wood for furniture making from, 137–*9*
plywood, specialist, 187
Podocarpus drouynianus (Emu Berry), 78
Poison Ivy, 98
Poison Oak, 98
polyethylene glycol (PEG), 201
Poplar Fungal Rust (*Melampsora medusa*), 185, *186*
Poplars (*Populus*), 184–202
    fodder value, 201
    market for, 186–7
    shrinkage rate, 35
    suitability for food packaging, 188
Populus See Poplars (*Populus*)
Populus alba (White Poplar), 188
Populus deltoides See American Cottonwood (*Populus deltoides*)
Populus nigra See Black Poplar (*Populus nigra*)
Populus nigra var. *italica See* Lombardy Poplar (*Populus nigra* var. *italica*)
Populus x euramericana See Hybrid Poplars (*Populus x euramericana*)
portable sawmills, 175, *248*
Potter Farmland Plan Project (Vic), 157–8, 160 *See also* Jigsaw Farms
Powder Post Borer, *See Lyctus*
Premier Slate, 148
pruning *See also* form-pruning
    Black Walnut, 206–8, 209
    Blackwood, 48
    Coast Redwood, 80–*1*, *81*
    Cricket Bat Willow, 194, 197
    double leaders and pre-emptive, 221
    effect on stability of Messmate Stringybark, 26–7
    English Oak, 249–50
    Hybrid Poplars, 190
    impact on fiddleback formation, 138–9
    Mountain Ash, *62*
    for sawlogs, 220
    Silky Oak, 93–4, 99
    stem, 222
    when to start, 220–1
pruning tools, 223
Prunus (Cherry cultivars), 215
Prunus africana (African Cherry), 96
Pseudotsuga menziesii (Douglas Fir, Oregon Pine), 74, 228, 236

Q

Quandong (*Santalum acuminatum*), 15
quartersawn boards, 29–30
    Blackwood, *47*
    English Oak, 99
    hardwoods, 178–9, *180*, *181*
    live-edge, 179
    Mountain Ash, *68*
    recommended wood for, 34
    River Sheoak, 154–5
    Shining Gum, *136*
    shrinkage, 34
    Sydney Blue Gum, 176
Queensland, native timbers, 75
Queensland Kauri (*Agathis robusta*), 75
Quercus, commercial value of, 246
Quercus alba (White Oak), 215, 246
Quercus bicolor (Swamp Oak), 247
Quercus coccinea (Scarlet Oak), 246
Quercus macrocarpa (Burr Oak), 246
Quercus palustris (Pin Oak), 246, *247*
Quercus petraea See Sessile Oak *(Quercus petraea)*
Quercus robur (English Oak) *See* English Oak (*Quercus robur*)
Quercus robur var. *fastigiata* (Cypress Oak), 247
Quercus rubra (Nothern Red Oak), 215

R

Race, Dr Digby, *284*
radial shrinkage, 30, 34-35, 155, 178
radial splits, 48, 65
Radiata Pine (*Pinus radiata*), 74, 75
    fodder value, 201
    F-rating, 226, *228*
    self-thinning lines, 88, *89*
    shrinkage rate, 35
    wood density, 145
rainfall, impact of land clearing on, 103–4
ray cells, 52, 99, *149*
reaction wood, 162, *163*
reclaimed timber, 226–9
Red Ironbark (*Eucalyptus tricarpa*), 80, 168, 226–42
    durability, 240
    F-rating, *228*
    in house building, 226–9
    pruning, *221*
    shrinkage rate, 35
Redhead matches, 185
Red-tailed Black Cockatoos, 148, 159
Reid, Tom, 39, 227, *237*
Reynolds, George, 28
Rhizobium bacteria, 40, 150
ring shakes, 26
riparian buffer strips, harvesting from, 130–2

River Cooba (*Acacia stenophylla*), 49–50
River Mint (*Mentha australis*), 264
River Red Gum (*Eucalyptus camaldulensis*), 80, 156–7, 227-8
    F-rating, *228*
River Sheoak (*Casuarina cunninghamiana*), 66, 148–64
    backsawn and quartersawn boards, *35*, *156*
    as boards, *152*
    colour change in heartwood, 154–5
    conservations status, 148
    resistance to *Lyctus*, 154
    shrinkage rate, 35, 155
    spacing trials, 160–1
Robinson-Koss, Mike, 120, 239
Rumex species (Dock), 120
Rutherford, Dr Ian, 132

S

Salix See Willows (*Salix*)
Salix alba var. *caerulea See* Cricket Bat Willow (*Salix alba* var. *caerulea*)
Salix fragilis See Crack Willow (*Salix fragilis*)
Salix nigra (Black Willow), 194–5
Saltbush (*Atriplex*), 14
Samuelson, Paul, 252
Sandalwood (*Santalum spicatum*), 15
Santalum acuminatum (Quandong), 15
Santalum spicatum (Sandalwood), 15
sapwood, 52
    cricket bat making, *193*
    durability, 240
    role of, 46
sawmills, 175–6, *248*
scarf, 53
Scarlet Oak (*Quercus coccinea*), 246
Sea Barley Grass (*Hordeum marinum*), 120
selective harvesting, 177, 234
self-thinning lines, 86–7, 88–9
Sequoia sempervirens See Coast Redwood (*Sequoia sempervirens*)
Sessile Oak *(Quercus petraea)*, use as wine barrels, 245–6
shade tolerant trees, 108, 292
Sharma-Luital, Parsuram, 258–9
sheep farms
    colonial, 16
    disease outbreak, 14
shelter belts, 124, 264–6, 272–*3*
    design, 276–7
    impact on wind and pasture production, 267
Sheoaks, fodder value, 201
Sheppard, Stephen, 288
shiitake mushrooms, 247, 248, 258–9
Shingle Oak, 156
shingles, 148
Shining Gum (*Eucalyptus nitens*), 128–46
    fiddleback grain, *136*–7, *223*
    F-rating, 226
    furniture making, 137–*9*
    guards for, 41
    harvesting, *141*
    pruning, 220
    for shiitake growing, 258
    shrinkage rate, 35
    susceptibility to borers, 135
    veneers from, *142*
    veneers market, 140–4
    wood density, 145
shrinkage *See also* radial shrinkage; tangential shrinkage

compression wood, 162
River Sheoak, 155
tension wood, 162
timber species and, 35
Silky Oak (*Grevillea robusta*), 92–108
    allergic reactions to, 98
    fodder value, 201
    pruning, 93–4, 99
    shrinkage rate, 35
    susceptibility to *Lyctus*, 98
    use in controlling soil erosion, 105
Sillett, Dr Stephen, 56, 58
Site Index, 212, 213, 217–18
site quality measures, 211–13
small cracks *See* checks (small cracks)
sodic soils, 76–7
    erosion control for, 78–9
Sodium Borate (Disodium Octaborate Tetrahydrate), 240
softwoods, 74, 152
    compression wood, 162, *163*
    epicormic shoots, *220*
    lignotubers in, 78
    plantations, 75
soil composition, 118–19
    effect of Black Walnut on, 213–14
    sodic, 76–9
soil erosion, 75–8 *See also* landslides
soil erosion (tunnel), 76, 77, 78, *80*
South Africa's Blackwood plantations, 46
Southern Blue Gum (*Eucalyptus globulus*), 118
    commercial value of, 264
    F-rating, *228*
    plantation schemes, 159
    salvaged from bush fire, 168–70
    for shiitake growing, 259
    shrinkage rate, 35
    tension wood, 153
    veneers, 140
Southern Boobook Owls, 79
splits *See* radial splits
Spotted Gum (*Corymbia maculata*), 168, 230, 238, 262–78
    bending properties, 228
    drought resistance, 272
    fire tolerance, 170
    F-rating, *228*
    planting tips, 296
    pruning, *260*
    shrinkage rate, 35
    veneers market, 232
Steadman model of apparent temperatures, 266–7
Stewart, Andrew, 255, *260*, 264–9, 272–3
Stewart, Jill, 268
Stewart, Lindsay, 272
Stewart, Sandy, 248
stocking rate in forests, 59, 60–1
    Coast Redwood, *82*, 87
    English Oak, 249
    impact on height of trees, 70–*1*
Strawberry Clover (*Trifolium fragiferum*), 120
Sugar Gliders, 99–100, 122
Sugar Gum (*Eucalyptus cladocalyx*)
    F-rating, *228*
    for shiitake growing, 258
Sugar Maple (*Acer saccharum*), 44, 140
summer branch drop, 31–2, 122
Summers, Jason, 46
sunburn, 286
swamp forests, 38
Swamp Oak (*Quercus bicolor*), 247
Swamp Sheoak (*Casuarina glauca*), 259
Sweden's historic English Oak plantation, 244, 246, 250–1
Swietenia mahagoni (West Indian Mahogany), 282, 283
Sydney Blue Gum (*Eucalyptus saligna*), 65, 166–82
    fire tolerance, 170
    F-rating, 226
    as lining boards, *176*
    quartersawn boards, 176
    shrinkage rate, 35

T

Tagasaste (*Chamaecytisus proliferus*), 200
Tallowwood (*Eucalyptus microcorys*), 221, 231
tangential shrinkage
    Messmate Stringybark, 30, 34
    Mountain Ash, *65*
    River Sheoak, 155
tannins, 43–4, 190 *See also* kino
    condensed, 24
    hydrolysable, 201
Tarago Reservoir catchment, 128–30
Tasmanian swamp forests, 39
Teak (*Tectona grandis*), 95
Tectona grandis (Teak), 95
tension wood, 152–4, 162–3
    Australian Red Cedar, 287
    Cricket Bat Willow, 198
    dangers of, 153
    shrinkage rate, 162
Terminalia ferdinandiana (Kakadu Plum), 15
thigmomorphogenesis, 41
through-and-through pattern, 178, *179*
Tibbits, Dr Josquin, 128, *129*, 134
tiger-stripe pattern *See* fiddleback grain
timber shakes, cutting techniques for, 148–9
Timor Leste's Ai-Kakeu (*Casuarina junghuhniana*), 149–50
tip moths, 285
Toona ciliata var. *australis See* Australian Red Cedar (*Toona ciliata* var. *australis*)
Toona sinensis, 283
Toxicodendron plants, 98
Tracy, Geoff, 101
tree bark *See* bark
tree branch failure *See* summer branch drop
tree trunk components, 52
tree-felling methods, 42–3 , 47, 53
tree planting tips, 294–7
Trifolium fragiferum (Strawberry Clover), 120
truewood, 52
Tuart (*Eucalyptus gomphocephala*), 276
Tubbo Station (NSW), 14, 16
tylosis, 246

U

Uganda
    Mount Elgon landslides, 102–3
    using Landcare principles for rehabilitation, 104–6
understoreys, 124
University of Guelph (Ontario), 208–9
University of Melbourne, 27

V

veneers market, 140–4, 232
Victorian Coroner's Court, 32
Virginia Agricultural Experiment Station, 214
visible stewardship, 288
Vitex keniensis (Meru Oak), 95

W

Washusen, Dr Russell, 128, 134, 136, 152–3, *273*
water quality in forested catchments, 128–9
watercourse rehabilitation, 128–31, 269
    buffer zone performance, *130*
    multipurpose planting conservation projections, 133–4
waterlogging, 120–1
Watson, Jack, 28
Wattles, fodder value, 201
Weatherstone, John, 50
Webb, Len, 101
weed control, 294–5, 297
West Indian Mahogany (*Swietenia mahagoni*), 282, 283
Western Australian fire towers, 28–9
Western Australian Sheoak (*Allocasuarina fraseriana*), 156
White Mahogany (*Eucalyptus acmenoides*), 231
White Oak (*Quercus alba*), 215, 246, 247
White Pine (*Pinus strobus*), 215
White Poplar (*Populus alba*), 188
wildlife
    dependence on sheoaks for food, 148
    protection from, 296
    providing natural habitats, 79, 100, 123, 124–5
wildlife corridors, 124
Wilkes, John, 240
Willows (*Salix*), 190–9, 201 *See also* Crack Willow (*Salix fragilis*); Cricket Bat Willow (*Salix alba* var. *caerulea*)
wind tunnels, 277
windchill factor, 266–7
windthrow, 26–7
wood density, 136, 144
    English Oak, 245
    table, *241*
    and tree age, 145
wood volume, 64–5, 83, 85
Wootton, Mark, 158, 160–1
World Agroforestry Centre (Nairobi), 18, 92–5, 96, 104–5
    Silky Oak planted in, *93*, *97*
World Congress of Agroforestry 2004 (Florida), 270–5
World Vision Australia, 21

Y

Yar (*Casuarina oligodon*), 149–51

Bambra Agroforestry Farm tree species list

Common Name	Scientific Name	Common Name	Scientific Name
Hickory Wattle	Acacia falciformis	Caucasian & Claret Ash	Fraxinus angustifolia
Blackwood	Acacia melanoxylon	Honey Locust	Gleditsia triacanthos
Black Wattle	Acacia mearnsii	Silky Oak	Grevillea robusta
River Cooba	Acacia stenophylla	Walnut	Juglans regia
Australian Kauri	Agathis robusta	Black Walnut	Julgans nigra
Drooping Sheoak	Allocasuarina verticillata	American Sweetgum	Liquidamber styraciflua
Bunya Pine	Araucaria bidwillii	Southern Beech	Lophozonia cunninghamii
Hoop Pine	Araucaria cunninghamii	Osage Orange	Maclura pomifera
Lemon Myrtle	Backhousia citriodora	River Mint	Mentha australis
Coast Banksia	Banksia integrifolia	Satinwood	Nematolepis squamea
Silver Banksia	Banksia marginata	Norway Spruce	Picea abies
River Banksia	Banksia seminuda	Stone Pine	Pinus pinea
Pecan	Carya illinoinensis	Radiata Pine	Pinus radiata
Chestnut	Castanea sativa	London Plane	Platanus x acerifolia
River Sheoak	Casuarina cunninghamiana	Brown Pine	Podocarpus elatus
Tree Lucerne	Chamaecytisus palmensis	Hybrid Poplar	Populus x euramericana
Hazelnut	Corylus avellana	Cherry	Prunus avium
Spotted Gum	Corymbia maculata	Pear	Pyrus communis
Leyland Cypress	Cupressocyparis x leylandii	Mandurian Pear	Pyrus ussuriensis
Mexican Cypress	Cupressus lusitanica	White Oak	Quercus alba
Monterey Cypress	Cupressus macrocarpa	Swamp White Oak	Quercus bicolour
Sugar Gum	Eucalyptus cladocalyx	Holm Oak, Holly Oak	Quercus ilex
Cut-tail, Brown Barrel	Eucalyptus fastigata	Burr Oak	Quercus macrocarpa
Southern Blue Gum	Eucalyptus globulus	Pin Oak	Quercus palustris
Flooded Gum	Eucalyptus grandis	Sessile Oak	Quercus petraea
Tallowwood	Eucalyptus microcorys	English Oak	Quercus robur
Yellow Stringybark	Eucalyptus muellerana	Red Oak	Quercus rubra
Shining Gum	Eucalyptus nitens	Deep Yellow Wood	Rhodosphaera rhodanthema
Messmate Stringybark	Eucalyptus obliqua	Aust. Sandalwood	Santalum spicatum
Otway Messmate	Eucalyptus obliqua x regnans	Coast Redwood	Sequoia sempervirens
Mountain Ash	Eucalyptus regnans	Aniseed Myrtle	Syzygium anisatum
Sydney Blue Gum	Eucalyptus saligna	Riberry	Syzygium luehmannii
Mugga Ironbark	Eucalyptus sideroxylon	Native Pepper	Tasmannia lanceolata
Red Ironbark	Eucalyptus tricarpa	Red Cedar	Toona ciliata
Manna Gum	Eucalyptus viminalis	Wollemi Pine	Wollemia nobilis